Early Modern Liveness

RELATED TITLES

British Black and Asian Shakespeareans: Integrating Shakespeare, 1966-2018
Jami Rogers
978-1-3501-1488-3

Early Modern Actors and Shakespeare's Theatre: Thinking with the Body
Evelyn Tribble
978-1-4725-7602-6

Lockdown Shakespeare: New Evolutions in Performance and Adaptation
Edited by Gemma Kate Allred, Benjamin Broadribb and Erin Sullivan
978-1-3502-4780-2

Playing Indoors: Staging Early Modern Drama in the Sam Wanamaker Playhouse
Will Tosh
978-1-3501-0950-6

Shakespeare and the 'Live' Theatre Broadcast Experience
Edited by Pascale Aebischer, Susanne Greenhalgh and Laurie Osborne
978-1-3501-2581-0

Studying Shakespeare Adaptation: From Restoration Theatre to YouTube
Pamela Bickley and Jenny Stevens
978-1-3500-6864-3

Early Modern Liveness

Mediating Presence in Text, Stage and Screen

Edited by
Danielle Rosvally and
Donovan Sherman

THE ARDEN SHAKESPEARE
LONDON • NEW YORK • OXFORD • NEW DELHI • SYDNEY

THE ARDEN SHAKESPEARE
Bloomsbury Publishing Plc
50 Bedford Square, London, WC1B 3DP, UK
1385 Broadway, New York, NY 10018, USA
29 Earlsfort Terrace, Dublin 2, Ireland

BLOOMSBURY, THE ARDEN SHAKESPEARE and the Arden Shakespeare logo are trademarks of Bloomsbury Publishing Plc

First published in Great Britain 2023
This paperback edition published in 2024

Copyright © Danielle Rosvally, Donovan Sherman and contributors, 2023

Danielle Rosvally and Donovan Sherman have asserted their right under the Copyright, Designs and Patents Act, 1988, to be identified as editors of this work.

For legal purposes the Acknowledgements on p. xi constitute an extension of this copyright page.

Cover image: *The Tempest* (© RSC, 2016)

All rights reserved. No part of this publication may be reproduced or transmitted in any form or by any means, electronic or mechanical, including photocopying, recording, or any information storage or retrieval system, without prior permission in writing from the publishers.

Bloomsbury Publishing Plc does not have any control over, or responsibility for, any third-party websites referred to or in this book. All internet addresses given in this book were correct at the time of going to press. The author and publisher regret any inconvenience caused if addresses have changed or sites have ceased to exist, but can accept no responsibility for any such changes.

A catalogue record for this book is available from the British Library.

A catalog record for this book is available from the Library of Congress.

ISBN: HB: 978-1-3503-1847-2
PB: 978-1-3503-1851-9
ePDF: 978-1-3503-1849-6
eBook: 978-1-3503-1848-9

Typeset by Deanta Global Publishing Services, Chennai, India

To find out more about our authors and books visit www.bloomsbury.com and sign up for our newsletters.

CONTENTS

List of figures vii
Contributors viii
Acknowledgements xi

Introduction *Danielle Rosvally and Donovan Sherman* 1

Part One Proximity 13

1 Liveness in virtual early modern theatre *Rebecca Bushnell* 15

2 Impressions of liveness in Shakespeare, at a distance *Stephanie Shirilan* 38

3 Medium specificity, medium convergence and aliveness in the chromakey (2018) and Big Telly Zoom (2020) *Macbeths Thomas Cartelli* 61

Part Two Performance 87

4 Liveness in VR and AR Shakespeare adaptations *Aneta Mancewicz* 89

5 Alive in the (early) modern repertory *Elizabeth E. Tavares* 111

6 Contemporary Turkish Shakespeares: New breath to old lives *Murat Öğütcü* 145

Part Three Premonition 171

7 Death draws down our curtain: Liveness beyond life in early modern Persianate Islam *Kenneth Molloy* 173

8 Signs of liveness: The blazing star in Renaissance drama *Gina M. Di Salvo* 196

9 The apparitional audience: Prophesizing live collectives in modern India and early modern England *Jonathan Gil Harris* 217

Index 239

FIGURES

2.1	Unsynchronized 'running man'	47
3.1	In the Porter's screening room from *Macbeth*, dir. Kit Monkman, 2018	66
3.2	Fleance sitting at the edge of the world from *Macbeth*, dir. Kit Monkman, 2018	71
3.3	Virtual spaces in Monkman's floating world from *Macbeth*, dir. Kit Monkman, 2018	73
3.4	Three officials morphed into witches with matching headpieces	78
3.5	Newly crowned Macbeth waving to supporters	79
3.6	Herdman modelling Macbeth's manic intensity	80
3.7	Nikki Harley as Lady Macbeth about to take her long walk into the Irish Sea	81
5.1	*Romeo and Juliet*, Willamette Park, 21 July 2017	117
5.2	*Julius Caesar*, Irving Park, 22 July 2017	120
5.3	*Much Ado About Nothing*, Irving Park, 23 July 2017	123
5.4	*Much Ado About Nothing*, Irving Park, 23 July 2017	125
5.5	*Much Ado About Nothing*, Irving Park, 23 July 2017	126
5.6a–6b	*Merry Wives of Windsor*, Irving Park, 22 July 2017	133
6.1	Macbeth (background), Mary (left), Warden (right), Kerem Kantarcı, *İkinci Katil*, 2017	148
6.2	From left to right: Fatma Fatih (standing), Ümmü Kurt, the angry villager, Cennet Güneş, Zeynep Fatih (from left to right), Pelin Esmer, *Kraliçe Lear*, 2019	154
6.3	Ghost and Karagöz Hamlet (left). Ophelia and Laertes (right), Ayhan Hülagu, *Dream of Hamlet*, Karagöz Theatre Company, 2021	161

CONTRIBUTORS

Rebecca Bushnell is the School of Arts and Sciences Board of Advisors Emerita Professor of English at the University of Pennsylvania. She is the author of books on subjects including Greek and Renaissance tragedy, early modern political thought, humanist pedagogy, early modern English gardening books and time in drama, film and video games. Her most recent book is *The Marvels of the World: An Anthology of Nature Writing before 1700*. She is a former president of the Shakespeare Association of America.

Thomas Cartelli is Professor Emeritus of English and Film Studies at Muhlenberg College. He is the author of *Marlowe, Shakespeare, and the Economy of Theatrical Experience* (1991) and *Repositioning Shakespeare: National Formations, Postcolonial Appropriations* (1999); co-author (with Katherine Rowe) of *New Wave Shakespeare on Screen* (2007); and editor of the *Norton Critical Edition of Shakespeare's Richard III* (2009) as well as of two additional single-text editions of *Richard III* for *The Norton Shakespeare 3*. His most recent book is *Reenacting Shakespeare in the Shakespeare Aftermath: the Intermedial Turn & Turn to Embodiment* (2019).

Gina M. Di Salvo is Assistant Professor of Theatre at the University of Tennessee, Knoxville. Her research focuses on medieval and early modern studies, theatre history and criticism, and dramaturgy. She is the author of the forthcoming monograph *The Renaissance of the Saints after Reform*.

Jonathan Gil Harris is Professor of English and Founding Dean at Ashoka University in India. He is the author of many books on Shakespeare, early modern literature and culture, and discourses of the foreign. His most recent books include *The First Firangis: Remarkable Tales of Healers, Heroes, Courtesans, Charlatans, and Other Foreigners Who Became Indian* (2015) and *Masala Shakespeare: How a Firangi Writer Became Indian* (2018). He is currently at work on a new critical edition of *Macbeth* for Cambridge and a book called *The Jewish Silk Road: Secrets from My Mother's Chinese Tea Chest*.

Aneta Mancewicz is Senior Lecturer in Drama and Theatre at Royal Holloway, University of London. Her research focuses on staging Shakespeare, digital technologies and European theatre. She is the author of *Hamlet after Deconstruction* (2022) and *Intermedial Shakespeares on European Stages* (2014). She also co-edited two collections of essays: *Intermedial Performance and Politics in the Public Sphere* and *Local and Global Myths in Shakespearean Performance*, both published in 2018. As an associate dramaturg, she supported virtual and augmented reality adaptations of Shakespeare, such as CREW's *Hamlet* (2017 and 2018) and Nexus Studios' *The Tempest* (2020).

Kenneth Molloy is a PhD candidate in the Department of Theatre Arts and Performance Studies at Brown University. His research brings pre- and early modern Islamic theories of performance into engagement with problems of ontology and epistemology in contemporary performance studies.

Murat Öğütcü is Associate Professor and he is currently working at Adıyaman University, Turkey. He is the general editor of the project Turkish Shakespeares, which aims to introduce texts, productions and research on Turkish Shakespeares to a broader international audience. He is also a researcher at the AHRC-funded project 'Medieval and Early Modern Orients', which aims to contribute to our understanding of the medieval and early modern encounters between England and the Islamic world. He has written book chapters and articles on his research interests, which include early modern studies, Shakespeare and cultural studies.

Danielle Rosvally is Clinical Assistant Professor of Theatre at the University at Buffalo. Her research investigates the intersection of performance, Shakespeare, American history, violence onstage and popular culture. She is an actor, dramaturg, fight director, and the author of a forthcoming monograph *Value and Worth: Buying and Selling Shakespeare in New York's Nineteenth Century.*

Donovan Sherman is Associate Professor of English at Seton Hall University. His research focuses on the intersections of early modern performance, philosophy and theology. His recent publications include *The Philosopher's Toothache: Embodied Stoicism in Early Modern English Drama* (2021) and the collection *Shakespeare and Virtue: A Handbook,* co-edited with Julia Reinhard Lupton, forthcoming from Cambridge University Press.

Stephanie Shirilan is Associate Professor of English at Syracuse University, where she teaches courses on early modern literature and affect, performance and environmental studies. Her research specializes in the literary and intercultural histories of science, medicine and philosophy. She is the author of *Robert Burton and the Transformative Powers of Melancholy* (2015). She is currently writing a book on air and breath in Shakespeare and a series of articles on the history of respiratory medicine. Her recent and related publications can be found in *Shakespeare's Audiences* (2020) and *Shakespeare and Virtue: A Handbook* (forthcoming).

Elizabeth E. Tavares is Assistant Professor at the University of Alabama with the Hudson Strode Program in Renaissance Studies. Specializing in early English drama, her research foci include playing companies, theatre history and Shakespeare in performance. Her award-winning research has appeared in *Early Theatre*, *Shakespeare Bulletin*, *Shakespeare Studies*, *The Map of Early Modern London*, among others, as well as several edited collections and academic blogs. Tavares is also a dramaturg and serves as the director of research for the Alabama Shakespeare Project.

ACKNOWLEDGEMENTS

The editors would like to thank Ian Downes for their help in preparing this manuscript. Thanks as well to Carla Della Gatta, Julia Fawcett and Louise Geddes for feedback on early materials and Lindsay Brandon Hunter for ongoing conversations regarding this book's subject matter. Finally, our most sincere gratitude to Mark Dudgeon and Lara Bateman at Bloomsbury for shepherding the project to completion.

Introduction

Danielle Rosvally and Donovan Sherman

In the spring of 2021, at the height of the global pandemic, the Royal Shakespeare Company (RSC) premiered *Dream*, a 'live interactive production inspired by the themes of *A Midsummer Night's Dream*'.[1] While traditional theatres around the world remained closed, vast swathes of people (sometimes over 7,000 per performance) from distant locations gathered in virtual spaces to communally witness the telling of a story. Audience members purchased tickets and, when the time came, accessed the play online. They were greeted with a brief introduction by a "real" person (the actor E.M. Williams, who played Puck), bedecked in motion-capture equipment, before plunging into a virtual world reminiscent of a sophisticated video game. The thin streams of the actual plot were more impressionistic than linear and involved familiar characters from Shakespeare's comedy – Puck, most prominently, but also more minor figures, like Moth, Mustardseed, Cobweb, and Peaseblossom, now afforded star turns – traipsing about the forest during a thunderstorm. Puck became lost and needed fireflies to light his way back home; spectators who had paid extra for their tickets (which is to say *paid* at all, since the performance was free for everyone else) could manipulate individual fireflies to help provide a path.

While the performance was bound to the digital realm and the audience/performer dynamic navigated solely via screens (since no audience members could be in the same room as the performers due to pandemic restrictions), it cannot be said that *Dream* lacked a quality of 'liveness'. The fairies were avatars of actual actors performing in real time; the music, provided by the Philharmonia Orchestra, was pre-recorded, as was the recognizable baritone of the rock musician Nick Cave; the performance was temporally bound within a specific frame; and the audiences could meet the cast and crew in the post-show Q and A session. In short, the performance carried with it the trappings of live performance even as it flouted performance's most traditionally assumed condition – that bodies be present together in space. This sense of liveness is a phenomenon explored in the influential book of the same name by Philip Auslander. For Auslander, liveness is not, contrary to the common understanding, something essential to or formally conditioned by performance but, rather, a historically contingent effect of the inextricable blending of the live and the mediated. 'How live and mediatized forms are used,' he explains, 'is determined not by their ostensibly intrinsic characteristics but by their positions within the cultural economy.'[2] Here, Auslander poses what appears to be a binary – the live and the 'mediatized', or that which is produced by technologies of reproduction – only to claim, as he does throughout the book, that the latter has cannibalized the former. All live performance creates a sensation of liveness, but it does so through the entanglement of the live and the mediated. In fact, for Auslander, the hallowed (some might say fetishized) qualities of live performance – its immediacy, intimacy and spontaneity – are often enhanced, not attenuated, by mediatization; technology ironically becomes a signal of liveness more than performance itself: 'Live performance thus has become the means by which mediatized representations are naturalized, according to a simple logic that appeals to our nostalgia for what we assumed was the im-mediate: if the mediatized image can be recreated in a live setting, it must have been "real' to begin with.'[3]

As this passage implies, the perception of reality itself is at stake when questioning the purity of the live event. The relationship between the 'real' and representational has been explored by many scholars over the years including, most relevantly, Peggy Phelan, who contends that the ephemeral power of live performance lies in its resistance to technological reproduction.[4] Lindsay Brandon Hunter, building off Auslander's theories, has analysed this quandary in performances where 'mediatization and mimesis compete and collude to represent what is *real* to audiences', thereby 'forcing a confrontation between the real and its representation, and between notions of authenticity, sincerity, and spontaneity, and their various, often copresent, others: the fake, the feigned, the staged, or the rehearsed'.[5] In the case of *Dream*, a similar confrontation emerged. Was it somehow more 'real' when Puck spoke with Mustardseed (an avatar that, we took on faith, moved in time to a performer's movements and spoke with their voice) than it was with the Wood (intoned by Cave's pre-recorded speech)? What of the moment the play ended, when the actors and masked crew appeared 'in person' to speak to the audience? One layer of mimetic scaffolding fell off, though what it revealed was, of course, another mediated image, beamed into computer screens worldwide.

Dream is merely one manifestation on a continuum of mediatized performance. Consider the RSC itself, where a 2016 stage production of *The Tempest* featured a CGI Ariel (a performance which, per the RSC, was the first play to incorporate live performance capture rendered in Unreal Engine – the technology which eventually produced the effects that underscore *Dream*).[6] But 'mediatization' does not necessarily implicate solely digital experimentations. As Auslander posits, *all* performance is, to a degree, the product of mediation. Even the most spare, minimal staging still relies on technological intervention. In fact, according to W.B. Worthen, the stage itself *is* a technology, one that mediates our experience of events just as a video camera or speaker or projection would. The theatre may, for Worthen, 'illustrate a crisis in the theatre as technology, but it cannot do so by posing a dichotomy between the technological and the theatrical. . . . As a technology, theatre has always represented this crisis, representing it with and through the technologies it appropriates, redefines, and represents as theatre.'[7] Theatre, in this understanding, becomes the site of its own struggle with technology – and it does so *as* a technological implement itself. Worthen's final tautology – that the theatre represents theatre – is not quite as paradoxical as it might first appear. The theatre is not some lost Edenic experience of communion, tainted by centuries of accreting sediments of mediatized interventions, but instead a mercurial, self-defining medium that produces an image of itself just as it does characters, settings and ideas. Sarah Bay-Cheng has taken this idea even further by suggesting that our understanding of the theatrical event needs to widen and encompass all surrounding media, not simply what is on stage: from liking a post on Facebook to talking to fellow audience members in the lobby to engaging with photographs of the production to writing a blog post about the play, performance constellates a series of events, only one of which is the experience in a particular structure at a particular time. Bay-Cheng provocatively suggests that '[w]e might characterize performance as the medium through which we perceive a series of interrelated events'.[8] In this view, performance – and with it liveness – is everywhere, a filter we place on the raw material of experience that grants it legibility. We are always live – we always experience liveness – because we are always in the present.

This book pursues these questions but aims them at the early modern theatre, a genre that often provides fodder for technological experimentation (as *Dream* demonstrates) while paradoxically also frequently representing the kind of nostalgic, 'purely' live theatre that media has eroded. For every Wooster Group *Hamlet*, there are legions of scholars and practitioners who attempt to reclaim the lost conditions of Shakespeare's theatre. Adherents of Original Practices (OP) (a field most prominently associated with the reconstruction of the Globe Theatre in London) have long believed that by recreating the material circumstances of early modern staging down to the smallest detail, they can experimentally learn more about, in the words of Andrew Gurr, 'what Shakespeare wanted from his performers'.[9] Gurr, the chief academic advisor to the Globe reconstruction, ties this endeavour directly to a desired feeling of liveness; in ventriloquizing the motivations of Sam Wanamaker, the American actor who led the Globe project for decades, Gurr demands that 'live theatre needs the unfamiliar, the frightening. People go to the theatre to be comfortably reassured, but reassurance is not what ought to happen. There must be an element of danger, of uncertainty, or the audience will sleep. More, extra invention was needed. . . . A new and disturbing Shakespeare would be created by taking the plays back to their original theatre.'[10] While this clearly wasn't his intention, it's hard not to note that (save for the last sentence) Gurr could be describing an experimental approach akin to Peter Brook's or Jerzy Grotowski's: a return to the primal frisson of the audience–actor interaction. This suggests that the end goals at the heart of the OP philosophy, this yearning for vital and vibrantly awake audiences at once in tune with the play in the past *and* present, could be equally accomplishable with a stripping down of theatrical elements. With only natural lighting, exposure to the elements and direct address to the audience – among countless other innovations – OP would gain a contemporary edginess by turning to the raw, romanticized, theatricality of the past.

David Crystal, the founder of the other OP (Original Pronunciation) similarly frames his efforts to reconstruct early modern speech as a reclamation of something vital and essential. Recounting the experience of witnessing an OP – in both senses – production of *Romeo and Juliet* at the Globe, Crystal notes that '[i]t was so electrifying to hear the accent *alive* again, in front of an audience, for a whole play', and, as a result, the audience listened intently, thus providing fuel for the actors in a feedback loop engendered by the recreated space and language. Attention, Crystal believes, 'is something which actors have a special sensitivity to, at the Globe, with groundlings all around your feet, a few inches away'.[11] In sum, for Crystal, Original Pronunciation 'reduced the psychological distance between speaker and listener, and to that extent presented a more immediate opportunity to access the speaker's thought'.[12] The implication is that *later* staging practices, far from their origin, have strayed from this immediacy and 'alive' quality; the psychological space has only widened between performer and audience. In a lighter vein, Rob Conkie recounts how his dabbling with 'original-ish practices' in a production of *Othello* yielded not immediate, revelatory brilliance but instead 'ridiculousness, inefficiency, and incompetence' – and yet, ironically, that self-same failure ended up affirming a new kind of theatrical 'magic'.[13] In one telling example, the performer playing Emilia (a man, in deference to the practice in the early modern English theatre of having boys play women) struggled to unpin Desdemona's corset; the stage business far exceeded the time of her speech, so she kept singing 'willow, willow' to cover the blunder. With little to no rehearsal time and no blocking – in keeping with OP conventions – this unforeseen technical mishap occurred for the first time in performance, but, as Conkie explains, it inadvertently 'highlighted Desdemona's beauty and serenity (against all odds) and vulnerability'; the slowdown of dramaturgical action let the play take 'a deep breath for what was about to unfold'.[14] In this moment, the liveness of Original Practices manifested as an explicit overlaying, for the audience, of the production's material reality (an actor is clearly struggling to complete his task) with the play's mimetic reality (a handmaiden pauses as if in uncanny anticipation of tragedy).

And yet to suggest that either OP can lead to a more 'live' experience is to deny the extent to which liveness in the early modern era was not essentialized as primarily theatrical – and to which the early modern theatre was itself *already* mediated. Because theorists of liveness tend to take up case studies from contemporary performance, scant attention has been paid to the experience of liveness in a past era – much less a past era so often held up as the standard-bearer for untrammelled, unmediated theatre. The present volume seeks to correct this oversight by examining early modern performances, in *both* their contemporary and early modern incarnations, to ask a simple question with complicated implications: how does the early modern theatre produce a distinct sense of liveness? After all, contemporary accounts of the theatre in Shakespeare's day do not praise it as a live and immediate art – that description would calcify only after a declinist narrative had been established, generations later. In fact, liveness was found in a much broader spectrum of poetic forms. In the first recorded use of the word 'mimesis' in English, Philip Sidney defines it as 'a representing, a counterfeiting, or figuring forth – to speak metaphorically, a speaking picture'.[15] Sidney's apologia, aimed at zealous Protestant censoriousness, frequently defends 'poesy' – inclusive of verse and theatre – as a more 'lively' art than philosophy or history, capable of a Horatian balance of education and entertainment. Poetry, in this formulation, indexes life itself. In one memorable example, Sidney imagines describing a rhinoceros to someone who has never seen one; such an effort would 'never satisfy his inward conceit with being witness to itself of a true lively knowledge' as much as a painting would; in the same way, poetry was needed to have wisdom 'illuminated or figured forth by the speaking picture of poesy'.[16]

Early modern liveness, then, was not tethered to particular material circumstances; it could emerge from hearing a poem or reading a text. It could also, of course, emerge from the theatre. Thomas Heywood's *Apology for Actors* – like Sidney's tract, a defence against Puritan charges of idolatry – similarly seizes on the salutary, patriotic power of producing a 'lively' effect on audiences. 'What English blood,' he asks, 'seeing the person of any bold English man presented and doth not hugge his fame' or offer 'to him in his hart all prosperous performance, as if the Personator were the man Personated, so bewitching a thing is *lively* and well spirited action?'[17] (sig. B4r, emphasis added). We might be tempted to ascribe a particular premium to theatrical liveness, but as Pascale Aebischer reminds us, the early modern theatre was itself already technologically complex. The nostalgia of a more intimate Shakespearean stage 'does not hold up to scrutiny: theatre buildings themselves are technologies of performance whose affordances have a determining impact on how plays may be staged and viewed within them'.[18] Heywood's celebrated lively impersonation is the result of a highly mediated space, not one more intimate because less adorned. Furthermore, the technological innovations of the past four centuries have in fact fostered *more* intimacy, not less: 'Technologies are deployed as a means of creating intense, and sometimes disturbingly visceral, individual and collective experiences that adapt the types of relationships possible in the early modern theatres for the digital age and a stratified neoliberal social environment.'[19] Aebischer's close examination of lighting techniques reveals how the rise of Stanislavskian acting methods paralleled the advent of technical innovations that can reveal exquisite and subtle details of inward life in the performing body – precisely the kind of 'live' intimacy that Gurr and Crystal ascribe to the early modern theatre's original conditions, not its afterlife.

There is a clear anachronism, as we have implied thus far, in discussing liveness in the early modern era. After all, as Auslander points out, 'live' logically arose in distinction to 'recorded' only when recording became viable.[20] Sidney and Heywood's use of 'lively' is not a temporal distinction so much as it is one of *life* – poetry, in a Platonic sense (but scrubbed of Plato's disapproval), carries with it a trace of the natural vitality it imitates. 'Lively' is closer to today's 'alive,' then; see, for instance, Sebastian, in *Twelfth Night,* recount his father's death by exclaiming 'O, that record is lively in my soul!'[21] However, as Sebastian's outburst indicates, the 'lively'/'live' distinction should not stop us from examining liveness in an era that predates recording technology. For a 'record' to become 'alive' for Sebastian, it takes on a quality of present-ness, of a cognitive life in opposition to his father's corporeal death. The era's use of 'lively' and 'alive' offers us a more capacious and even radical understanding of liveness, one that allows for mediated presence to exist in a variety of experiences. Liveness, in this sense, remains an *effect* of engagement, not an unattainable horizon; just as *Dream* can produce the sensation of liveness, so too can a play or a text.

The literature of the era was alive to this possibility, toying with the temporal and phenomenological affects of the ever-present *now* created in the interaction of art and subject. Thus Lear's famous lament for Cordelia: 'O thou'lt come no more, / Never, never, never, never, never' marks the passage of time, each foot notching another moment in which she cannot come back to life, even though the text itself exists in no fixed temporality.[22] The lines keep track of the *listener's* experience of time by creating the illusion of time passing in the fictional world. More playfully, Jonson's induction to *Bartholomew Faire* operates with the conceit that the play itself is delayed due to a rip in one actor's stockings; the first line is from the exasperated Stage-Keeper: 'Gentlemen, have a little patience, they are e'en upon coming, instantly.'[23] More than simply metatheatrical – though it is that too – the moment makes the audience complicit in feeling like they are privy to the *true* present moment, just as 'real' as the furtive actions of Emilia biding time while unpinning Desdemona: a liveness-effect produced through the technology of the stage.

It is this effect, broadly construed across different media, that concerns the chapters contained here. The recent pandemic has made this exploration all the more timely, though, as we have shown, this concept has long been debated, since the early modern era itself. As for that term, we interpret 'early modern' to include non-Western and non-traditional performance practices, asking how they employ embodiment, materiality, temporality and perception to impress on audiences a sensation of presence – a term that, like liveness, originates not in an essential or formal make-up of a work but through the alchemy of performative contact. The volume's contributors vary in their approaches. Some seek to recover the material texture of the original event; others explore performative legacy in multimedia adaptations; others still see how a global, capacious and open rethinking of the period challenges our understanding of what it means to be 'live' at all.

In Part One, 'Proximity', contributors grapple with how perceived physical distance between an audience and a performance cements or shifts conceptions of liveness. Rebecca Bushnell examines virtual performances of early modern plays and how liveness might be interpreted in these digital spaces. Stephanie Shirilan unpacks the potential of shared breath as memory by using early modern natural philosophy and Cleopatra's speech as keys to understanding contemporary virtual performance. Thomas Cartelli uses two recent versions of *Macbeth* – Kit Monkman's 2018 film and Big Telly's 2020 Zoom production – as examples of encounters with the boundary between acting in an analogue past and a digital future.

Part Two, 'Performance', considers liveness as a function of theatrical production, in either virtual or actual spaces. Aneta Mancewicz confronts liveness through an analysis of – and recounting of dramaturgical experience with – virtual and augmented reality Shakespeare adaptations. Elizabeth E. Tavares examines OP in action at the 2017 WIL festival, which employed early modern rehearsal methods in its productions. Murat Öğütcü considers the presence of Shakespeare in the contemporary Turkish theatrical repertoire and how Turkish adaptations resonate with contemporary politics.

Part Three, 'Premonition', presents the possibility that liveness is an interaction between the past, present and future and that the experience of liveness may reveal glances, whether perceived or actual, into that future. Kenneth Molloy considers the theatricality of early modern Islamic conceptions of life, exemplified in the hagiography Kāshifī's *Rawḍat al-Shuhadāʾ*, a source of the *taʾziyeh* play. Gina Di Salvo traces the development – and speculates as to the audience's experience – of the 'blazing star' as both a stage effect and a plot element that presages as an omen onstage. Jonathan Gil Harris considers the profane religiosity of Hindi film audience behaviours in India and this dynamic's relationship to early modern theatrical audiences.

Taken as a whole, these essays, rather than focus on either dramatic texts or theatrical events as primary sites of interpretive authority, examine the intimate and ephemeral experience of early modern theatre in its diverse manifestations. Liveness, as we have implied here, is not a phenomenon unique to the brick-and-mortar theatre experience but instead drafted by a feeling of copresence, which can be sparked at any moment when an audience encounters a piece of art.

Notes

1 'Dream Q&A', *Royal Shakespeare Company*, https://www.rsc.org.uk/support/supporters-room/get-closer/dream-q-a, accessed 15 January 2022.

2 Philip Auslander, *Liveness: Performance in a Mediatized Culture* (New York: Routledge, 1999 [2008]), 56.
3 Ibid., 43.
4 Peggy Phelan, *Unmarked: The Politics of Performance* (New York: Routledge, 1993), esp. 146–66.
5 Lindsay Brandon Hunter, *Playing Real: Mimesis, Media, and Mischief* (Evanston: Northwestern University Press), 2021, xiv.
6 'Live Performance and Gaming Technology Come Together to Explore the Future for Audiences and Live Theatre', *Royal Shakespeare Company*, https://www.rsc.org.uk/press/releases/live-performance-and-gaming-technology-come-together-to-explore-the-future-for-audiences-and-live-theatre, accessed 15 January 2022.
7 W. B. Worthen, *Shakespeare, Technicity, Theatre* (Cambridge: Cambridge UP, 2020), 15.
8 Sarah Bay-Cheng, 'Theatre Is Media: Some Principles for a Digital Historiography of Performance', *Theater* 42, no. 2 (2012): 35.
9 Andrew Gurr, 'Staging the Globe', in *Shakespeare's Globe Rebuilt*, ed. J. R. Mulryne and Margaret Shewring (Cambridge: Cambridge University Press, 1997), 168.
10 Andrew Gurr, 'Shakespeare's Globe: A History of Reconstructions and Some Reasons for Trying', in *Shakespeare's Globe Rebuilt*, ed. J. R. Mulryne and Margaret Shewring (Cambridge: Cambridge University Press, 1997), 27–50, 3232.
11 David Crystal, *Pronouncing Shakespeare: The Globe Experiment* (Cambridge: Cambridge University Press, 2019), 136, emphasis added.
12 Ibid., 142.
13 Rob Conkie, '*Othello*, Original Practices: A Photographic Essay', *Critical Survey* 28, no. 2 (Summer 2016): 137.
14 Ibid., 142.
15 Philip Sidney, 'The Defence of Poesy', in *The Major Works*, ed. Katherine Duncan-Jones (Oxford: Oxford University Press, 2002), 217.
16 Ibid., 222.
17 Thomas Heywood, *An Apology for Actors* (London, 1612).
18 Pascale Aebischer, *Shakespeare, Spectatorship, and the Technologies of Performance* (Cambridge: Cambridge University Press, 2020), 13.
19 Ibid., 3.

20 Philip Auslander, 'Digital Liveness: A Historico-Philosophical Perspective', *PAJ: A Journal of Performance and Art* 34, no. 3 (September 2012): 5.
21 William Shakespeare, *Twelfth Night*, ed. J. M. Lothian and T. W. Craik (London: Arden Shakespeare, 2007 [1975]), 5.1.244.
22 William Shakespeare, *King Lear*, ed. R. A. Foakes (Walton-on-Thames: Arden Shakespeare, 1997), 5.3.305–6.
23 Ben Jonson, 'Bartholomew Faire', in *The Alchemist and Other Plays*, ed. Gordon Campbell (Oxford: Oxford University Press, 1995), Induction 1.

PART ONE

Proximity

1

Liveness in virtual early modern theatre

Rebecca Bushnell

As the Covid-19 pandemic was easing during the summer of 2021, Anglo-American theatres returned to performing Shakespeare in place and in person. As a first step, to stage *The Comedy of Errors*, the Royal Shakespeare Company (RSC) built the Lydia and Manfred Gorvy Garden Theatre, a temporary outdoor structure on the banks of the Avon. The director Philip Breen spoke then about the value of being in a 'shared space', with the 'actors being able to see the audience as well as hearing them. Sharing the same weather and the same sky. It might make the audience feel differently about their relationship with the play when they are not sat in a dark room merely observing it, but more actively participating in it'. He also contrasted spectating in this theatre with the experience of 'digital realities'. In digital realities, he insisted, spectators are 'gods' but alone, whereas in the physical world we are together: the play needs an audience, for 'We can't make it make sense without you, the audience'.[1] Breen thus implied that in-person performance makes meaning through shared experience, whereas meaning fails in a digital one, where the passive spectator is disconnected from the performers and other audience members.

One may agree with Breen when joyfully returning to collective in-person events, whether in small family groups or massive gatherings. That said, his assumptions about virtual versus physical performance can certainly be questioned by more deeply investigating live Shakespeare performances during the pandemic.[2] When physical theatres were closed, the RSC itself laboured mightily to connect audience and performers in 'digital reality'. For example, in *Dream*, a virtual performance inspired by *A Midsummer Night's Dream*, the company attempted to recreate a sense of liveness by having viewers synchronously interact with a screened performance by creating digitally generated 'fireflies' to lead Puck through the forest and 'seeds' to restore a landscape devastated by a storm.[3]

In staging *Dream*, the RSC drew on many precedents of virtual Shakespeare performance that involved both live streaming and synchronous interaction between players and spectators through social media commentary or gamelike interaction. These earlier moves to incorporate digital technologies into live performances of early modern plays had already blurred many distinctions between what is real and virtual, reminding us, as Sita Popat has argued, that 'Theatre has always been a space of virtuality. The action on the stage exists as neither what it is actually nor what it is pretending to be; instead, it bridges the actual and the imaginary to create a virtual world in which performers and viewers are complicit'. New technologies extend the theatrical imaginary beyond 'physical restrictions', with 'people, environments, and objects interacting and interlacing with the action onstage, or even replacing the stage altogether'.[4]

Responding in 1999 to Peggy Phelan's claims that only embodied or physical performance could be considered 'live', in *Liveness: Performance in a Mediatized Culture* Philip Auslander questioned the distinction between what we usually think of as live and mediatized performances in film, video and digital platforms. Long before the explosion of the Internet and live streaming, Auslander understood that liveness can be reproduced in what he calls 'a technologically mediated relationship among human beings', as well as interactions with non-human agents like machines: he observed that 'To the extent that websites and other virtual entities respond to us in real time, they *feel* live to us, and this may be the kind of liveness we now value'.[5] Following Auslander and more recent theorists of liveness, this chapter focuses on how different modes of virtual Shakespeare have sought to generate liveness through interaction. In particular, I will argue that in these modes of interaction, versions of virtual Shakespeare have reflected or at least gestured towards the circumstances and interactive practices of early modern English theatre performance. These factors include, among others, the spatial features of the indoor and outdoor stages, early modes of inviting audience participation and the temporality of performance. In this sense, the transformation of early modern theatre into digital forms pushes Auslander's thinking further by aligning historical theatrical practices with virtual modalities.

I will first briefly consider the general arguments about liveness in virtual performance, beginning with Auslander and Phelan and extending to present theorists of liveness. I will then review different virtual modes of interaction with Shakespeare plays from the recent past, including live broadcasts and filmed versions, uses of social media, video game adaptations and experiments with virtual reality (VR), focusing in particular on how these modes hark back to aspects of the interactivity and sense of liveness that characterized early modern English stage performance. I will then explore what happened during the pandemic when all performances moved to virtual platforms that sought to evoke liveness through engagement or interaction when there were no alternatives.

Virtual theatre and liveness

Current discussions of liveness usually begin with Peggy Phelan's insistence in *Unmarked: The Politics of Performance* that 'Performance's only life is in the present. Performance cannot be saved, recorded, documented, or otherwise participate in the circulation of representations: once it does so, it becomes something other than performance'. For Phelan, 'live' 'implicates the real through the presence of living bodies' and involves how 'a limited number of people in a specific time/space frame can have an experience of value which leaves no visible trace afterward'.[6] That is, liveness is exclusive to in-person, singular performances done by physical bodies in a particular place and time. As discussed elsewhere in this volume, in contrast, Auslander attributes liveness to a wider range of digital and analogue events. In an essay published in 2021, he clarified this claim:

> To summarize my argument: some technological artifact – a computer, Website, network, or virtual entity – makes a claim

on us, its audience, to be considered as live.... In this analysis, liveness ... is an interaction produced through our engagement with the object and our willingness to accept its claim.[7]

Auslander here thus moves away from the ontological claims about liveness that have characterized much of this debate and instead locates liveness in a relationship with or experience of an 'object'. Many recent scholars on liveness have similarly rejected a binary of performance by human bodies in a shared space versus a recording or digital event to focus instead on interaction as well as immediacy.[8]

Centring liveness in experience or interaction as opposed to physical presence evokes the image of early modern English theatres that emphasized audience responsiveness rather than just passive watching. Many scholars of early modern theatre have drawn on Robert Weimann's influential idea of the early modern stage as divided conceptually (and to some extent physically) between the *locus*, the area in which the fictive action appears happening in another place and time, and the *platea*, the space where the actors speak to or interact with the audience.[9] Pascale Aebischer describes the *platea* as 'located in the here and now of the performance [for] a specific set of emancipated spectators ... who, through their collaborative engagement with the performers and responsiveness to technologies of performance, are able [to interact within] an event for which they share responsibility'.[10] Following Weimann, many critics have written about the ways in which the early modern English stage thus functioned as an interactive playing space.[11] Gina Bloom argues that 'encouraging audiences to feel as if they were active participants in the fictions staged before them was vital for London's first commercial theaters, which had to introduce their audiences to a relatively new way of consuming drama', even while they technically remained just spectators of the action played out before them.[12]

Weimann's notion of the *locus* and *platea* also draws attention to the specific temporal conditions of performance in these stages, where the action that takes place in the present world of the *platea* is simultaneously mapped on the 'other place and time' represented in the *locus*. The spectator's dizzying experience of what constitutes the past and present at once opens up a space for engagement in the interstices of time. That is, 'liveness' connected to the notion of the present does not exclude the experience of other senses of time.

While early modern theatre may appear to envelop us in the present moment, in Matthew Wagner's words, its power lies in 'its marked constitution of past and future, its trumpeting of its beginning and end not as they line up sequentially, but as they stack simultaneously'.[13]

Many scholars and practitioners see the recreated Globe Theatre in London producing those effects of connection, interaction and temporal complexity posited for these early stages. In recounting the theatre's history, Joe Falocco argues that 'Part of the Globe's success is due to the power and responsibility it grants audience. The proximity and visibility of playgoers connects them to the performers in a way not possible in traditional venues, and the absence of lighting effects and elaborate sets means that no production can proceed without the consent and participation of the public'.[14] William Worthen has offered an important critique of these assumptions,[15] but commercial amphitheatres like the Globe surely did blur the boundaries between audience and actors, through both the open air setting and the audience members' proximity to the stage.

Contrary to Breen's insistence that we are isolated in our 'digital realities', I think that virtual Shakespeare productions do indeed make live demands on the spectator, insofar as, in Gabriella Giannachi's words, 'Virtual theatre constructs itself through the interaction between the viewer and the work of art which allows the viewer to be present in both the real and the virtual environment'.[16] That said, the modes of interaction do vary. As Matthew Reason and Anja Mølle Lindelof have put it, audience attention and 'processes of materializing in acts of performance, acts of making, acts of archiving and acts of remembering' may themselves constitute forms of engagement.[17] Audiences of a virtual performance may also be afforded more intentional participation, for example, with live streaming combined with chat or tweeting. Spectators of virtual theatre productions have also been engaged using practices adapted from gaming that invite them to be actors as well. The rest of this chapter explores the affordances of all these modes that can make virtual theatre feel intensely live.

Live streaming, gaming and VR

In pursuing liveness in virtual Shakespeare, scholars have most closely studied broadcasts of in-person productions, primarily by the RSC and the National Theatre in the UK; NT Live began in 2009, and the RSC started live-streaming productions in 2013. They first produced these films as synchronous broadcasts to cinemas that were then archived and streamed later to both cinemas and homes.[18] Currently, most critics of these productions agree that they are experienced in some way as live, when 'digitised and remediated' performances 'carry on performing in the present of the online environment even as the live event to which it is related has receded into the past'.[19] In particular, Erin Sullivan has argued that both the original streaming of theatrical productions into cinemas and their transition to home screens generated 'their own sense of eventful connectedness among audience members, even when they are physically distant from one another',[20] as an important feature of liveness. More recently, live streaming has been accompanied by synchronous chat and Twitter, which further connect the audience members with both the production and each other, creating a sense of not only presence and immediacy but also collectivity, where, in the words of Eirini Nedelkopoulou, 'liveness is regarded as an encounter, a gathering'.[21]

Interactive video games offer another form of live digital engagement with Shakespeare. Critics writing about Shakespeare video games mostly look at them as forms of adaptation that also allow for the gamer to transform the plays.[22] Here I will focus on the ways in which that engagement produces liveness as an effect of performance. Adapting early modern plays into games makes more sense than it might appear at first glance, given what some scholars have described as the centrality of games to this period's theatre.[23] Gina Bloom makes a powerful case for the ways in which games and gaming informed that theatre, since 'The overlap between games and theatrical plays was a foregone conclusion for premodern people'.[24] Bloom reminds us that gamelike interactivity preceded digital gaming, when 'early modern theaters, even as they appeared to restrict physical forms of interaction, encouraged their audiences to play with, around, and through the dramas presented onstage'.[25]

Whether in a physical theatre or on the screen, gaming is all about living in the present, while possibly knowing both the past and future. As Christopher Hanson has observed, 'Games require constant input from the player to sustain a continuous feedback loop between the player's interaction and the game's mechanics.

This mode of liveness is characterized not just by the game's operative state but also by the player's active involvement via the game's interface and play mechanics'.[26] While sometimes video game present time feels slow, it speeds up further when a player encounters a 'quick-time event' and must act immediately, whether in dialogue or deadly conflict, to move the game forward.[27] Jesper Juul describes such moments as an intense 'sense of happening *now* when you play. Pressing a key [or a button] influences the game world, which then logically and intuitively has to be happening in the same now'.[28] At the same time, however, the player may be offered an opportunity to go back in game-time to repeat an event, especially if one's panicked responses have resulted in death, in order to correct mistakes and direct future actions. In these passages, present time is thus layered with past and future time, when the player acts knowing the outcome of an action or choice.

Of the Shakespeare video games created to date, the most temporally complex that makes liveness a theme is *Elsinore*, a game developed by Katie Chironis and designed by Connor Fallon and their team at Golden Glitch. In this game the play's avatar is Ophelia, who is given the opportunity to avert *Hamlet*'s catastrophes. As the website describes the game:

> On a summer night, the Danish noblewoman Ophelia awakens from a terrible vision: in four days, everyone in Elsinore Castle will be dead. Even worse, she's been thrown into a time loop from which she cannot escape. Forced to relive the same four days over and over again, Ophelia determines to do everything in her power to change the future. *Elsinore* is a time-looping adventure game set in the world of Shakespeare's *Hamlet*. *Elsinore* combines strong social simulation elements, a dynamic story that reacts immediately to player decisions, and a world full of diverse characters with secrets to uncover. Can Ophelia prevent the tragedy that lies before her?[29]

Here the gameplay involves the spectator in an experience redolent of liveness while also intertwined with the past. In the gameplay, one is always acting in the present since each iteration of Ophelia's action is unique. Over the course of the simulated four days (considerably speeded up), Ophelia dies, and the game returns to a moment in which she awakes to begin again. At each awakening, the player/Ophelia retains the information learned from her previous day, which is then used to influence future actions. The player is always in the present, acting live, while at the same time accessing the past to change the future. In this sense, video game performance does echo the temporality of performance of early modern theatre established in Weimann's ideas of the temporality of the *locus* versus the *platea*, especially if the audience comes to the theatre knowing something of the play's plot.

The temporality of video game Shakespeare finds its parallel in recent experiments in VR Shakespeare, which offer spatial as well as temporal immersion in ways that evoke precedents of early theatrical performance. To date, forays into VR Shakespeare have been rare since this is both a costly and difficult undertaking. What has been done shows how VR theatre can enhance interaction and presence, further transforming what it means to be engaged live in a performance of an early modern play. As Peter Rubin has asserted, 'Presence is the absolute foundation of virtual reality, and in VR, it's the absolute foundation of connection – connection with yourself, with an idea, with another human, even connection with artificial intelligence.'[30] Once you don your VR headset, you are immersed in another world while still present in your own. You become a part of the world that is represented while also a spectator of it.[31] In VR, one experiences the illusion of being embodied in a virtual world inhabited by other simulated bodies; when transformed into an avatar, your own body is both real and unreal, both your own and not your own.[32]

The most basic applications of VR to early modern theatre performance have involved representing theatre spaces. For example, the American Shakespeare Center has created a 360-degree immersive documentary introduction to their Blackfriars playhouse that puts the viewer in the position of a spectator of a play in action.[33] In this setting, viewers can turn around 360 degrees, although overall their positions are fixed. This virtual experiment provides a sense of the proportion and sight lines of this stage, meant to evoke the stages of indoor performances in Shakespeare's London; however, as it stands now, the viewer is limited to witnessing two *Hamlet* soliloquies.

In contrast, Steven Maler's hour-long 2019 VR film *Hamlet 360: Thy Father's Spirit*, produced by Sensorium and featuring the Commonwealth Shakespeare Company for WGBH Boston, offers a full-scale, if significantly redacted, VR version of *Hamlet* that invites a spectator into a performance.[34] This one-hour version of the play is set in a ruined theatre littered with hundreds of random objects, including an old car, toys and dozens of lamps. Furniture is loosely grouped into room-like spaces that serve as the settings for individual scenes. As with other 360 VR experiences, once spectators don their headsets, they are placed in the middle of the action. They can move their viewpoint in 360 degrees by turning around or just moving their heads where they may see other characters conferring or spying – for indeed action may be happening behind them as well as in front. The director controls overall changes of location about the stage, marking changes of scene with a fadeout in a dissolve of mist. Thus, the director and cinematographer partially influence point of view and the viewer's orientation in the playing space, but the spectator also has some freedom. While the production itself is a film, each iteration of *Hamlet 360* feels live, not only in the sense that viewing filmed or live-streamed version of Shakespeare happens 'live' but also because the viewer can direct the perspective on the action and thus produce a unique event.[35]

In inviting a spectator into a fully realized illusion of three-dimensional space, *Hamlet 360* tempts the spectator into trying to engage with objects and people there. While the makers of *Hamlet 360* did not aspire to gamelike interactivity, they did attempt to draw the viewer into the action. Seeing *Hamlet* very much as 'a father and son story',[36] the creators decided to make the viewer literally inhabit 'Thy Father's Spirit' as the omnipresent ghost of King Hamlet, who interjects his presence and his words at decisive moments. At perhaps five discrete moments, the otherworldly voice of the ghost emanates from the viewer, addressing characters (usually Hamlet alone) who react in amazement and wonder. The ghost also makes at least three appearances to the viewer's eye: two reflections in mirrors during his speeches and one wordless sequence at the play's close, when we witness him walking among the dead, seemingly reflecting on the carnage his vengeance has wrought. Further, two significant moments in *Hamlet 360* seem to go beyond just observation or presence to grant the ghost and thus the spectator a kind of agency, even though there is no real interaction with the play world. In one moment in the final scene of the duel, Laertes is distracted, apparently by a vision or at least a sense of the ghost's presence. This hesitation allows Hamlet to stab him (while it is not the final blow). When Gertrude drinks the poison, she also looks directly at the spectator as the ghost, implying a kind of awareness or connection. In these two instances as the ghost, the spectator feels a connection with the action, and even a kind of effect on it, thus enhancing liveness through the illusion of interactivity.

Hamlet 360 thus reminds us that a virtual performance can be understood as 'live' insofar as it allows a spectator to feel involved, whether with other spectators or with the events of the play performed. Live streaming of productions and the synchronous use of social media create that sense of shared experience in the present, even when what is being seen is a recorded performance. In turn, gaming or presence in a VR production offers the possibility of real-time interactivity. That interactivity may be illusory, indeed, but it feels real and locates the spectator in the present of performance.

Virtual early modern theatre in a time of pandemic

During the pandemic, streaming of recorded and Shakespeare productions onto screens escalated as companies struggled to remain relevant when all theatres were closed. The Globe Theatre in London soon made its full repertoire of recorded performances available on demand, and the RSC allowed viewing of six of their recorded plays on the BBC IPlayer. As the pandemic period progressed, theatre companies experimented with creating new Shakespeare performances using film, Zoom, VR and gamification, striving to reproduce the sense of immediacy and interactivity associated with in-person early modern theatre performance. This chapter focuses on a few examples done by theatre companies in the United States and the United Kingdom that I attended, but they represent only a fraction of the work that was made at this fraught time.[37]

Some companies created original filmed Shakespeare productions designed to generate a sense of presence and immediacy even when not broadcast live. For example, during the spring of 2020, the Wilma Theatre in Philadelphia produced an adaptation of *Hamlet* called *Fat Ham*, written by James Ijames and co-directed by Morgan Green. Performed by an all-Black cast, this version reimagined the play as a family barbecue set in the American South, transforming it from a tragedy of revenge to a celebration of Black and queer identity and resistance to authority. The Wilma had originally intended to stage this performance in person but pivoted to create a filmed version on site. The camerawork contributed to a sense of audience presence by following the actors through the garden and the exterior of the house where the scenes took place: for example, travelling up the stairs behind the actors onto a deck as if one were joining the barbecue feast. The actors also performed their soliloquies by directly addressing the camera, framed by the full screen, thus implicitly locating the viewer in the playing space, as if in dialogue with the audience in the *platea*.

While of course such moves are established cinematic techniques meant to create a sense of presence and liveness in filmed performance, what made *Fat Ham* distinctive was its being recorded outdoors. As Morgan Green recounts the story of how it was acted and filmed:

> Twenty-four of us travelled to Schuyler, Virginia in the tail end of winter to rehearse and film this piece for five weeks, becoming intimate with the challenges of the eleven long takes that constitute this film. Rather than filming each scene over and over until we achieved what we wanted (as would happen on a traditional film set), we filmed the entire play continuously each time we captured, progressing with the setting sun in order to maintain the feeling of continuous action as you would experience in the theater.[38]

Through this mode of continuous filming, they aimed to reproduce something like 'theatrical time', in which the flow of the action feels like lived time but was also aligned with the time of day, 'progressing with the setting sun'. In doing so, *Fat Ham* thus also evoked the temporality of performances in the early modern amphitheatres, foregrounding the time of the *platea*, as if the story were happening in a lived moment of time. That temporality, in turn, emphasized the contemporary feeling of the plot itself in its radical rethinking of *Hamlet*'s plot. That said, the viewers of this filmed version did not experience the performance synchronously: rather, it was to be seen 'on demand', and so in that sense, the contemporaneity was an illusion.

Other theatre companies took a different approach to generating filmed pandemic performance using Zoom and other web-based conferencing software to produce synchronous rather than asynchronous performances in virtual space.[39] In most of these performances, the actors were each confined to their own homes but interacted with each other to create the illusion of their being together, while the spectators still perceived them as inhabiting their Zoom 'boxes' on the screen. However, during the 2020–2021 season, the San Francisco Shakespeare Festival company pushed Zoom further by performing *King Lear* and *Pericles* using the technology of 'unified virtual space'. In this process, the actors each played their parts in their own homes against green screens; having first laboriously rehearsed the blocking and body movements to simulate interaction, they were brought together simultaneously in one screen space against a virtual background.[40] As the company's website describes the process, when the actors' live performances 'were composited in real time onto digital scenic backgrounds and broadcast to the audience', they created 'the thrill of viewing a live, ensemble performance on our YouTube channel, Facebook Live, and Twitch'.[41] Liveness here was thus linked to synchronicity through the broadcast medium, while, as with *Fat Ham*, the production also used the familiar techniques of direct address adapted from the conventions of Shakespeare performance as well as film, linking liveness to proximity as well as immediacy.[42]

Aware of the challenges of still generating liveness through film, the SF Shakespeare Festival began each of its similar virtual performance of *Pericles* with a live trivia game, gesturing towards audience participation in the 'live event'. This prequel was just one version of what other theatre companies have tried to generate liveness through audience input, beyond the use of social media or chat accompanying a performance. Direct address in live broadcast may generate liveness by drawing the spectator through the frame of the screen, and live chat may create a sense of audience presence, but increasingly, virtual theatre has employed forms of gaming to create the kind of interactivity that has been said to generate liveness. In one example, in collaboration with Manchester International Festival, Marshmallow Laser Feast and the Philharmonia Orchestra, as well as Epic Games, in March 2021 the RSC presented their *Dream*, a live-streamed virtual adaptation of *A Midsummer Night's Dream* in which actors in motion capture suits were transformed into animated avatars inhabiting a forest.[43] In this adaptation, the plot amounts to following Puck through that forest in search of the other *Midsummer* fairies; in the process, Puck passes through a storm that devastates the landscape. During the performance, the spectator's viewpoint alternated between watching Puck and perceiving the forest from Puck's point of view, which did help to create a sense of immersion in the playing space. In an effort to enhance that effect, the production involved the audience further at certain points by offering them first the chance to join in as a 'firefly' and later to plant a seed (both generated using a drag-and-drop mechanism in a sidebar on the screen). The premise was that activating one's firefly would light Puck's path through the forest; then in the end, the audience was asked to use their seeds to help revive the natural world. Most reviewers of the production found this gamelike interaction underwhelming; not only did it distract from an otherwise compelling production, but it also struck me as a little too much like the audience's clapping to revive Tinkerbell in *Peter Pan*.[44] Of course, that interaction did not really affect the play's events, other than generating the visible spots of light. However, the opportunity for the spectator to interact in real time with the live streaming did represent a step towards creating the sense of acting in the 'now' connected with game-time.

The tentative gesture of being an active 'firefly' in *Dream* makes the experiment undertaken in the VR 'Under Presents' *Tempest* more striking, insofar as there the spectator participated in the performance as an actor.[45] The innovative games studio Tender Claws already created a VR multiplayer game called 'The Under Presents', in which spectators as avatars interact live with both each other and actors.[46] In 2020–2021, they pivoted to stage an adaptation of *The Tempest* using the same platform. The fictional premise was that it was a version of Shakespeare's play moved online because of the pandemic. As the 'final script' describes it:

> While sheltering in place in the Hollywood Hills, an actor, who was to play 'Prospero' in a postponed production of *The Tempest*, takes the audience through the highlights, dreams, and private imagining of the show. The line between reality, virtual reality, and fiction blurs as players are 'cast' as Prospero's spirits. The players must interact with the actor, magic, and the set to help realize a virtual version of the play.[47]

Each ticketed performance of *Tempest* took place at a distinct time and lasted approximately an hour.[48]

The Tender Claws' 'Under Presents' *Tempest* was certainly the most absorbing virtual performance I have ever experienced. At the appointed time I donned my Oculus Quest headset and entered a virtual theatre, called 'The Decameron'. I was attending in the persona of my avatar, a conical body with stretchy black hands and a mask that was a means of casting spells; I could not speak, but I could move through the space, gesture and manipulate objects. I first wandered around the theatre lobby, interacting with the other audience members and objects in the lobby, and then entered into the performance itself, encountering the actor as well as my fellow spectators. The actor, who spoke both in her (assumed) personal identity and increasingly as Prospero, assigned each audience member a name and taught us to do spells with our hands and masks. We were then transported to *The Tempest*'s island.

Once on the island, the spectators participated in four *The Tempest*-derived scenes in which they played an active role when called upon to interact with the virtual environment and with each other. In the first, in Prospero's cell, they had to pick up an object which triggered a memory related to *The Tempest*'s backstory. In the second episode, the spectators were assigned the roles of Miranda and Ferdinand (I was Ferdinand) and asked to play out a scene of their first encounter (while the Prospero actor voiced the dialogue). In the next scene, called the 'Feast/Harpy scene' and associated with *The Tempest* Act 3.3, the audience members were given visible neck ruffles that linked them with Alonso and his followers, and devoured the banquet; then the actor transformed into a gigantic harpy who 'roasted' the players' actions saying, 'Prospero's justice has been served'. In the ensuing episode called 'The Celebration', while two of the actor-spectators resumed their roles as the lovers, the other players became 'spirits', and 'Prospero invite[d] the spirits (players) to put on a Masque for the young lovers as Greek gods. The theme of the masque is fertility, bounty . . . players use restoration magic to restore the bounty of the land'. The performance ended when 'everyone ha[d] a dance party and [got] sauced around the fire in the Hollywood Hills. Prospero [said] a meaningful epilogue about setting the players (his spirits) free and giving up his magic: this is double speak for virtual actor/audience'.[49]

These events produced liveness intensely not only by happening synchronously but also because they required the audience members to act or interact at Prospero's insistence. There was no such thing as passively watching this *Tempest*. As Erin Sullivan has commented on her own experience of a performance:

> In this brave new world, the person who most surprised me was *me*, and the thing that most astonished me was the deep, magnetic focus I felt as I became a spectator both to the show in front of me and my own presence within it. Visiting 'The Under Presents: *Tempest*' reminded me of what it feels like to stop paying attention to everything a little bit and to submit to a single work of art totally and unreservedly.[50]

When I had to respond to my 'Miranda' when we met, I was acutely conscious of my being in that moment, pressured to improvise a means of communicating with her in my avatar's body. Further, since the two Miranda/Ferdinand pairs were competing as to whom would be chosen to play them in the final Celebration scene, I was conscious that my acting was being judged. At this point this play was indeed very much a game as well as a performance, with all the temporal immediacy experienced in video gaming.

These kinds of encounters in *Tempest* enhanced the sense of liveness not only because they demanded attention but also because they provided the illusion of physical connection. I did find the presence of my Miranda uncanny, when we stared into each other's face/mask and 'grasped' each other's hands; in the Celebration scene, we embraced each other. As Popat has observed, 'Touch is identified as a contributing factor in the establishment of presence, yet it is the action involved in reaching out to touch rather than in the achievement of contact that provides the constituting effect';[51] that is, in VR, the actual sensation of touch is not as important as the gesture itself in contributing to a sense of being in the moment in a place and time. In this sense, the 'Under Presents' *Tempest* approximated the kind of embodiment that is more traditionally associated with liveness, that is, with bodily presence.[52] If VR can provide a sense of presence through immersion in a simulated environment, it can also transform your sense of your body in place, not just through seeing but also through doing and connecting.

The use of my body and hands, of course, was complicated, because the relationship of my body and that of my avatar was not a natural one. My hands were transformed through the mechanism of the Oculus Touch controllers into my avatar's hands, which had a life of their own; since I was mute, I had to speak with those hands. Tara Ahmadinejad, a consultant to *Tempest,* has described this kind of 'acting in VR as closer to puppetry or commedia dell'arte'.[53] Thus, not only can VR performance adumbrate the conditions of occupying the stage through locating a body in three-dimensional space, but it can also mimic the vocabulary of gesture theatre historians have associated with early modern acting styles.[54]

Tender Claws is a gaming studio, not a company devoted to producing early modern theatre. To what extent then is their *Tempest* significant as a version of Shakespeare's play, as opposed to just a Shakespeare-themed VR multiplayer game? Its most powerful connection to *The Tempest* lies in its evoking magic, when it grants the audience members the capacity to produce their own effects, far beyond *Dream*'s mechanical generation of fireflies and seeds. The final script for the performance identifies both magic and control as key themes of the project and the play itself: both 'The power of the magician/trickster guide and what control they have over the experience/agency of the audience', and 'illusion/reality, magic created from the beholders perspective of reality'.[55] Erin Sullivan writes that 'The result was a *Tempest* that not only made me feel part of the magic in a way I hadn't before, but also made me feel part of myself in a way that was at once estranging and remarkable'.[56] Like the RSC *Dream* and Shakespeare-based video games, this *Tempest* gamified Shakespeare's play, but the gaming itself became part of what we understand as the ineffable creative power of performance, that power that Shakespeare's play attributes to Prospero and Ariel alone.

In a review of 'Under Presents' *Tempest*, Alexis Soloski asks, 'Is this a brave new world for live performance? Or just another app?'[57] The same question can be asked about the future of virtual Shakespeare performance. In the short term, virtual performance in platforms like VR will certainly be constrained by the limited access that people have to the technology that allows them to participate and the sophistication of that technology. However, as this brief survey has suggested, the pandemic crisis spurred creators to innovate and adapt technology to new ways of theatre-making, and surely there is no going back, even when people are eager to return to physical theatres. The experience of pandemic theatre has accustomed audiences and actors alike to what it means to feel live in virtual space and to connect with each other there. Virtual theatre has shown itself to be adaptable to the performance of early modern theatre in particular, in its ability to produce at least the illusion of close proximity and interaction that, along with synchronicity, have been identified as essential to liveness. The use of new technologies has taken Auslander's insights about the relationship of interaction and a sense of liveness to another level, insofar as they have enabled forms of interaction that can transcend just 'feeling' to become 'real' in new ways.

Notes

1 Phillip Breen, 'An Opening Night Like No Other', https://www.rsc.org.uk/news/an-opening-night-like-no-other.

2 While the topic of this chapter more broadly is virtual early modern theatre, all of my examples will be taken from Shakespeare.

3 See Martin Barker, 'Coming a(live), A Prolegomenon to Any Future Research on "Liveness"', in *Experiencing Liveness in Contemporary Performance: Interdisciplinary Perspectives*, ed. Matthew Reason and Anje Mølle Lindelof (New York and London: Routledge, 2017), 22–3, on notions of what makes up liveness: copresence, simultaneity, risk and audience-impact.

4 Sita Popat, 'Missing in Action: Embodied Experience and Virtual Reality', *Theatre Journal* 68, no. 3 (2016): 357–78; 357.

5 Philip Auslander, *Liveness: Performance in a Mediatized Culture*, 2nd edn. (New York: Routledge, 2008), 79.

6 Peggy Phelan, *Unmarked: The Politics of Performance* (New York: Routledge, 1993), 146–9.

7 Philip Auslander, 'Digital Liveness: A Historico-Philosophical Perspective', *PAJ: A Journal of Performance and Art* 34, no. 3 (2012): 3–11; 9.

8 See, for example, Thomas Cartelli, *Reenacting Shakespeare in the Shakespeare Aftermath: The Intermedial Turn and the Turn to Embodiment* (London: Palgrave Macmillan, 2019); Susan Davis, 'Liveness, Mediation and Immediacy: Innovative Technology Use in Process and Performance', *RiDE: The Journal of Applied Theatre*

and *Performance* 17, no. 4 (2012): 501–16; David Cameron, Michael Anderson, and Rebecca Wotzko, *Drama and Digital Arts Cultures* (London: Methuen, 2017), 29, 'Liveness, digital or otherwise, is not an objective or natural condition in the world but a subjective experience'.

9   Robert Weimann, *Shakespeare and the Popular Tradition in the Theater: Studies in the Social Dimension of Dramatic Form and Function*, ed. Robert Schwartz (Baltimore: Johns Hopkins University Press, 1978).

10 Pascale Aebischer, *Shakespeare, Spectatorship, and the Technologies of Performance* (Cambridge: Cambridge University Press, 2020), 17.

11 For some examples of the uses of Weimann's work, see Phyllis Rackin, *Stages of History: Shakespeare's English Chronicles* (Ithaca: Cornell University Press, 1990); Erika T. Lin, *Shakespeare and The Materiality of Performance* (New York: Palgrave Macmillan, 2012), especially 25–7, where she revises Weimann.

12 Gina Bloom, *Gaming the Stage: Playable Media and the Rise of the English Commercial Theatre* (Ann Arbor: Michigan University Press, 2018), 10.

13 Matthew Wagner, *Shakespeare, Theatre, and Time* (New York: Routledge, 2014), 34. See also Rebecca Bushnell, *Tragic Time in Drama, Film and Videogames: The Future in the Instant* (London: Palgrave Macmillan 2016), 24; and Bloom, *Gaming the Stage*, of the temporality of the theatre in comparison with that of chess in her analysis of *The Game of Chess*.

14 Joe Falocco, *Reimagining Shakespeare's Playhouse: Early Modern Staging Conventions in the Twentieth Century* (Cambridge: D.S. Brewer, 2010), 139–40; see also *Shakespeare's Globe: A Theatrical Experiment*, ed. Christie Carson and Farah Karim-Cooper (Cambridge: Cambridge University Press, 2008), chaps. 8 and 9; *Imagining the Audience in Early Modern Drama: 1558–1642*, ed. Jennifer A. Low and Nova Myhill (New York: Palgrave Macmillan, 2011); also Bloom, *Gaming the Stage*, Introduction.

15 William B. Worthen, *Shakespeare, Technicity, and Theatre* (Cambridge: Cambridge University Press, 2020).

16 Gabriella Giannachi, *Virtual Theatres: An Introduction* (New York: Routledge, 2004), 11.

17 Reason and Lindelof, *Experiencing Liveness*, 1.

18 See Lindsay Brandon Hunter, *Playing Real: Mimesis, Media, and Mischief* (Evanston: Northwestern University Press, 2021), 12: 'In

the case of NT Live, a constellation of choices shapes a mediatized product so that it may showcase the vestiges and marks of liveness: synchronous, local, public consumption (in cinemas), a gesture toward theater's seemingly constitutive newness.' See also Claire Read, '"Live, or Almost Live. . .": The Politics of Performance and Documentation', *International Journal of Performance Arts and Digital Media* 10, no. 1 (2014): 67–76; Martin Barker, *Live to Your Local Cinema: The Remarkable Rise of Live Broadcasting* (London: Palgrave Macmillan, 2013); and the report by NESTA from 2010) 'Beyond Live: Digital Innovation in the Performing Arts', found at: http://www.nesta.org.uk/about_us/assets/features/beyond_live.

19 Pascale Aebischer, *Screening Early Modern Drama* (Cambridge: Cambridge University Press, 2014), 146.

20 Erin Sullivan, 'Live to Your Living Room: Streamed Theatre, Audience Experience, and the Globe's *A Midsummer Night's Dream*', *Participations: Journal of Audience & Reception Studies* 17, no. 1 (2020): 92–119; 1.

21 Eirini Nedelkopoulou, 'Reconsidering Liveness in the Age of Digital Implication', in *Experiencing Liveness*, ed. Reason and Lindelof, 215–28: 215. See Erin Sullivan, *The Audience Is Present: Aliveness, Social Media, and the Theatre Broadcast Experience* (London: The Arden Shakespeare, 2018), 62: 'Liveness in such context is about being art of an event that is 'a-live' with experience, engagement and possibility – and while other people are certainly part of that process, they don't necessarily have to be physically co-present actors on the stage'. Several scholars have written about the RSC's now decade-old social media adaptations of Shakespeare in *Such Tweet Sorrow* (2010) and *A Midsummer Night's Dreaming* (2013). See, for example, Erin Sullivan, 'Shakespeare, Social Media, and the Digital Public Sphere: *Such Tweet Sorrow* and *A Midsummer Night's Dreaming*', *Shakespeare* 14, no. 1 (2018): 64–79; Stephen Purcell, 'The Impact of New Forms of Public Performance', in *Shakespeare and the Digital World: Redefining Scholarship and Practice*, ed. Christie Carson and Peter Kirwan (Cambridge: Cambridge University Press, 2014), 212–25.

22 Bushnell, *Tragic Time*; Rebecca Bushnell, 'Videogames and *Hamlet*: Experiencing Tragic Choice and Consequences', in *Games and Theatre in Shakespeare's England*, ed. Tom Bishop, Gina Bloom and Erika T. Lin (Amsterdam: Amsterdam University Press, 2021), 229–54; Geoffrey Way, 'Shakespeare Videogames, Adaptation/Appropriation and Collaborative Reception', in *Games and Theatre*, 255–75; Peter S. Donaldson, 'Game Space/Tragic Space: Julie

Taymor's *Titus*', in *A Companion to Shakespeare and Performance,* ed. Barbara Hodgdon and W. B. Worthen (Oxford: Blackwell, 2005), 457–77; Katherine Rowe, 'Crowd-Sourcing Shakespeare: Screen Work and Screen Play in Second Life', *Shakespeare Studies* 38 (2010): 58–67; Gina Bloom, 'Videogame Shakespeare: Enskilling Audiences Through Theater-Making Games', *Shakespeare Studies* 43 (2015): 114–27; Laurie Osborne, 'iShakespeare: Digital Art/Games, Intermediality, and the Future of Shakespearean Film', *Shakespeare Studies* 38 (2010): 48–57; Matthew Harrison and Michael Lutz, 'South of Elsinore: Actions that a Man Might Play', in *The Shakespeare User: Critical and Creative Appropriations in a Networked Culture*, ed. Valerie M. Fazel and Louise Geddes (London: Palgrave Macmillan, 2017), 23–40.

23 See. Bishop, Bloom and Lin, eds., *Games and Theatre*.
24 Bloom, *Gaming the Stage*, 2.
25 Ibid., 6.
26 Christopher Hanson, *Game Time: Understanding Temporality in Video Games* (Bloomington: Indiana University Press, 2018), 12.
27 See Bushnell, *Tragic Time*, 69.
28 Jesper Juul, 'The Game, the Player, the World: Looking for a Heart of Gameness', in *Level Up: Digital Games Research Conference Proceedings*, ed. Marinka Copier and Joost Raessens (Utrecht: Utrecht University, 2003), 30–45; 132. https://www.jesperjuul.net/text/gameplayerworld/.
29 From the *Elsinore* website, Golden Glitch Studios, http://elsinore-game.com/ *Elsinore* was released by Golden Glitch in July 2019.
30 Peter Rubin, *Future Presence: How Virtual Reality Is Changing Human Connection, Intimacy, and the Limits of Ordinary Life* (New York: Harper Collins, 2018), 4; see also Nick Kaye and Gabriella Giannachi, 'Acts of Presence: Performance, Mediation, Virtual Reality', *TDR: Drama Review* 55, no. 4 (2011): 88–95; on virtual reality connected with Shakespeare and pedagogy, see Stephen Wittek and David McInnis, eds., *Shakespeare and Virtual Reality* (Cambridge: Cambridge University Press, 2021).
31 As Giannachi observes, 'In a way that resembles the involvement of a player in a videogame, 'Virtual reality offers fluid and open forms that allow for the viewer simultaneously to be inside and outside the work of art' (*Virtual Theatres*, 12).
32 The following three paragraphs are adapted from an essay on 'Shakespeare and Virtual Reality' that I co-authored with Michael

Ullyot, published in *The Routledge Handbook of Shakespeare and Interface*, ed. Cliff Weirer and Paul Budra (Cambridge: Cambridge University Press, 2022) (in press). I am grateful to them all for permission to use them here.

33 https://americanshakespearecenter.com/vr/.

34 *Hamlet 360: Thy Father's Spirit* (2019), the Commonwealth Shakespeare Company in Boston in collaboration with Google and Sensorium. https://www.youtube.com/watch?v=Jc88G7nkV-Q.

35 Danielle Rosvally has noted to me, 'Having attended many CSC productions: the VR experience is, likely, a way the spectator can more clearly see and hear the company's work (i.e. preferable in some ways to a live experience). CSC works outdoors, usually, in a giant park space with audiences on blankets (often very far away from the stage). It's basically impossible to get "up close and personal" with these plays as they are conventionally performed by CSC – the VR experience may, in some ways, be more "lived" than the live one'.

36 '*Hamlet 360*: Virtual Reality Shakespeare'. Interview with Barbara Bogaev, Steven Maler and Matthew Niederhauser, https://www.folger.edu/shakespeare-unlimited/hamlet-virtual-reality.

37 On lockdown theatre in general, see Barbara Fuchs, *Theater of Lockdown: Digital and Distanced Performance in a Time of Pandemic* (London: Methuen, 2021); on Shakespeare specifically, Pascale Aebischer, *Viral Shakespeare: Performance in the Time of the Pandemic* (Cambridge: Cambridge University Press, 2021); *Lockdown Shakespeare; New Evolutions in Performance and Adaptation*, ed. Gemma Kate Allred, Benjamin Broadribb and Erin Sullivan (London: Bloomsbury, 2022); in that volume, Gemma Allred offers a fascinating essay on 'Notions of Liveness in Lockdown Performance', in which she covers a number of pandemic-era performances (65–86).

38 https://wilmatheater.org/fat-ham-wilmabill/.

39 On other uses of Zoom theatre, see Aebischer, *Viral Shakespeare*; Fuchs, *Theater of Lockdown*; Allred, 'Notions of Liveness'; Thomas Cartelli, 'Medium Specificity, Medium Convergence, and Aliveness in the Chromakey (2018) & Big Telly Zoom (2020) *Macbeths*', in this volume; and Pascal Aebischer and Rachel Nicholas, 'Creation Theatre and the Big Telly *Tempest*: Digital Theatre and the Performing Audience', in *Lockdown Shakespeare*, 87–106.

40 See Allred, Aesbischer, and Cartelli on Big Telly's *Macbeth*, which used a similar technology, vMix Open Broadcaster Software (OBS).

41 In a webinar recording about the making of *King Lear*, Director Elizabeth Carter described the advantages of performance with

this technology as direct address and closeness, as well as the static background http://www.sfshakes.org/performances/free-shakespeare-at-home-reflections-on-summer-2020. For clips from the *Lear* performance see https://www.nealormond.com/uvs?pgid=kkbu7f161-88bd522d-4183-494d-bd7f-05d81adfedf4

42 https://www.youtube.com/watch?v=iZ3B4EYrdJgi. This video is paywall-protected. For a discussion of this production, see Fuchs, *Theater of Lockdown*, chap. 4.

43 Up until recently, a recorded version was now available to watch on demand, but that link no longer functions: it was at https://www.rsc.org.uk/news/dream-on-demand.

44 For reviews, see: https://www.britishtheatreguide.info/reviews/dream-19791; https://www.theguardian.com/stage/2021/mar/21/dream-review-rsc-royal-shakespeare-company-nick-cave-the-litten-trees-fuel; https://www.nytimes.com/2021/03/17/theater/review-dream-royal-shakespeare-company.html

45 https://tenderclaws.com/tempest. For another analysis of the performance, see Erin Sullivan, 'Immersion in a Time of Distraction: The Under Presents *Tempest*', in *Lockdown Shakespeare*, 107–26; also Alex Coulombe, 'Let's Dive into the Underpresents *Tempest*', https://medium.com/alive-in-plasticland/lets-dive-into-the-under-presents-tempest-pt-1-2d1ef2168c5f

46 https://tenderclaws.com/theunderpresents.

47 'Final Script'. https://drive.google.com/file/d/15oI7Py4ELjAG2ZKH8KMgX8BLijgTEunz/view

48 I experienced the show at 1:00 p.m. EDT, on Sunday, 21 March 2021, with Oculus Quest; also https://www.filmindependent.org/blog/tender-claws-uses-vr-to-re-imagine-immersive-theater-during-lockdown/.

49 This is all from the 'Final Script' for the performance.

50 Sullivan, 'Immersion in a Time of Distraction', 122.

51 Popat, 'Missing in Action', 360–1.

52 See Popat, 'I will argue, on the contrary, that this emphasis on experiences and interactions in, and with, VR environments can enable us to relocate ourselves as embodied beings rather than distancing us from our bodies' (359).

53 Alexis Soloski, 'Theater's Next Act? A Show That's All in Your Head', https://www.nytimes.com/2020/07/08/theater/virtual-reality-the-tempest.html

54 See Farah Karim-Cooper, *The Hand on the Shakespearean Stage: Gesture, Touch and the Spectacle of Dismemberment* (London:

Bloomsbury, 2016); see also Gina Bloom, Nick Toothman, Sawyer Kenp and Evan Buswell, on 'presenting gesture in digital terms', in '"A Whole Theatre of Others": Amateur Acting and Immersive Spectatorship in the Digital Shakespeare Game *Play the Knave*', *Shakespeare Quarterly* 67 (2016): 408–30.

55 'Final Script'.
56 Sullivan, 'Immersion in a Time of Distraction', 122.
57 Soloski, 'Theater's Next Act'.

2

Impressions of liveness in Shakespeare, at a distance

Stephanie Shirilan

A little over a year after the outbreak of the virus, I set out to teach a course on Shakespeare in the age of Covid-19 alongside a course I regularly teach on breath in Shakespeare. The new course sought to examine the ways that pandemic theatre has challenged the premise of the latter course, which is that shared air, or pneumatic community, as I refer to it elsewhere, is vital to the experience of liveness in Shakespeare's theatre.[1] The observations and arguments developed in this chapter emerged out of questions posed in both classes: What sort of respiratory or pneumatic exchange takes place in the absence of physical copresence, when we are not trading motes and molecules, not inhaling and exhaling the same trace chemicals, hormones, minerals, viruses, bacteria (or miasma and effluvia, to use early modern terms), not assimilating the same airborne sensory data or species, not inspiring and respiring the same pneumatic spirits concentrated by the presence of one another's living and decaying bodies in real time and place?[2] What kind of shared experience of air and atmosphere is possible at a distance? Further, how has a renewed sense of the dangers of respiratory proximity, and the inequality of such precarity, reshaped our affective relationship to the physical atmosphere of 'live' theatre and the feeling of liveness itself?[3]

While my students are trained sceptics of binary oppositions between the real and the virtual in the theatre or anywhere else in their cybernetic lives, social distance under the pandemic prompted new awareness in the virtual classroom of the constructed and mediated nature of liveness and presence in Shakespeare.[4] Studying distance as a theme and as our own pedagogical modality, class discussions repeatedly remarked on the imaginative production of physical and atmospheric presence in the plays. We observed the ways that Shakespeare primes the audience to feel 'live' through a variety of rhetorical and dramatic techniques, perhaps most notably through a species of ekphrasis I refer to as pneumatic energeia – the evocation of an unseen, spatially and/or temporally distant atmosphere whose instrumental distance this chapter seeks to theorize.[5] Pneumatic energeia produces presence 'at a distance', a term used in early modern natural philosophy to designate the capacity of one body to affect another at a spatial or temporal remove. This chapter surveys the range of this concept in early modern thought and explores its parallels in contemporary scholarship on 'telematic' theatre in order to reconsider the instrumentality of distance to the perception of liveness and presence in Shakespeare.[6] I suggest that socially distanced theatre re-exposes the production of presence and proximity in live, 'in-person' theatre as, itself, an effect of aesthetic distance. My approach is guided by Pascale Aebischer's argument that 'Digital technologies of performance . . . reactivate older forms of spectatorial engagement and offer enhanced, intensified and accelerated ways of experiencing the shared response-ability/ responsibility of performers and spectators'.[7] Borrowing from Aebischer, I argue that pandemic theatre exposes pneumatic energeia as a rhetorical technique that mobilizes temporal or spatial distance to 'enhance[e], intensif[y], and accelerat[e]' the visceral experience of presence.[8]

The Derridean argument that absence produces symbolic rather than material presence (that the trace only signifies indexically and has no *real* presence of its own) has exerted an outsized influence in performance scholarship on liveness.[9] But the sharp ontological distinction between presence and absence on which this formulation relies is largely incompatible with early modern theories of presence rooted in Christian metaphysics and natural magic, central to which is the principle of action at a distance: the capacity of bodies and objects to wield transformative influence over one another by communicating or transmitting information remotely. In what follows, I suggest not only that remote or telematic theatre underscores the necessity of distance to the 'magical' perception of presence in live, in-person theatre but that it highlights the function of distance as crucial to the experience of atmospheric liveness as a theatrical effect in Shakespeare. Distanced theatre, in other words, reveals how distance, both temporal and spatial, compels the recollection of liveness that 'bodies forth' the memory of presence by activating the faculties of the imagination that 'make it real'.[10]

Feeling for presence at a pandemic distance: we were never proximate or synchronous

It takes me at least twice as long to teach on Zoom as it does in person, an effect I attribute to many disorienting aspects of the platform, the most frustrating being the diminished impact of signals I rely on to communicate presence and attention. When I lean forwards, there is no perceivable displacement of the physical air, no registration of the risk or reward of many physical gestures so key to classroom proxemics. On Zoom, my attempt to 'get close' falls flat (I seem to compensate by getting louder). Flatter still is the fall of my gaze.[11] There is no direct address of the visible audience, only the illusion of such. In the parlance of early modern faculty psychology, the beams of information that travel (intromissively or extramissively) between my audience and me are displaced by the rendering of this very skewed camera obscura.[12] My students and I observe that even with optimal signal strength and bandwidth, the lag in transmission of sound and image over Zoom interrupts simulated synchrony.[13] This is more obvious when attempting synchronized speech or singing but no less disorienting than the micro-lags between a question, comment or joke and the confirmation of its hearing that precipitates response. These deaths by a thousand delays make me yearn for the liveliness of in-person teaching and theatre, or what we might instead regard as a better command of the illusion of synchrony therein. But an illusion it is. We were never synchronous. Fast as sound travels, the time of my speaking is not the time of your hearing, even 'in person'. The impression of my liveness and presence as vital heat, breath, subtle movement and subtler vibrations is mediated – and delayed – by the media of its transmission and the modes and senses of perception, chief among them, to use the early modern vernacular, the faculties of the imagination.[14]

Remote theatre, and the remote study of theatre, renews the delight of old theatrical tricks that expose the experience of proximity and synchrony in live theatre as illusions amplified by the powers of the imagination. Take 'Catch', for instance. This is a version of a popular performance exercise that prepares the actor to deliver and respond to the text with heightened agility by passing a ball while trading lines. In the version my students and I play in our Zoom classroom, we recourse to mimicry almost immediately to compensate for distance.[15] A different kind of game emerges. The students and I pantomime the gestures of rearing up to launch an invisible projectile. We comically strain backwards in task chairs or lurch sideways to 'catch' a phantom object outside the frame, outdoing one another to surprise and delight in the variety of ways we can approximate (by exaggerating) the gestures of live and proximate physical interaction. One might say that the exercise activates the neural pathways of spatial reasoning and proprioception that organize impressions of presence and copresence.[16] Another way of putting this would be to say that the exercise generates the feeling of liveness by recruiting the spatio-temporal faculties of the imagination that produce illusions of presence through the evocation of proximity and synchrony. This conspicuousness of the illusion of presence *qua* illusion, I argue, is central to the affective experience of liveness at a distance.

Zoom 'catch' elucidates pneumatic enargeia as a procedure that relies on similar kinds of pantomime to conjure atmospheric presence telematically, across a distance or gap that this chapter seeks to theorize. The gap (between the sign and the signifier, the percipient and the perceived) to which Derrida's *différance* refers reflects a phenomenological approach that places absence at the centre of the experience of presence. But the gap between bodies in a telematic theatre is less one that gestures at ontological absence than a span that situates presence across and between percipients/spectators and the objects of their perception.[17] It is not a void but a space or *span* that connects as it separates.[18] It is across this span that one *longs* – a verb that invokes both spatial and temporal distance and the desire it generates.[19] Jean-Luc Nancy characterizes the gap or space between bodies in the theatre as the space that makes presence possible. Drawing on the Stoic theory of the incorporeals (void, time, place and the sayable/expressible), he underscores that this spacing 'is not an inert interval . . . the void between bodies is not a negative thickness' but a combination of void and place: 'the void permits the distinction of places, and time is nothing else but the spacing of sense, the extension by which it stretches toward itself . . . by which the signifier stretches towards the signified'.[20] Nancy's attribution of presence to disposition or extension provides a useful tool for theorizing liveness at a distance, particularly as a complement to attempts by performance scholars to theorize liveness in the digital age.

In their research on new media forms of theatrical presence, Gabriella Giannachi and Nick Kaye draw on the etymologically implied anteriority, posteriority and prepositionality of the word 'presence' to show how '"being there" . . . is implicitly associated with dynamics of relation, separation and proximity'.[21] This, they argue, helps to explain how and why phenomena of 'presence' are frequently produced counter-intuitively.[22] They note that experiments in virtual theatre have generated a new awareness that 'the more . . . objects tend to lose their material essence . . . the more their "presence" gains ground' – a paradox that Jon Erikson has described as fundamental to the experience of theatrical presence as 'a physicality in the present that at the same time is grounded in a form of absence'. Presence, says Erikson,

> is something that has unfolded, is read against what has been seen, and presently observed in expectation as to what will be seen. It means that the performer is presenting herself to the audience, but at the same time holding something back . . . not only does the notion of presence in performance imply an absence, but that absence itself is the possibility of future movement; so paradoxically, presence is based not only in the present, but in our expectation of the future.[23]

Erikson's formulation of theatrical presence as an effect of the tension between what has been shown and what is held in reserve will be particularly germane to our analysis of Cleopatra's atmospheric presence. What I wish to point out here is how it revises

Derridean approaches to the gap or delay in the signifying process to reveal how 'the phenomena of presence may emerge in layering, in veiling, in the very operation of the sign and representation' such that '*difference* is also a locus for presence'.[24]

Early modern presence at a distance

The emphasis on asynchronous or diachronic presence in the scholarship on inter/mediated presence brings us closer to concepts of presence more contemporary to Shakespeare, concepts that relied upon cosmic powers of sympathy and the faculties of the imagination (or faith) to explain the capacity of objects and bodies to affect one another at a distance. Natural magic and pre-modern natural philosophy explained that such transactions harness subtle affinities (sympathies and antipathies, attractions and repulsions) either in matter itself (which, for Bacon, was capable of desire) or by the sensory and imaginative faculties of the percipient that similarly seek to make connections between like and like.[25] In such thinking, the span or gap between bodies is what makes their *occult* (literally, hidden) correspondence wondrous.[26] Indeed, the registration of wonder and marvel as affective responses to action at a distance in early modern natural philosophy provides a useful if underutilized tool for theorizing affective experience and the production of presence and liveness in the early modern theatre.

In Renaissance natural magic, action at a distance not only reveals but also activates the cosmic forces (love, desire, world-soul, divine presence) that order the universe, and in so doing it makes these forces knowable to sense. Occult philosophers of the late sixteenth and early-mid seventeenth centuries explained phenomena such as the attractive power of the loadstone and the efficacy of the weapon salve as evidence of the dynamic, interactive relationship between the celestial and sublunary world. According to Paracelsian iatrochemist Jan Baptiste Van Helmont, 'material nature does uncessantly by its secret Magnetism, suck down forms from the brests of the superior Orbs, and greedily thirst after the favor and benign influence of the celestial Luminaries'. Recognizing this truth, he says, one would have to concede that 'there is a . . . reciprocal return from each to other, and one harmonious concord, and conspiracy of all parts with the whole universe'.[27] Helmont's 'harmonious concord' is a descendent of Ficino's world soul, which connects and is 'equally connected with everything, even with those things which are at a distance from one another, because they are not at a distance from her'.[28] Natural magic amplifies the copresence of objects and bodies, separated by distance, through the intermediating force of a world soul and makes that power more manifest by demonstration. The illusion of proximity at a distance in telematic or remote theatre invokes these pre-modern scripts of action at a distance invested with the power to manifest sympathy in the cosmos and the felt presence of its maker.

The increased presence of a thing or person *in absentia* is, of course, a central concern and chief objective of early modern poetics. The work of the Renaissance poet is to evoke – and preserve – through lively or vivid imagery the presence of a subject that not only outlives its physical referent but also becomes more live at a distance. The *visiones* or *phantasiai* in Quintilian's oft-quoted formulation of *enargeia* are the 'means by which images of absent things are represented to the mind . . . such that we seem to see them with our eyes and to be in their presence'.[29] The Scottish poet and historian Henry Adamson puts it succinctly: 'In poetrie . . . Things absent you can present make appear/And things far distant; as if they were near/Things senselesse unto them give sense can yee,/And make them touch, taste, smell, and heare, and see.'[30] The beloved addressed in Sonnet 55 shall not only 'shine more bright' in the poet's 'powerful rhyme' than in 'gilded monuments' but more than they did in the flesh, or 'in-person'.[31]

The paradox of presence-in-absence, and the instrumentality of distance to the experience of divine presence, is paramount to Christian metaphysics and sacramental theology. To use contemporary performance terminology, the Eucharist is a presencing technique whose capacity to produce real feelings of presence was underscored by the very Reformers who disputed its materiality. Protestant commentators emphasized that faith enhances one's ability to perceive divine presence, not despite but because of its distance from the world of physical sense. 'So quycke of sight is faith,' says Erasmus, 'that she seeth euen those things as present whiche are farre distant from the bodely senses.'[32] The clergyman John Prime describes faith as a telematic tool for bridging the physical gap between the Eucharistic sign and signified, or the real and the virtual: 'Faith hath an eye, an hande & a wing, wherby it pearceth, reacheth and flyeth vp to heauen it selfe. To fayth, thinges absent are present, things distant are conioyned.'³³ The leaping of the mind to 'conjoin' distant things both requires faith and rewards it, holding out the promise of eternal life in the apprehending or 'taking' of such communion. Peter Martyr Vermiglii suggests that it is distance itself that generates saving faith:

> what impediment shall now the spaces of places be, which are betwéene heauen, where Christ abideth, and vs [here in earth]. . . . Surelie nothing at all, if we haue faith, whereby our minds . . . may be carried vp into heauen, and there be refreshed with the spirituall meate and drinke of the bodie and bloud of Christ, and be restored vnto eternall life.³⁴

Faith makes possible the 'flight' of the mind up to heaven, but it is the 'spaces of places' between heaven and earth that generates the faith (or imaginative capacity) to traverse it.³⁵ The perception of liveness and copresence in remote theatre recalls the logic of this paradox and its vital implications. In the Reformist tradition, the longing for copresence generates its perception at a distance whose *imaginative* traversal is what restores 'unto eternall life'.

Mimetic distance as the presencing technique

As in Vermigli's sacramental theology, the experience of presence in the remote theatre requires the reminder of distance through the conspicuousness of the delay or asymmetry of the illusion of presence and proximity. Big Telly Theatre's early 2021 *Recipe for Disaster* provides a rather striking contemporary illustration. *Recipe* is a piece of online interactive comedy in the style of *Tony and Tina's Wedding*.³⁶ Along with their access link tickets, audience members receive ingredient lists for dishes and drinks to be prepared during the performance. The conceit is that the guests will help to furnish the refreshments in an effort to ease the financial burden of the wedding. Part zany dinner-theatre and part interactive cooking show, *Recipe* works to recruit feelings of community and commensality for an audience in lockdown through the collective work of imagining impossible proximity at a conspicuous distance. Audience members are encouraged by the MC/Best Man to keep their cameras on as they follow step-by-step cooking demonstrations by real-life chef Paula Macyntyre, who plays a friend of the couple. Performers and audience members alike appear in their own Zoom tiles, 'together apart' to use a catchphrase of the pandemic. The plot is simple: the groom gets cold feet (he asks about remedies for sweaty palms in the chat box) and resorts to staging a burglary to avoid tying the knot. The couple, each in their separate locations, retreats 'off-stage' to a supposed Zoom room of their own to work things out, which they do, and the show culminates in revels. The audience is invited to join the actors on an imaginary dance floor, composed of the many kitchens and living spaces pictured in individual Zoom frames, and enjoined to dance by the antic choreography of the players' pantomime of an 80s dance party. Virtuosity and verisimilitude are swapped for slapstick and mime, not unlike that of my students' Zoom game of 'Catch', the *piece de resistance* of which involves a split-screen, digital version of the 'helping hands' improv game, this one with legs. The four principal players create the illusion of a single couple's body, doing the 'running man' dance (two of the characters animate the top 'halves' of the couple and the other two play their legs; Figure 2.1). The delightfully crude trick indulges the generic expectation of a happy ending not only for the nuptial couple but also for the lonely MC and the chef, who lets slip her attraction to him. These secondary characters supply the faces and torsos for the bride and groom's feet. The obvious failure of this illusion, comically exaggerated by the asynchrony and asymmetry of the top and bottom images, is precisely what makes the gag work as a proxemic device. The failed, baldly anti-mimetic attempt to collapse the space between the distanced players (and audience members) ap-proximates (*makes proximate*) copresence as an imagined but more keenly felt liveness at a distance.

Unlikely as the comparison may seem, something similar is at work in the evocation of presence across the vast distances of time and place in *Antony and Cleopatra*. The play performs a particularly magisterial instance of this in Enobarbus's recollection of Cleopatra's appearance and the sumptuousness of her presence on the Cydnus River.[37] What *Recipe for Disaster* exposes in *Antony and Cleopatra* is the way that mimetic failure is recruited in the service of emphasizing a distance that elicits the feeling of liveness and proximity. The perspectival asymmetry of this scene's structure

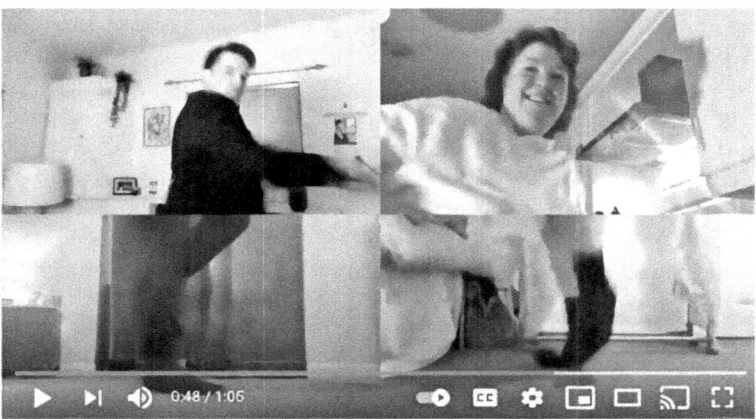

FIGURE 2.1 *Unsynchronized 'running man'*. MC and Best Man (Chris Robinson) plays head and torso to the groom's (Tom Richardson's) feet. Paula Macintyre, playing herself, is the dancing top half to black-socked feet of the bride (Nicky Harley). Recipe for Disaster *(dir. Zoe Seaton, Big Telly Theatre 2021; screengrabs from promotional video clips from interactive live stream, 30 January 2021).* Reproduced with permission of Big Telly Theatre Company, Northern Ireland.

is multifold. Enobarbus depicts a scene memorialized by Plutarch and others as the first encounter not just between Antony and Cleopatra but also between a familiar West and an exotic East. The play, however, has already granted the audience access to the queen at almost too close a range, exposing her fits, insecurities and pettiness in a close-up at times so unflattering that it serves, rather than undermines, her apotheosis by suggesting that only someone larger-than-life could survive such exposure and retain their mystique. The rapacious curiosity displayed by Enobarbus's onstage Roman audience serves as a pretence for the narrator to elaborate upon Cleopatra's presence at an artificial distance or perspectival gap that cultivates the (impossible) desire for its transcendence.

The enlivening effect of mimetic failure is achieved through the asymmetry or gap between life and that which is larger than life, a gap exaggerated by the audience's desire for Cleopatra's (and by extension, the East's) enormity.[38] Tell us, Agrippa and Maecenas beg, how much is her overmuch? Egypt's legendary excess, however, is beyond measure. It can only be approximated as a differential of scale: 'but as a fly' to 'an eagle'.[39] The Roman appetite for Egyptian surfeit ('Eight wild boars roasted whole at a breakfast / and but twelve persons there. Is this true?' [2.2.190]) establishes the telematic procedure of Cleopatra's evocation as one activated by unsatisfiable desire ('she makes hungry/ Where most she satisfies' [2.2.247-8]) and expressed as rhetorical impossibility: her 'person … beggared all description' (2.2.207-8). The diegetical invocation that commences Enobarbus's speech ('I will tell you') functions as a proxemic device that brings the audience closer by underscoring its distance from the imagined scene (2.2.200). The audience's desire to hear what follows is intensified by mimetic example in Enobarbus's listeners and the poetics of erotic imitation, the longing call and response, of the scene's ekphrastic imagery:

> Purple the sails, and so perfumed that
> The winds were love-sick with them; the oars were silver,
> Which to the tune of flutes kept stroke, and made
> The water which they beat to follow faster,
> As amorous of their strokes. (2.2.203-7)

Cleopatra's presence is created as an effect of the audience's longing, at a distance, for access to a scene brought closer through its internal depictions of longing.[40] Longing, affective and dimensional, begets the paradoxical presence that Giannachi and Kaye describe as '[a] theatrical relation, a function of representation'.[41]

The poetic evocation of airy atmosphere – pneumatic enargeia – intensifies the sense of both distance from and desire for an object that evades capture by virtue of its ephemeral qualities. Cleopatra's presence is pictured as wind, heat, breath (anticipating the images of fire and air by which she will apotheosize herself). Her attendants, who '[w]ith divers-coloured fans, whose wind did seem / To glow the delicate cheeks which they did cool, / And what they undid did' mimetically swell a pneumatic theme that becomes its own nadir at its apogee (2.2.213-15). The 'strange invisible perfume' that wafts '[f]rom the barge' and 'hits the sense / Of the adjacent wharfs' sucks the people from the marketplace, leaving Antony to 'sit alone, / Whistling to th'air, which but for vacancy / Had gone to gaze on Cleopatra, too' (2.2.222-7). On the one hand, Enobarbus's poetic anemography endows this legendary encounter with a haptic and proprioceptive dimensionality that makes it imaginatively proximate. On the other, it accentuates the elusiveness of its object, even to the near point of vanishing. The audience is told that Cleopatra's presence *would* have drawn the air along with the people out of the market 'but for vacancy', which we may read as a statement either of impossibility or of fact – either the air would have quit the marketplace, if such a thing were possible, or perhaps it already has, making it impossible as repetition (and if so, more poignant as a meta-commentary on the ephemerality of performed presence). In either case, the presencing effect of this pneumatic ekphrasis hangs on the failure of the imagined attempt to foreclose the gap between the audience and the recollected scene. The imagined vacancy (hypothetical or real) at the centre of the recollection seems paradoxically to imply that distance cannot be collapsed without creating a gap in nature. But the paradox is lessened by recalling that the gap is decidedly not a vacuum.[42] The air, notwithstanding its desire to quit the marketplace and 'gaze on Cleopatra, too' remains at a distance from the imagined spectacle, forming a pneumatic interval or gap between the represented scene and its audience that is not absent presence, not the trace of presence, but pneumatic presence: the animate air itself. As so often in Shakespeare, air is the uncanny witness to that which positively remains of performance.

Pneumatic presence and breathless power

In the wake of the barge speech comes the suggestion that the mysterious source of Cleopatra's enigmatic power is her breath, or, more precisely, her power of respiratory self-replenishment. After a rather crude interruption by one of his listeners (who intimates that Cleopatra's command is more calculating, and calculated, than numinous), Enobarbus continues his ethopoeia:

I saw her once
Hop forty paces through the public street
And, having lost her breath, she spoke and panted,

That she did make defect perfection,
And, breathless, pour breath forth. (2.2.238-242)

Another auditor laments that '[n]ow Antony/Must leave her utterly', in response to which Enobarbus delivers perhaps the play's most memorable line: 'Age cannot wither her, nor custom stale/Her infinite variety' (2.2.245-6). The epitaph is paradoxical, immortalizing in the manner of eulogy a spirit who is still living, at least within the dramatic fiction of the play.

Many critics have remarked the disjunctive temporality of this scene as a heightened instance of paradox that works throughout the play to destabilize its mimetic projects.[43] Harald Fawkner suggests that Cleopatra's 'over-picturing' in the barge speech liberates the mind 'from the mimetic dimension' and 'resituates us in the hyperontological gestalt of the play', wherein 'paradoxical images of voiding and filling, leaving and following create a central hyperontological figure of an absence that presences'.[44] Cleopatra's breathless power is, in his view, the play's central paradox: the 'breathing *power* of breathlessness is tied to the notion of *leaving in general*', not just the leave-taking of erotic abandonment that Maecenas predicts (and with which Cleopatra is obsessed) but death, which 'precisely because it is treated in terms of its own deferral' becomes 'the infinitely protracted performance of its own possibility'.[45] In other words, Cleopatra's breathless breath discursively establishes her aesthetic immortality through the infinite deferral of her death. However, even as the play presents the possibility of such a procedure, it gives voice to the prospect of its failure. The prediction of some future boy actor diminishing Cleopatra's greatness with his vocal (and respiratory) defect points exaggeratedly to the scandal of the speaking (squeaking) body as an instrument of spiritual impersonation and, in so doing, underscores the impossibility of the mimetic task that Enobarbus establishes for him.

In Enobarbus's epitaph, Cleopatra's liveness is invoked through what Hans-Thies Lehman calls the 'erosion of slippage and presence' that is characteristic of the postdramatic mode.[46] To speak in more materialist terms, her imagined vitality gains intensity through its paradoxical and seemingly superhuman replenishment through expenditure. The social and political realities of pandemic theatre draw renewed attention to the power dynamic that undergirds the slipperiness of this enargeic technique. The pandemic casts a particularly harsh light on the mystification of power that the play itself highlights in the ambivalent paranomasia of the word 'powre', which is alternately represented by editors as 'power' and 'pour'.[47] The enigmatic source of Cleopatra's presence is linguistically imagined as a capacity to regenerate respiratory spirit through thriftless exertion. The recollection of Cleopatra's more proximate pneumatic presence, her presence in breathlessness, provides a striking counterpoint to the image of the marketplace she cannily avoids when she leaves Antony alone to whistle to the air. Whereas Cleopatra would not come to Antony, she comes to the audience by way of pneumatic enargeia, pouring/powering breathless breath in sport. The savour of her atmosphere, at once magnetic and elusive in the barge scene (emanating from and drawing its percipients towards its source), remains at a distance. In this first recollection, the audience is affectively placed with Antony, longing for Cleopatra's presence from afar. In the recollection a moment later, the immediacy of her panting in the public streets – and her perfect defect as breathless power in this display – brings her closer to the audience only to establish her greater remove. The hypothetical gap in nature of the airless marketplace is replaced by the unimaginable proximity and ineffable mystery of the queen's breathless power itself.

The distance of pandemic theatre renews the affective capacity of pneumatic enargeia as a rhetorical strategy that amplifies the liveness of the act of recollection but does so with a renewed sense of poignancy that reflects the risk that compels such distance and the violence of its unequal protections, indeed the unequal extension of life and the feeling of liveness at a distance. The memory of Cleopatra's inimitable spirit is evoked in the particularity of her capacity not for superhuman longevity, nor by the inexhaustibility of her physical spirit (indeed, her exhaustibility is the mark of defect that perfects), but for the 'triumph' of her survival as the memory of pneumatic presence through the poetics of distance. The memory of Cleopatra's 'panting' invokes (via its French etymon, *pantiser*) the connection between breath and imagination, or *phantasia*.[48] The laboured breathing that is the mark of respiratory lack is converted fantastically in the memory of her numinous presence into the sign of immortal respiratory plenitude. Reflecting in pandemic on the enargeic liveness of Cleopatra's presence-in-absence, a presence made more potent by its failed mimesis, we might ask: whose *liveness* is made more manifest at a distance? In the wake of racial and other justice movements that have decried the inequality of respiratory security,[49] we must ask: whose breath and historical presence is made more powerful by its diminishment, indeed, by the very anoxia that serves as a relief for respiratory *qua* spiritual abundance?[50]

Distanced theatre, particularly in asynchronous performance, underscores the fugitive presence of the theatrical present. It intensifies a sense of liveness that theatre scholars have long associated with the actor's mortality, rather than vitality. Hans Lehman, quoting Heiner Muller, describes this as the liveness of presence that 'has more to do with death than with the often evoked "life" of theatre'.[51] The abstract sense of presence that is always 'floating, fading . . . already leaving', that 'crosses out dramatic representation' in Lehman's terms, is made sharper by the material realities of a historical moment that has both compelled distance as a strategy of plague management and, through technological mediation, allowed for an elaborated fiction of presence at this distance. Even as remote theatre has sustained and, indeed, expanded the range of community and connectivity between theatre makers and audiences,[52] its figuring of distance as redemptive (saving artists, saving theatres, saving lives by staying home) is double-edged. Participation in pandemic theatre at a distance rewrites the rhetoric of theatrical risk, subversion and contagion as threats averted by the prophylaxis of an imagined proximity. The uncanniness of this inversion of conventional theatrical language may, however, be rendered more familiar when we reconsider the proxemics of imagined presence – at a distance.

Notes

I wish to express my gratitude to Sally Barnden and the members of her 2021 SAA seminar on archives and performing memory for providing the first impetus and audience for this project; Danielle Rosvally and Donovan Sherman for nurturing this chapter and collection with great patience and generosity, despite the distance and delays of the pandemic; Pascale Aebischer, Gina DiSalvo and Ryan Howlett for their invaluable feedback and support; Morgan Shaw for help with manuscript preparation; and the Israel Institute for Advanced Studies for supporting this research.

1 Stephanie Shirilan, 'Respiratory Sympathy and Pneumatic Community in Shakespeare', in *Shakespeare's Audiences*, ed. Matteo Pangallo and Peter Kirwan (New York: Routledge, 2021), 27–44. For a brief history of the classical concept of co-breathing or conspiration, see Phillip Sidney Horky, 'Our Common Breath: "Conspiration" from the Stoics to the Church Fathers', in *The Life of Breath in Literature, Culture and Medicine: Classical to Contemporary*, ed. David Fuller, Corinne Saunders, and Jane McNaughton, Palgrave Studies in Literature, Science and Medicine (Cham: Springer, 2021), 55–68.29/12/2021 13:50:00.

2 For accounts of species as sense data, see Robert Pasnau, *Theories of Cognition in the Later Middle Ages* (Cambridge: Cambridge University Press, 1997); Stuart Clark, *Vanities of the Eye: Vision in Early Modern European Culture* (Oxford: Oxford University Press, 2007); Leen Spruit, *Species Intelligibilis: From Perception to Knowledge*, vol. 1, 2 vols. (Leiden: Brill, 1994). Mary Hesse's summary of debates on the multiplication of the species is particularly useful given her emphasis on action at a distance: Mary B. Hesse, *Forces and Fields: The Concept of Action at a Distance in the History of Physics* (London: Nelson, 1961), 79–82.

3 At the time I was preparing the course, very little scholarly work had yet been published on the subject. The following are some of the early blog posts, articles and performance reviews that my students read and which helped to generate the conversations described earlier. Barbara Fuchs and Jared Mezzocchi, 'Reverse-Engineering Zoom with Isadora: Site-Specific Performance for the Internet', *HowlRound Theatre Commons*, https://howlround.com/reverse-engineering-zoom-isadora, accessed 4 October 2021; Gemma Allred, 'Acting in Lockdown: Midsummer Night Stream', *'Action Is Eloquence': (Re)Thinking Shakespeare* (blog), 7 August 2020, https://medium.com/action-is-eloquence-re-thinking-shakespeare/acting-in-lockdown-midsummer-night-stream-5ec399822789; Benjamin Broadribb, '"A Vision of the Island": Immersion Meets Isolation in Creation Theatre's The Tempest', *'Action Is Eloquence': (Re)Thinking Shakespeare* (blog), 21 May 2020, https://medium.com/action-is-eloquence-re-thinking-shakespeare/a-vision-of-the-island-immersion-meets-isolation-in-creation-theatre-s-the-tempest-935bb01a44fa; Alice Saville, 'Does Online Theatre Really Need to Be Live?', *Exeunt Magazine*, http://exeuntmagazine.com/features/theatre-online-liveness-livestream/, accessed 4 October 2021; Kate Bergstrom, 'Sometimes the Best Technology Is Relationships', *HowlRound Theatre*

Commons, https://howlround.com/sometimes-best-technology-relationships, accessed 4 October 2021; TDR Editors, 'Forum: After Covid-19, What?', *TDR: The Drama Review* 64, no. 3 (2020): 191–224. I am indebted to Pascale Aebischer for her direction to a number of resources she compiled for the use of her students and to her generosity with her research on this topic more generally.

4 For Philip Auslander's extensive critique of this binary in performance studies, see Philip Auslander, *Liveness: Performance in a Mediatized Culture*, 2nd edn. (New York: Routledge, 2008).

5 On enargeia, see Ruth Webb, *Ekphrasis, Imagination, and Persuasion in Ancient Rhetorical Theory and Practice* (Farnham: Ashgate, 2009), Chap 4; Terence Cave, '"Enargeia": Erasmus and the Rhetoric of Presence in the Sixteenth Century', *L'Esprit Créateur* 16, no. 4 (1976); Heinrich F. Plett, *Enargeia in Classical Antiquity and the Early Modern Age: The Aesthetics of Evidence* (Leiden: Brill, 2012).

6 'The use of computing, information technology, and telecommunications for the long-distance transmission of information' ('telematics, n.', *OED Online*, December 2021, Oxford University Press). For definitions of the term in media studies, see Sarah Bay-Cheng, Chiel Kattenbelt and Andy Lavender, *Mapping Intermediality in Performance* (Amsterdam: Amsterdam University Press, 2010), 93–4; 99; David Casey, 'Telematics | The Chicago School of Media Theory', https://lucian.uchicago.edu/blogs/mediatheory/keywords/telematics/, accessed 27 December 2021. See also Roy Ascott, *Telematic Embrace: Visionary Theories of Art, Technology, and Consciousness* (Berkeley: University of California Press, 2003).

7 Pascale Aebischer, *Shakespeare, Spectatorship and the Technologies of Performance* (Cambridge: Cambridge University Press, 2020), 10.

8 Ibid., 9.

9 This influence is felt largely through the work of Peggy Phelan. See *Unmarked: The Politics of Performance* (New York: Routledge, 2003). On the Derridean inheritance in performance studies more broadly, see Gabriella Giannachi and Nick Kaye, *Performing Presence: Between the Live and the Simulated* (Manchester: Manchester University Press, 2011), 13–16.

10 Lina Perkins Wilder borrows the terminology of 'bodying forth' from Joseph Roach's work on effigy (*Shakespeare's Memory Theatre: Recollection, Properties, and Character* [Cambridge: Cambridge University Press, 2010, 2]). The phenomenology of liveness in remote theatre underscores the role of the imagination in the production and

activation of memory in the early modern playhouse as described by Perkins Wilder, Marvin Carlson (*The Haunted Stage: The Theatre as Memory Machine* [Ann Arbor: University of Michigan Press, 2003], and Andrew Sofer) (*The Stage Life of Props* [Ann Arbor: University of Michigan Press, 2003]).

11 Performance scholars have largely remarked such absences as confirming the essentiality of physical proximity to an experience of liveness and copresence rooted in sensory immediacy. See, for instance, Carla Neuss, 'Going "Live" Again: Reflections on Zoom, Copresence, & Liveness in a (Post)Pandemic World', *Theatre Survey* 62, no. 3 (2021): 336–9.

12 Clark, *Vanities of the Eye*; David C. Lindberg, *Theories of Vision from Al-Kindi to Kepler* (University of Chicago Press, 1981), chaps. 2, 4.

13 Articles on 'Zoom fatigue' were among the earliest to appear on the modality. Those my students discussed include Evan Malater, 'The Logical Time of Ending a ZOOM Session as a Metaphor for the Terror of the Current Situation', *European Journal of Psychoanalysis*, https://www.journal-psychoanalysis.eu/the-logical-time-of-ending-a-zoom-session-as-a-metaphor-for-the-terror-of-the-current-situation/, accessed 4 October 2021; Geert Lovnik, 'The Anatomy of Zoom Fatigue', https://www.eurozine.com/the-anatomy-of-zoom-fatigue/, accessed 4 October 2021; Betsy Morris, 'Why Does Zoom Exhaust You? Science Has an Answer - WSJ', https://www.wsj.com/articles/why-does-zoom-exhaust-you-science-has-an-answer-11590600269, accessed 4 October 2021.

14 On the lags and delays that suggest 'theater can never be "live". Or, never only live', and the denial of such mediation in claims to 'liveness' in 'real-time' performance, see Rebecca Schneider, *Performing Remains: Art and War in Times of Theatrical Reenactment* (New York: Routledge, 2011), 92–3.

15 Gorman et al describe a similar experience playing a telematic version of a game they call 'whoopah'. See Tom Gorman, Tiina Syrjä and Mikko Kanninen, 'There Is a World Elsewhere: Rehearsing and Training through Immersive Telepresence', *Theatre, Dance and Performance Training* 10, no. 2 (2019): 218. See also Tracy Davis, 'Teaching Performing Arts During the Pandemic', *HowlRound Theatre Commons*, https://howlround.com/teaching-performing-arts-during-pandemic, accessed 4 October 2021.

16 Among performance scholars, dance theorists have explored these issues most analogously in terms of 'virtual touch'. See Sita Popat, 'Virtually Touching*: Embodied Engagement in Telematic and Virtual Reality Performance', in *Contemporary Choreography*, 2nd edn.

(New York: Routledge, 2017). https://www.taylorfrancis.com/chapters/edit/10.4324/9781315563596-40/virtually-touching-sita-popat; Naomi P. Bennett, 'Telematic Connections: Sensing, Feeling, Being in Space Together', *International Journal of Performance Arts and Digital Media* 16, no. 3 (2020): 245–68; Susan Kozel, *Closer: Performance, Technologies, Phenomenology* (Cambridge: MIT Press, 2008).

17 Tom Gorman, Tiina Syrjä and Mikko Kanninen, theorizing the intimacy effects of what they refer to as their 'telemetric' production of *King Lear* (produced as a remote collaboration between students in Coventry and Tampere, Finland, pre-pandemic), suggest that 'the need to overcome peculiar qualities of distance experienced in telepresence acting connects us to what Harri Laakso calls 'the technology of yearning'. The telemetric experience makes the distant things forcefully and sometimes painfully present. This leads us to a world 'where the virtual is no longer anything remote, where distance is something we can touch' ('There Is a World Elsewhere: Rehearsing and Training through Immersive Telepresence', *Theatre, Dance and Performance Training* 10, no. 2 [2019]: 225).

18 Early uses of the word refer to the distance from the thumb to forefinger, that is, a handsbreadth, which suggests a distance that is both short and graspable, hence the verb 'to grasp, lay hold of, seize' and to 'make a span *over* something: to reach with or as with a span; to stretch or range *from* one place or point *to* another'. See 'span, n.1 and v.1', *OED Online*, September 2021. The English 'gap' suggests an 'opening or breach in an otherwise continuous object; a chasm or hiatus'. It derives from the Old Norse *gapa* 'to open the mouth' or gape ('gap, n.1', *OED Online*, September 2021).

19 'long, v.1', OED Online, September 2021. See also Anatoly Liberman, 'The Long Arm of Etymology, or, Longing for Word Origins', *OUPblog* (blog), 13 September 2006, https://blog.oup.com/2006/09/the_long_arm_of/.

20 Jean Luc Nancy, 'Body Theatre', in *Figures of Touch. Sense, Technics, Body*, ed. Mika Elo and Miika Luoto (Helsinki: University of Fine Arts Helsinki, 2018), 21.

21 Giannachi and Kaye, *Performing Presence*, 4.

22 Giannachi and Kaye, *Performing Presence*, 10–13. Philip Auslander's use of the term 'mediatized' performance (adapted from Baudrillad) as 'performance that is circulated on television, as audio or video recordings, and in other forms based in technologies of reproduction' continues to serve the field even as scholars are increasingly concerned with 'other forms' of reproduction and replay, such as web-performance and simulcast (Auslander, *Liveness*, 3). See Lindsay

Brandon Hunter, *Playing Real: Mimesis, Media, and Mischief* (Evanston: Northwestern University Press, 2021), 7. Pascale Aebischer prefers the term 'technologically mediated' (Aebischer, *Shakespeare, Spectatorship and the Technologies of Performance*). Gemma Allred and Benjamin Broadribb mark the distinction from analogue with the term 'digital theatre'. See Gemma Kate Allred, Benjamin Broadribb and Erin Sullivan, eds., *Lockdown Shakespeare: New Evolutions in Performance and Adaptation* (Arden, forthcoming, 2022).

23 Erikson in Giannachi and Kaye, *Performing Presence*, 18.
24 Ibid., 20.
25 On desiring matter, especially in Bacon, see Guido Giglioni, 'Introduction: Francis Bacon and the Theologico-political Reconfiguration of Desire in the Early Modern Period,' in Guido Giglioni, James A.T. Lancaster and Sorana Corneanu, eds., *Francis Bacon on Motion and Power*, International Archives of the History of Ideas 218 (Dordrecht: Springer, 2016), 1–40.
26 On sympathies and antipathies, see Mary Floyd-Wilson, *Occult Knowledge, Science, and Gender on the Shakespearean Stage* (Cambridge: Cambridge University Press, 2013), 1–27.
27 Johannes Baptista van Helmont, *A Ternary of Paradoxes: The Magnetick Cure of Wounds*, trans. Walter Charleton (London, 1650), 8.
28 Marsilio Ficino, *Three Books on Life*, ed. and trans. Carol Kaske and John Clark (Binghamton: Medieval & Renaissance Texts & Studies in conjunction with the Renaissance Society of America, 1989), 243.
29 Quintilian, *The Orator's Education, Volume III: Books 6–8*, ed. and trans. Donald A. Russell, Loeb Classical Library (Cambridge: Harvard University Press, 2002), 60–1.
30 He continues: 'What Can Not Poets Do? They Life Can Give/And after Fatall Stroke Can Make Men Live' (Henry Adamson, *The Muses Threnodie, or, Mirthfull Mournings,* [Edinburgh, 1638], 28).
31 William Shakespeare, *Shakespeare's Sonnets: Revised*, ed. Katherine Duncan-Jones, Arden Third Series, (London: Bloomsbury, 2010), 221.
32 Desiderius Erasmus, *The Seconde Tome or Volume of the Paraphrase of Erasmus Vpon the Newe Testament* (London, 1549), fol. XXv.
33 John Prime, *A Short Treatise of the Sacraments Generally, and in Speciall of Baptisme* (London, 1582), D6r.
34 Pietro Martire Vermigli, *The Common Places of the Most Famous and Renowmed Diuine Doctor Peter Martyr* (London, 1583), 140.
35 For a comprehensive account of enargeia and the rhetorical work of imagining presence in Reformation theology and poetry, to

which my thinking is indebted, see Yaakov A. Mascetti, 'Tokens of Love: Part 1: Renaissance and Reconnaissance', *Common Knowledge* 27, no. 1 (2021): 1–39.

36 The wildly popular immersive dinner-theatre production, which debuted in 1985, ushered in an age of commercialized environmental theatre that appropriated such techniques previously associated with the avant-garde. See Arnold Aronson, *The History and Theory of Environmental Scenography* (London: Bloomsbury, 2018), 4.

37 This scene is frequently cited as the definitive example of enargeia in Shakespeare (i.e. Plett, *Enargeia in Classical Antiquity and the Early Modern Age*, chap. 3) and in early modern writing more broadly (i.e. Claire Preston, 'Ekphrasis: Painting in Words', in *Renaissance Figures of Speech*, ed. Gavin Alexander, Katrin Ettenhuber, and Sylvia Adamson [Cambridge: Cambridge University Press, 2007], 115–30).

38 See Alison V. Scott, *Literature and the Idea of Luxury in Early Modern England* (New York: Routledge, 2016), chap. 2.

39 William Shakespeare, *Antony and Cleopatra*, ed. John Wilders, Arden Third Series (London and New York: Bloomsbury, 1995). All references to this play henceforth cited parenthetically in the text.

40 Later twentieth-century readings of the elusiveness of presence in *Antony and Cleopatra* have sought to populate or fill these gaps by identifying the bodies that lie outside of the frame of representation and invest the representation of absence with their affective and seductive power (mainly as objects of queer and/or Orientalized desire). See Catherine Belsey, 'Cleopatra's Seduction', in *Alternative Shakespeares: Volume 2*, ed. Terence Hawkes (London: Routledge, 1996); Jonathan Gil Harris, '"Narcissus in Thy Face": Roman Desire and the Difference It Fakes in Antony and Cleopatra', *Shakespeare Quarterly* 45, no. 4 (1994): 408–25. Catherine Belsey remarks Cleopatra's seduction as one of strategically deferred presence. The play, she says, 'locates her at a distance ... her erotic power is seen as mysteriously elsewhere, deferred, indefinable, irreducible to language, identified only as a transcendent and thus inevitably absent presence' (44–5). Belsey's analysis both draws on a Derridean account of absent presence and suggests that this absence gestures at the presence of the boys whose desirability invests Cleopatra with her unimaginable seductiveness.

41 Giannachi and Kaye, *Performing Presence*, 20.

42 On the debates surrounding the (im)possibility of the vacuum in early modern thought, see Edward Grant, *Much Ado about Nothing: Theories of Space and Vacuum from the Middle Ages to the Scientific Revolution* (Cambridge: Cambridge University Press, 1981).

43 On paradox in *Antony and Cleopatra*, see Benjamin T. Spencer, 'Antony and Cleopatra and the Paradoxical Metaphor', *Shakespeare Quarterly* 9, no. 3 (1958): 373–78; Janet Adelman, *The Common Liar: An Essay on Antony and Cleopatra* (New Haven: Yale University Press, 1973); Peter G. Platt, *Shakespeare and the Culture of Paradox* (Farnham: Ashgate, 2009). On temporality, see David Kaula, 'The Time Sense of Antony and Cleopatra', *Shakespeare Quarterly* 15, no. 3 (1964): 211–23; J. K. Barret, *Untold Futures: Time and Literary Culture in Renaissance England* (Ithaca: Cornell University Press, 2016), chap. 5.

44 Harald William Fawkner, *Shakespeare's Hyperontology: Antony and Cleopatra* (Rutherford, NJ: Fairleigh Dickinson University Press, 1990), 55.

45 Ibid., 60.

46 Hans-Thies Lehmann, *Postdramatic Theatre*, trans. Karen Jurs-Munby (New York: Routledge, 2006), 144.

47 'breathless power breath' F1; 'breathlesse power breath F2; breathless power breathe F3 and F4; 'breathless, pour breath' Oxford.

48 'pant, v.', *OED Online*, December 2021. Oxford University Press.

49 On the racial disparity of Covid-19 mortality rates, see William Mude et al., 'Racial Disparities in Covid-19 Pandemic Cases, Hospitalisations, and Deaths: A Systematic Review and Meta-Analysis', *Journal of Global Health* 11 (26 June 2021): 0501; Ralph Lawton et al., 'A Longitudinal Study of Convergence between Black and White Covid-19 Mortality: A County Fixed Effects Approach', *The Lancet Regional Health – Americas* 1 (1 September 2021). On gendered impacts, see Alexandra N. Fisher and Michelle K. Ryan, 'Gender Inequalities during Covid-19', *Group Processes & Intergroup Relations* 24, no. 2 (1 February 2021): 237–45; Jewel Gausman and Ana Langer, 'Sex and Gender Disparities in the Covid-19 Pandemic', *Journal of Women's Health* 29, no. 4 (1 April 2020): 465–6. On socioeconomic disparity of risk, see Gonzalo E. Mena et al., 'Socioeconomic Status Determines Covid-19 Incidence and Related Mortality in Santiago, Chile', *Science* 372, no. 6545 (28 May 2021).

50 My questions here are inspired by emerging work on respiratory in/security and in/justice in and between the fields of critical human geography, disability studies and critical race studies. See Marijn Nieuwenhuis, 'The Politics of Breathing: Knowledge on Air and Respiration', in *Atmospheres of Breathing*, ed. Lenart Skof and Petri Berndtson (Albany: State University of New York Press, 2018), 78–95; Marijn Nieuwenhuis, 'Atmospheric Governance: Gassing as Law for

the Protection and Killing of Life', *Environment and Planning D: Society and Space* 36, no. 2 (2017): 78–95; Jasbir K. Puar, *The Right to Maim: Debility, Capacity, Disability* (Chapel Hill: Duke University Press, 2017); Lundy Braun, *Breathing Race into the Machine: The Surprising Career of the Spirometer from Plantation to Genetics* (Minneapolis: University of Minnesota Press, 2014); Rob Nixon, *Slow Violence and the Environmentalism of the Poor* (Cambridge: Harvard University Press, 2011).

51 Muller argued that 'the specificity of theatre is . . . not the presence of the live actor but the presence of the one who is potentially dying' (quoted in Lehmann, *Postdramatic Theatre*, 144).

52 Allie Marotta, 'The Ableist Effects of Creating "Post-Pandemic Theatre" During a Pandemic', *HowlRound Theatre Commons*, https://howlround.com/ableist-effects-creating-post-pandemic-theatre-during-pandemic, accessed 6 October 2021; Pascale Aebischer and Rachael Nicholas, 'Digital Theater Transformation: Digital Toolkit', *University of Exeter*, October 2020, https://creationtheatre.co.uk/wp-content/uploads/2022/01/Digital-Theatre-Transformation.pdf, accessed 28 July 2022.

3

Medium specificity, medium convergence and aliveness in the chromakey (2018) and Big Telly Zoom (2020) *Macbeths*[1]

Thomas Cartelli

In the first half of this chapter, I use specific features of Kit Monkman's recent chromakey *Macbeth* (2018) to ask a series of questions about what I take to be a transitional stage in the evolution of screen Shakespeare, one poised between an analogue, cinematic past and a digital, virtual future. Some of these questions are: What are the affordances of reproducing Shakespeare on screen when the reproductive apparatus unmoors Shakespeare from grounding in a conventionally realistic cinematic environment? How do – or should – actors and acting conform to the aesthetic of a floating world that not only lacks fixed framings and grounding but repeatedly calls attention to its discontinuities and constructedness? What practices are best suited to encourage the engagement and interactivity of such a film's viewers? How can the rarefied atmosphere conjured by such a film convey a sense of *aliveness* that actively engages its viewing audience? If, as some media theorists contend, a work of art is successful insofar as it fulfils its medium specificity, how do we apply such formulas to artworks in an intermediate stage of development? May we legitimately derive from what the artwork lacks what successor artworks require in order to fulfil the promise of medium specificity? Or would we do better to resist the boundary-policing tendency of such 'media scripts' in favour of exploring how 'the traffic, recycling, and cross-pollination between screen and other arts' – which Katherine Rowe identifies with media *convergence* – 'expand our sense of the formal properties specific to a given medium'?[2]

In the second half of this piece, I ask related questions regarding the opportunistic use of the Zoom teleconference platform in the Big Telly Theatre Company's *Macbeth* (2020), one of the more provocative productions of lockdown Shakespeare, which was presented in a hybridized mix of live and recorded formats for a few weeks in the fall of 2020. Given the recent resumption of live theatre performance in many parts of the globe, the deployment of Zoom as a performance medium is already in decline. Hence, rather than marking a transitional moment in live and/or recorded theatrical production, Zoom may merely occupy a provisional or fallback position in any future economy of performance and reception transactions. That said, the number, quality, resourcefulness and frequent *aliveness* of even fully recorded performances enabled and mediated by the Zoom platform, and the ability of the medium to help socially distanced individuals inhabit (however briefly) virtual communities during the pandemic, suggests that future space may well be afforded for theatre practitioners to develop newer, technically adept strategies to make Zoom theatre less of an ephemeral, provisional phenomenon and more of a creative alternative to conventional in-person, digital or cinematic production.

Unlike most theatre performances created and distributed by means of Zoom technology during the first phase of the global Covid-19 lockdown, Big Telly's *Macbeth* was presented *live* and occasionally integrated the spotlighted reactions of its self-selected auditors to its five performers who, like the auditors, were effectively spotlighting themselves from the privacy of their own homes. As a rather singular case in comparison with other, largely pre-recorded Zoom lockdown productions, the Big Telly *Macbeth* may prompt one to ask to what extent its condition of (semi-)liveness makes its performance comparable to the live performances of the early modern stage, always recognizing, with Philip Auslander, that there could be no *acknowledged* condition of liveness in the days before recorded performance.[3] But this question involves conflating what is merely a performance condition (liveness) with a performance effect (aliveness). I've poached my twist on *aliveness* from an intriguing essay by Martin Barker where he writes that 'we should understand "alive" experiences as *emergent,* that is, as they are experienced they are felt . . . to open up new possibilities', whether these be immersive in orientation or more casually open-ended.[4] I particularly endorse Barker's decision to 'rethink' liveness as aliveness on the grounds that it offers an experience-based way of substituting moments in time when memorable contact is made between artwork and audience in place of a concept – liveness – that doesn't in isolation supply a specific value-added charge to a shared physical or temporal condition. As we shall see, the interruptive shifts between the often seamless editing of its live and recorded sequences, the roughness and intensity of its face-on presentational style, and its generally awkward embedding of live auditors in its virtual performance space position Big Telly's *Macbeth* at a stylistic remove from Monkman's technically adept, formally distanced but generally more immersive chromakey *Macbeth*. At the same time, Big Telly's shifting modes of address arguably contribute an *effect* of *aliveness* that obviates the search for residual indicators of live performance in the fully recorded version of the production that serves as my primary point of reference.

The chromakey *Macbeth*

Kit Monkman is possibly the first film director since Peter Greenaway to employ a multi-windowed, super high-tech-savvy cinematic approach to an adaptation of Shakespeare, in this instance enabled by chromakey (green screen) film-making technology. Taking full advantage of the affordance 'that allows you to take your subjects out of the real world and [place them] into a completely new world', Monkman generates a dramatic/cinematic environment that is everywhere and nowhere at once.[5] Though plot, language and highly accented speech establish its Shakespearean provenance, the film often floats free of its theatrical moorings and the stylings of cinematic realism alike. Scenes don't so much end as slip into a kind of vertically oriented re-routing, as if the search function on one's laptop were scrolling through a panel of possibilities, some collateral with what we've already seen, some seemingly summoned by accident from a tributary database stream. But though it browses a tempting array of cinematic spaces before choosing one on which to land, the film always re-sets in a compartment that is recognizably *Macbeth*.

How Monkman deploys chromakey to generate this cinematic environment is described in this excerpt from Judith Buchanan's programme notes distributed at the film's London premiere on Tuesday, 13 March 2018:

> The film's drama is contained within a floating world [that] features multiple layers of playing space presented as empty rooms or wider arenas awaiting occupation. The camera roams around these, exploring the multiple architectural compartments and coming, *as if by happenstance*, upon dramatic moments in the playing spaces it enters. Each time *it chooses* the next zone for its focused investigation and moment of sustained observation, *that space becomes what it needs to be as the site of the action it is hosting*. . . . This unformed-ness is a product of the post-production business of replacing green screen with a digitally built world. The decision to leave visible the traces of its own construction and to resist communicating a definitive sense of sealed completion, however, *signals the quasi-theatrical laws by which these spaces operate*. . . . each scene claims only as much full defined space as is required for that piece of action to play out. *The rest is merely bare boards*, or indicative construction lines, awaiting the next narrative claim on it to become what it then needs to be [emphases mine].[6]

Buchanan – co-author of the film's screenplay and a leading Shakespeare-on-film scholar – supplies here a telling account of how the 'digitally built world' that replaces 'green screen' offers viewers a constantly evolving backdrop, which ranges from the occasional conventionally propertied space of tables and wall hangings to something considerably more fluid on shifting stages that seem to float like satellites in outer space. Her remarks, however, may not be entirely reliable guides to how viewers respond to how the film moves through its allotted space-time. As my italicized phrases indicate, whatever claims to formal singularity this trailblazing chromakey *Macbeth* may advance or embody are qualified by the passage's repeated likening of the film's protean playing spaces to the differently protean features of the considerably more grounded, barebones fixed stage, most often associated with early modern playhouses. These comparisons indicate an effort to recoup or recover the aura of what is regrettably lost or diminished in the process of making a film that is, technically speaking, light years removed from original practices. Indeed, the rhetorical likening of the film's playing spaces to theatrical space, with each scene playing out on essentially the same minimally propertied soundstage, belies the fact that the *filming* of these scenes involves a roaming camera that puts them into unprecedented motion and a post-production artistry that re-sets them in fluidly fluctuating spaces unimaginable in early modern playhouses or, for that matter, in more conventionally rendered films of *Macbeth*.

Monkman and Buchanan, of course, have nothing to say about medium specificity – which is *my* preoccupation, not theirs – and readily acknowledge the 'quasi-theatrical laws' that govern how their playing 'spaces operate', which suggests that it is actually medium *convergence*, particularly with established theatrical and cinematic practices, that informs this film's aims and design: a factor amplified by the film's grounding on, and occasional projection of extracts from, a 1909 silent film version of *Macbeth* directed by Mario Caserini. These extracts, screened in a cinematic ground floor identified as the Porter's lodge, literally anchor this film's tracings of a virtual future to foundational substructures of the cinematic past. In Monkman's narrative framework, Caserini's film is gifted to the Porter by a child associated with a beneficent-seeming but presumably otherworldly woman (identified only as 'Mother' in the programme notes), the reels awaiting release from the old film can in which they have been interred, thus making the silent film projected against the lodge's wall seem as much the product of supernatural agency as Macbeth's drive to make himself king (Figure 3.1).

But if medium convergence and a concomitant tendency to engage in media allegory – in a manner pioneered by Olivier's *Henry V* (1944) and differently mined in later Shakespeare films ranging from Greenaway's *Prospero's Books* (1991) to Michael Almereyda's *Hamlet* (2000) – are primary touchstones of Monkman's film, in what other quarter of technical development can its singularity be located or found? In his own opening section

FIGURE 3.1 *In the Porter's screening room from* Macbeth, *dir. Kit Monkman, 2018.*

of programme notes, Monkman states that he wants 'to make films that reignite the imaginative participation of the audience; films that celebrate theatricality and thrive on the viewers' co-creation of what unfolds'. This page concludes with Monkman suggesting that his *Macbeth* constitutes just such 'an opportunity to present a new type of experience on film, one that . . . treats the audience as active participants in the creative endeavour'.[7] The interactivity of audiences functioning as co-creators of imaginative experiences has an aspirational basis in places as different as the great Iranian filmmaker Abbas Kiarostomi's theories about 'an unfinished cinema' and the core interactive experiences on offer in virtual reality (VR) apps and video gaming sessions.[8] Indeed, one of Kiarostomi's later films, *Shirin*, concentrates entirely on the presumed responsiveness of an audience comprising 113 women to the screening of a film that *Shirin*'s presumptive audience never actually sees, such that we read the film (and the ghosted film-within-the-film) by assessing their presumed responses.[9] I cite this example because compared to the interactivity supplied by VR apps and video gaming, the 'cocreation' of cinematic experiences by audiences of films is almost always more aspirational than evidential. Buchanan persuasively highlights the 'unformed-ness' of the cinematic world Monkman puts on display, which suggests the availability of virtual spaces of 'unfinished cinema' for audiences to access and fill in. But as my italicizing of 'as if by happenstance' and 'it chooses' in the programme note suggests, *how* the succession of scenes progresses and *where* Monkman's camera lands are never serendipitous or subject to audience intervention, both deriving from the film-maker's conscious choice to have scenes play out in and as reasonable facsimiles of the play's settings and events, however creatively crucial plot-points and speeches have been restructured, reassigned and reordered.[10]

Invitations to 'finish' or refine what the film leaves unfinished or doubtful are, nonetheless, occasionally on offer to viewers, beginning with the film's opening moments as the screen frame is filled by the serious, sympathetic face of 'Mother' (Wunmi Mosaku) and then filled out as the image widens to embrace the rest of her hooded and robed body and two closely held children. We watch as she whispers to them and they deliver Caserini's silent film to the lighted dwelling on the edge of the soundstage, prompting us to ask: Who are these surrogates for the playtext's witches, and why are they presented in so differently charged a manner than in virtually all other reproductions of the play? Who is this so-called Porter (Dai Bradley), who is able to screen the film on his own projector in a matter of minutes and seems delighted by it? And what relationship does Monkman expect us to draw between the silent film and his own film of *Macbeth*, which commences in earnest after this mysteriously engaging prelude? Each of these questions offers an opportunity for interactive audience engagement, as does a later, distinctly disorienting sequence that displaces and elides most of *Macbeth* 4.1 and consists of a series of visions that substitute for Macbeth's second encounter with the witches. As Buchanan describes it:

> the visions that Mark Rowley's Macbeth 'sees' appear to him in his sleeping world, and they take the form of the conjurations depicted in the 1909 film, projected on to the pillars around him. . . . The film that seemed to start life with an identifiable singularity, tightly locked inside a containing film canister, gradually permeates the imaginative spaces of this world . . . perhaps such viral levels of uncontainable permeation are precisely what does happen when a powerful story . . . is introduced into a new eco-system.[11]

This two-minute sequence starts with Macbeth still seated drinking at the head of the same, now-disordered table set for his deranged encounter with Banquo's ghost (3.4) and conjuring the witches in voice-over. Without any obvious signposting to viewers, the screen begins to scroll vertically through several unclearly designated settings before settling on a space that resembles the undercroft of a church defined by pillars on which, as Buchanan writes, projected images from Caserini's silent film are synched to additional voice-over responses to Macbeth's conjurations. Images from this film briefly take charge of the entire screen right before the scene shifts to Macbeth awakening in his bed from the troubled dream that has presumably hosted his second encounter with Monkman's surrogates for Shakespeare's witches.

In offering opportunities like these to viewers to make sense of 'such viral levels of uncontainable permeation', Monkman's *Macbeth* may well be making, in Philip Auslander's terms, 'a claim on us to engage with them as live events' – or possibly not, given Auslander's contention that 'some real-time operations of digital technology make [such] a claim [...] and others do not'.[12] What kind of claim, if any, does Monkman's *Macbeth* make on us and how can that claim prompt us to engage with an artfully assembled film as a live event? Again according to Auslander, whatever claim 'some technological artifact – a computer, Website, network, or virtual entity', or, by extension, a film may make upon us,

> we, the audience, must accept the claim as binding upon us, take it seriously, and hold onto the object in our consciousness of it *in such a way that it becomes live for us*. In this analysis, liveness is neither a characteristic of the object nor an effect caused by some aspect of the object such as its medium, ability to respond in real time, or anthropomorphism. Rather, liveness is an interaction produced through our engagement with the object and our willingness to accept its claim.[13]

Monkman's express claim is to '[treat] the audience as active participants in the creative endeavour' such that it becomes co-creators of 'what unfolds'. Does this, can this, happen for viewers of the Monkman *Macbeth*? It certainly *can* happen with respect to viewer interrogation of the film's opening interpolation and effort to negotiate meaning out of the unusually benign-looking women and children who serve as surrogates for *Macbeth*'s typically more malign witches. And co-creation can, of course, happen for *any* auditor sufficiently engaged by other moments of the film to try to 'fill in' what the film chooses to leave out, as in the film's powerfully compressed re-staging of *Macbeth* 4.1. But audience efforts to co-create 'what unfolds' as the film proceeds to rehearse (however discontinuously) the play's established plot are often discouraged by the closed circuit within which that plot is routed. For example, as the opening credits roll and a series of unscripted actions (pillage, rape, burial, all connected to the violence and chaos of war) are presented on vertically scrolling, digitally produced panels, we may be tempted to expect that something outside the parameters of the text of *Macbeth* will be disclosed or set into motion. But by the time the credits conclude, the 'bloody man' who can 'report . . . of the revolt/the newest state' (*Macbeth* 1.2.1-3) has become centred in the film frame, and as he approaches a stunning, photographically posed silent tableau of Duncan and his court, the play of *Macbeth* snaps to attention, with questions left to be asked largely concerning the silent film, the benign-looking witches and children, and the elliptical way in which scenes like 4.1 are presented and performed. Such mysteries and several additional visualized but unexplored scrolled settings *suggest* the possibility that alternative paths to the *Macbeth* narrative could be made available to the venturous auditor. But as an effectively closed artefact – in terms of dramatic structure if not style of address – the film forecloses on that possibility by reproducing the play's plot, however resourcefully restructured and re-presented.

It isn't, however, only its repeated association of cinematic representation with 'quasi-theatrical laws' and foreclosure of 'live' hypertextual options that inhibit the film's effort to dematerialize *Macbeth* and thereby elevate it above and beyond conventional cinematic realism. This effort is weighed down by distractingly naturalistic, overly casual 'presentist' acting in several of the film's primary roles, primarily by Mark Rowley and Al Weaver in the roles of Macbeth and Banquo. It is also rendered earthbound by the frequently leaden delivery of lines, which clash with qualities better attuned to the fragile economy of chromakey film-making, such as the cooler, more stylized manner in which Akiya Henry undertakes the role of Lady Macbeth. The economy of this kind of film-making – an electronic ecosystem that positions real-life actors in computer-generated environments – is fragile to the extent that it depends on the seamless convergence of the immaterial and the material, the semi-constructed framings of abstract space and gravity-bound actors.

Such seamless convergences occur often enough in this visually arresting, boundary-breaking film to occasion regret when they do not, which is not to say that technical solutions need exclusively be sought in the enhanced immateriality of the holographic projections Gregory Doran manufactured using live motion-capture technology in his 'tech-enabled' RSC *Tempest* (2016).[14] Clashes of the material and immaterial are to be expected in the early stages of such work. More regrettable is the film's foreclosure of dramatic options for the visual possibilities it puts on offer, its failure to entertain alternative pathways for characters and spectators to explore or inhabit in order (as noted earlier) to enhance 'engagement with the object'. The rooms upon rooms, animatronic books, angelic *putti* urinating into the Roman bath in which John Gielgud's Prospero holds forth in Greenaway's *Prospero's Books* offer models of spatially expansive, intriguingly paratextual options Monkman might have pursued had he allowed actors and auditors to off-ramp the plot of *Macbeth* instead of allowing the film to settle back into a replication of the play's established design. Similarly speculative pathways are on offer in the inspired materializations of the Macduffs' sitting room and Macbeths' bedchamber, a densely furnished herbalist shop and forbiddingly austere asylum ward, and the largely non-representational dance performances that seem to wait around every corner of the McKittrick Hotel in the once seemingly forever run of *Sleep No More* in New York.

It may have been Monkman's effort to make a largely faithful film of *Macbeth* that clogged its digital arteries in the first place. Richer affordances might have been generated by an open-ended *Macbeth* website, which could have made alternative pathways available to all comers, either of the pre-scripted, pre-staged, pre-filmed variety or by a VR undertaking, which could have better exploited the visual pleasures evoked when this film isn't busily going about the business of successively rehearsing *Macbeth* plot-points. Indeed, it is in those in-between moments, when Monkman's camera seems to be aimlessly searching for a landing place in a floating world that resembles an unmoored space station, that this film seems to find what it is looking for: a freely associative space beyond drama and narrative alike. At some moments, just before the camera's landing, we hear a succeeding scene drawn from the *Macbeth* playtext start speaking itself before characters appear in their delegated compartment, as if the drama were floating free of

FIGURE 3.2 *Fleance sitting at the edge of the world from* Macbeth, *dir. Kit Monkman, 2018.*

its plot moorings and constraints. Several times the film makes use of its nowhere/everywhere atmospherics to have characters sitting or standing at the edge of a cliff that overhangs empty space as if the set itself and setting of the film were an inside-out spaceship or satellite or vagrant chip of a crescent moon (Figure 3.2).

In many ways, the most exciting prospect opened up by the film encourages viewers to feel as if they are entering an immersive, genuinely virtual realm. As someone who has, during a VR experience, felt the dizzying effect of a stairway opening up under me that I seemed capable of descending, I was able to experience something of the same vertiginous promise when tracings of seemingly endless virtual stairways offered the same invitation here. The film generates multiple spaces like these out of a large database of possibilities but fails to offer viewers pathways that make those spaces as much a part of their experience as the always already experienced plot of *Macbeth*. In a word borrowed from Doreen Massey by way of N. Katherine Hayles, the cyberspatial prospects opened up by Monkman's film are not sufficiently 'lively' to entertain possibilities apart from those redundantly on offer.[15]

It's in this circuitous way – considering what the Monkman *Macbeth isn't* doing that it *could* be doing – that we return to earlier concerns about medium specificity and medium convergence. Questions about medium specificity have been posed about every successive form of dramatic storytelling over the last 125 years, beginning with silent film's challenge to live theatre, then moving on to television's challenge to motion pictures and live theatre in the 1950s, and now focusing on cyberspace's tentacular, multi-mediated challenge to television, live theatre and conventional film-making practices alike. Indeed, I've recently come across a 1915 defence of silent film that, in many particulars, could well serve as a précis of the medium specificity of silent black-and-white film at the moment it transitioned from an emergent to a dominant medium of dramatic expression. As Henry MacMahon writes in the 6 June 1915 edition of *The New York Times*:

> The film play, compared with its rival, the stage play, has certain serious defects, notably the absence of sound and color. But on the other hand, it has certain compensating qualities of its own and producers are very wisely laying more stress on these instead of imitating what the stage can always do better. For instance, the film playwright can use all outdoors for his background instead of a painted and rumpled back drop. He can change the scene oftener than the Elizabethan dramatist. He can dip into the future or the past as though he were in Wells's time-machine.... *He can reveal the mind of his characters in two ways, neither of them possible on the stage, first by bringing the actor so close that the spectator can read his facial expression, and second, by visualizing his memories or imaginings* [my emphases].[16]

MacMahon was a research consultant and publicist for D.W. Griffith's *Birth of a Nation* (1915) and hence served in the formal vanguard of film's evolution, which is perhaps why his distillation of film's specific qualities and potentials seems so acute. But I've italicized his insight into how film can 'reveal the mind of [its] characters' precisely because 103 years later, Monkman brings Macbeth into sustained, unflattering close-up while he runs Macbeth's 'sound and fury speech' in voice-over (while the temporarily out-of-frame Macduff patiently waits for Macbeth to finish so he can chop off his head). What MacMahon isolates out as a defining feature of silent film is thus regressively rehearsed by Monkman's close-up, abetted by the 70-year-old Shakespearean voice-over convention he inherits from Olivier's Hamlet soliloquies. We are likely meant to witness this moment's privileging of media

FIGURE 3.3 *Virtual spaces in Monkman's floating world from* Macbeth, *dir. Kit Monkman, 2018.*

convergence as a kind of *hommage* to silent film itself, which grounds its media allegory. But I rather see it – as before – as a recursive drag on the film's hypertextual potential.

At its best, the Monkman *Macbeth* demonstrates what digital film-making may do when it becomes unmoored from the media – filmed theatre, analogue film – it is convergent with, most notably in its suggestive 'transporting of scenes into the inside of a vast globe which simultaneously sits on Macbeth's desk and envelops the dramatic space'.[17] It is not until his film is ending that Monkman gives us a macrocosmic view of this 'vast globe' itself, presented as a floating world in which we can make out tiny figures possibly enacting virtual scenes we've not been able to access more directly. In so doing, he leaves us with a glimpse of what differently formatted *Macbeths* might afford future Shakespeare users once the play is liberated from its endlessly recurring repetition (Figure 3.3).

Big Telly's *Macbeth*

No one could anticipate that the global pandemic, which shut down most theatrical and filmic commerce with the Bard in 2020 and 2021, would generate, by means of the emergent Zoom platform, so wide an array of experiments in live and recorded performances, including a medium-specific version of *Macbeth* that is also (predictably) medium convergent. Directed by Zoë Seaton with deft technical support supplied by Sinéad Owens, Big Telly's *Macbeth* premiered under the auspices of the Belfast International Arts Festival from 14 to 17 October 2020 and went on to enjoy an additional ten-day virtual run hosted by the Creation Theatre box office and platform in Oxford, concluding on Halloween, 31 October. Unlike almost all theatrically centred Zoom productions in the first plague year – a conspicuous exception being Big Telly's *The Tempest*, a 'digital immigrant' co-produced with Creation Theatre Company in April 2020 – *Macbeth* was 'digitally native' and transmitted live, enabling the incorporation of a considerable amount of auditor spotlighting in a skilfully orchestrated hybrid mix of live and pre-recorded performance.[18] (The live auditors were prompted to keep their cameras on four times during performances so that they might be incorporated into the proceedings.) Like highlights of earlier Zoom-enabled theatrical productions such as Richard Nelson's three additions to his growing body of plays about the Apple family of Rhinebeck, New York, the acting in the BT *Macbeth* was almost entirely face-on presentational in the style J.L. Styan long ago identified with the non-illusory theatre of the Elizabethans. But whereas the Apples are presented in four separate, adjacent panels in Zoom's gallery format, Seaton generally isolates her characters within a single, exclusive speaking frame, adapting film's continuity editing technique of shot-reverse-shot to a software-enabled frame-reverse-frame approach in order to stage remotely performed dialogic interactions. As Amy Borsuk observes in a review of the production:

> The show runs from multiple accounts, including one just for sharing sound, and another 'Hecate's' account onto which all the special effects are compiled to create the full composite effect. To make the eerie encounter between Macbeth and Banquo's ghost, for example, Macbeth stands in his own screen looking to the right, Banquo in his own screen sat looking left, and on the shared screen Hecate brings these two together into the banquet hall, with Banquo sat at the table and Macbeth standing beside him in fear.[19]

In her own recent trailblazing account of the *Tempest* collaboration and the Big Telly *Macbeth*, Pascale Aebischer asks the following larger question of such digital platform manoeuvres: 'To what extent does the medium of a videoconferencing platform facilitate the remediation of early modern spatial dramaturgies and audience participation and deal with the vexed questions of copresence and liveness when performers and audiences are all geographically dispersed?'[20] A short answer to Aebischer's question is that the dispersion of the audience, and their subjection to externally managed spotlighting, inhibits their ability to exercise responsive agency when prompted to do so, which in turn forecloses the similarly dispersed actors' ability to play to or against a copresent audience. Indeed, in those parts of the production when the liveness of the actors themselves is captured once and for all and distilled in a single recorded performance, we have the odd circumstance of an absent audience being more lively present than the actors themselves. However, when Seaton's cast of five actors – who had never met each other before in person – *synchronously* Zoom themselves in from five different locations (Belfast, Deptford, Dublin, Kent and London) to perform their parts *live*, we entertain something very different, which recalls the early days of 1950s live TV when performing and viewing conditions were at least analogous to the high-wire do-or-die acts that obtain in live theatre performance. In this and other respects, as Aebischer observes, Zoom

> is similar to theatre broadcasts insofar as it lends itself to replicating the technological proximity to a character, and the creation of an intimate and emotional bond with a performer that does not necessarily depend on direct address to the audience. Instead, the audience's affective investment in a character may simply be the result of the 'camerawork' of the performer, as they frame themselves and change their position vis-à-vis their webcam to create the equivalent of mid-shots and close-ups.[21]

These 'on air' performances are often stitched together skilfully enough to resemble a professionally edited film, though they also often generate considerably rougher Zoom footage, such as when all five actors need to be seen in the narrow third-floor hallway of Lady Macbeth's tightly packed home in the performance of *Macbeth* 2.3. However awkward such moments appeared, making so many characters visible within the same frame could also be accounted an improvement on 'the early days of Zoom theatre (March 2020)', when, as Crissy O'Donovan recounts, 'we were screensharing', which 'added moments of disruption to the action'. Thanks to the employment of vMix software, O'Donovan adds, Big Telly's technical manager, Sinéad Owens, was able to 'pull performers' screens into the software and share it back through her screen' and 'to blend filmed and live performances', making them seem 'much more continuous and seamless'.[22]

Technical advances apart, Seaton is experimenting with the available technology in an open-ended, audience-friendly manner. As she states in an interview, 'One of the biggest reasons I love game theatre and why I think it translates so successfully to Zoom is that it is absolutely about focusing on the audience experience. And that means both inviting people to be playful while respecting people's right to choose how far they want to go.'[23] Some commentators are not persuaded that such claims carry over from the earlier Big Telly/ Creation Theatre *Tempest* to the Big Telly *Macbeth*. As Benjamin Broadribb writes in an online review of the latter, 'Whilst certainly "playful" . . . these elements also had a sinister edge: whether they were aware of it or not, audience members featured on screen were part of the witches' charade.'[24] That said, inducting audiences virtually into 'the witches' charade' in the lead-up to a lockdown Halloween performance could also be construed as offering viewers theatrical fare that was just as topically timely as performances of *The Merchant of Venice* or *Bartholomew Fair* on the early modern stage. As Philip Auslander observes, 'in order for a work to be meaningful, we must experience it as *contemporaneous*', adding the qualifier that 'Contemporaneity in this sense is not a characteristic of the work itself [but] a description of how we choose to engage with it'. Going on to contend that when we 'grasp it as contemporaneous', a 'work of art from a past of which we have no direct experience becomes fully present to us', Auslander suggests that 'in order to experience interactive technologies as live, we similarly must be willing to experience and take seriously their claims to liveness and presence: an entity we know to be technological that makes a claim to being live becomes fully present to us when we grasp it as live'.[25] In this respect, the thoroughly collaborative *in the moment* attitude Seaton and her ensemble bring to their project often generates a sense of shared presence with their audience in which an effect of *aliveness* could be said to compensate for whatever deficit of liveness is recorded or experienced.[26]

It should not, on this account, be assumed that *presence* is only generated in the expressly live patches of the Big Telly *Macbeth* production, or mainly when Seaton injects audience-friendly dollops of humour, camp, schlock and implausibility into her production. Indeed, a sense of presence or aliveness often emerges from the pre-recorded sequences, one of which in particular delivers an unqualifiedly serious theatrical experience. This is the edited passage of live and recorded material that has the 'onstage' Macbeth speaking the sound and fury speech in voice-over as we watch a carefully assembled montage of Lady Macbeth wading into the Irish Sea to achieve a death by drowning. For Lady Macbeth's resolute walk to the sea, Seaton uses a range of digitally recorded close-up, medium and long shots, including even an artfully superimposed transparency that doubles our view of Nicky Harley's Lady Macbeth, mixing and matching the affordances of the Zoom platform with conventional film-making technology. She mixes these shots with Dennis Herdman's evocative voice-over in a way that doubles down on our investment in characters, who, in more conventional productions of *Macbeth*, audiences would have long before divested themselves of any affective connection.

The topical way Seaton chooses to begin her production, however, could hardly be less predictive of its closing movement. Seaton starts by positioning her three multiple role-playing actors – Aonghus Og McAnally (Witch, Duncan, Macduff), Dharmesh Patel (Witch, Banquo), and Lucia McAnespie (Witch, Malcolm, Lady Macduff) – as government officials and having them deliver a cleverly scripted spoof of the frequent televised reports all of us endured during the Covid-19 crisis from varying casts of politicians, medical experts and authorities, real and imagined. The sequence culminates in a moment of live audience participation as auditors initially identified as witches (by way of superimposed conical witch-hats on their unassuming spotlighted heads) are re-identified as 'false positives'. In signalling contemporaneous connections between politically motivated misrepresentations of Covid-19, the opportunistic identification and victimization of witches in the past, and the formative role played by *Macbeth*'s witches in generating the play's tragic effects, Seaton attempts both to lighten the load of (re)performing *Macbeth* in the darkest of days while calling out the viral role played by untrustworthy political actors in making us all suffer for their sins of commission and omission alike.

Once performance of the play-proper begins, Seaton transposes her political actors into the witches of *Macbeth,* wearing

FIGURE 3.4 *Three officials morphed into witches with matching headpieces. Reproduced with permission of Big Telly Theatre Company, Northern Ireland.*

home-made cardboard headpieces that help mitigate the deeply sinister manner in which the lead-witch, played by McAnespie, speaks (Figure 3.4). After Seaton has McAnespie bitterly record the refusal of 'a sailor's wife' to share her chestnuts, she demonstrates the witches' vindictive power and agency when a (recorded) news report Lady Macbeth is watching ('live') on her laptop (also voiced by McAnespie) confirms the catastrophic loss of an argosy named *The Tiger* in the vicinity of Aleppo ('where the earth was feverous and did shake'), whose master became 'drained of blood' prior to the disaster. This interpolated scripting of the fruition of their curse against the sailor and his wife anticipates the power that the variably playful and predatory witches will command against the Macbeths and their victims throughout.

The 'darkness' of this reading of the play is one reason Aebischer found this lockdown production less hopeful in mitigating the strains of the pandemic than Big Telly's and Creation Theatre's earlier *Tempest*.[27] But it became for me a critical means of supplementing Herdman's performance as an emotionally isolated but unusually self-assured Macbeth and of recalibrating the formal 'glitches' of the production that are vetted in Aebischer's *Viral Shakespeare*. In the end, the predictable consequences of having actors record themselves in physical and tonal isolation from one another converge to generate a home-movie aesthetic that takes the chill out of the coolness of a medium founded on remoteness. The casualness of Seaton's approach to integrating live and recorded material encourages auditors to take pleasure in the variable archness and artlessness of her multiple role-playing actors while allowing her performers to express themselves in a range of styles. In an atmosphere of anything goes, anything went, among the highlights being Macbeth bouncing along to his coronation in a virtual carriage to a performance of Queen's 'We are the Champions' adapted to the anachronistic orchestration and beat of a 1920s British music hall recording (Figure 3.5). This appeared to be one sequence in which auditors fully enjoyed the opportunity to be spotlighted, cheerfully returning Macbeth's performatively royal waves from within the breached privacy of their home-viewing spaces, matching his delight with their own.[28]

Another creative convergence of face-on presentational Zoom recording and computer-generated imagery occurs when the Macbeths are dressing for the banquet (3.2), with Macbeth speaking directly to the camera, which does double dramatic duty here as his mirror. This scene literally takes flight when Macbeth's incantation beginning 'Come, seeling night', appears to summon a flock of

FIGURE 3.5 *Newly crowned Macbeth waving to supporters. Reproduced with permission of Big Telly Theatre Company, Northern Ireland.*

computer-generated bats who fly towards us, over and around and through Macbeth's face before dissolving into the presumptive mirror. What also distinguishes this moment from so many others in recent *Macbeth* productions is the pleasure verging on manic delight Herdman's Macbeth takes in plotting his way forward even as he fumbles with his collar and tie, something the actor never loses touch of even towards the bitter end of his fatal encounter with Macduff (Figure 3.6).

Arguably less successful was Seaton's setting of 4.1 in an actual theatre, with the witches pulling the theatre curtain up and down and thinly masking their amplified voices in order to include us in the deception of Macbeth, who sits 'virtually' alone in the orchestra. This scene highlights the convergence of Zoom film-making with traditional theatrical machinery and chromakey scene-setting alike, offering split-screen renderings of the witches' staged performance of their prophecies and Macbeth's reactions. Having this sequence '[s]eemingly conjured from within a Covid-19 closed theatre' also highlights the extent to which 'the loss of in-person theatre was at the core of the production'.[29] But the effort of stitching live actors into a virtualized 'real' theatre where the witches are compelled to do their own heavy lifting rather too glibly burlesques both

FIGURE 3.6 *Herdman modelling Macbeth's manic intensity. Reproduced with permission of Big Telly Theatre Company, Northern Ireland.*

their own and Macbeth's established claim to seriously sinister intent. And the virtual positioning in the royal box of the largely indifferent auditors who have turned their cameras on in response to a captioned invitation to a 'gala performance' belies the fact that the witches themselves are the only ones having a good time. Indeed, this scene – which concludes with virtual crowns being placed on the heads of the auditors by means of augmented reality filters – fails to sustain the aura of engagement generated by Herdman's intense and intelligent line readings and Harley's embodied affect.

In marked contrast, Seaton's evocative staging and filming of Lady Macbeth's walk into the Irish Sea while Macbeth rehearses the sound and fury speech perfectly conveys the two actors' different ways of inhabiting their characters: the one, full-bodied and expressive; the other, bitterly articulate but also unrepentant about the path he has chosen (Figure 3.7). This is, perhaps, not what viewers might have expected from a production that is otherwise eager to please in any number of cleverly offhand ways. But it appears to be what Seaton and her actors set out to achieve in their tonally promiscuous but almost always compelling Zoom project, darkly repurposed for dark days.

FIGURE 3.7 *Nikki Harley as Lady Macbeth about to take her long walk into the Irish Sea. Reproduced with permission of Big Telly Theatre Company, Northern Ireland.*

Coda

In a video essay on the Monkman *Macbeth*'s website, Akiya Henry (Lady Macbeth) describes the extent to which performing on an empty soundstage in front of a green screen closely resembled acting in a theatre rehearsal space while also requiring unusual leaps of imagination. Actors would often have to adjust to speaking in isolation to other absent actors who might appear in the same frame in the final edit. Not knowing how the space around them would ultimately be formed, actors would have to imagine how to walk through empty spaces that would eventually become filled with virtual framings and furnishings. Big Telly's actors faced considerably more isolating challenges. Instead of coming together to meet and interact on spacious soundstages with their director and fellow actors, they were stuck at home filming themselves and sharing footage by way of Zoom, having little to no knowledge of how any of this would play out. Both projects thus turned upon challenges that were not dissimilar from those early modern actors faced in preparing to perform roles sketched out in character-specific scripts whose only concession to the whole cloth of a play were their entrance cues.

A greater challenge the two projects faced was how to move from a position of distance or remoteness, exacerbated, respectively, by the chromakey film-making process and Zoom platform, to one of engagement with an audience of invisible lookers-on. Fortuitously, the word I've chosen to use for those moments in these productions when such contact was likely on offer, *aliveness,* complements Herbert Blau's wonderfully candid way of reframing what he calls a 'failing distinction' between acting in 'live' or 'living' theatre and on film or television. '[T]here were times', he recounts, when 'the presence of live actors made no real difference: stage or screen, the effect and/or affect was very much the same', indeed, times when 'the felt actuality was such . . . that the quotient of liveness seemed more in the transparency of film', adding that 'it was apparent that the factitious reality of the figures on a screen could have considerably more vitality, as if they were truly alive, than the flesh-and-blood actors up there on the stage'.[30]

Reversing the evaluative flow from the 'aura' of live performance to that of the electronically mediated 'body or face' of actors on screen has not been my agenda in this chapter. But while we are rethinking liveness as aliveness, it remains worth considering whether privileging the presence or immediacy of live actors on the modern or early modern stage makes one too quick to conflate a specific condition of performance with the powerful effects all manner of differently transmitted performances aspire to have – and often do have – on their audiences.

Notes

1. I owe Judith Buchanan a debt of gratitude for inviting me to the Monkman *Macbeth*'s premiere screening in London on 13 March 2018; another to Pascale Aebischer for acquainting me with Big Telly's *Macbeth*, for supplying advance access to her *Viral Shakespeare* MS and for generously sharing notes and corrections for this evolving MS; and a third to Crissy O'Donovan for making the Big Telly *Macbeth* recording, production photos and screen captures available to me upon request.
2. Katherine Rowe, 'Medium-Specificity and Other Critical Scripts for Screen Shakespeare', in *Alternative Shakespeares*, ed. Diana Henderson, vol. 3 (London and New York: Routledge, 2007), 37.
3. In his ground-breaking study of liveness, Auslander proposes that before 'the advent of [recording] technologies (e.g., sound recording and motion pictures), there was no such thing as "live" performance, for that category has meaning only in relation to an opposing possibility'. *Liveness: Performance in a Mediatized Culture* (London and New York, 1999), 51.
4. Martin Barker, 'Coming a(live): A Prolegomenon to Any Future Research on "Liveness"', in *Experiencing Liveness in Contemporary Performance*, ed. Matthew Reason and Anja Molle Lindehof (New York and London: Routledge, 2016), 29. Cf. Erin Sullivan: 'as broadcasting initiatives have diversified, liveness as a temporal and spatial entity, and aliveness as an experiential and affective quality, have begun to uncouple', 'The Audience is Present: Aliveness, Social Media, and the Theatre Broadcast Experience', in *Shakespeare & the 'Live' Theatre Broadcast Experience*, ed. Pascale Aebischer, Susan Greenhaigh and Laurie E. Osborne (London: Arden Shakespeare, 2018), 62.
5. Chuck Peters, 'Green Screen – How Does It Actually Work?' https://www.videomaker.com/article/c10/17026-how-does-green-screen-work, accessed 17 December 2021.

6 Judith Buchanan, 'Some Reflections on the Film'. Program Notes. *Macbeth: A Cinematic Experience*, 2018, unpaginated.

7 'A Cinema of the Imagination'. Program Notes. *Macbeth: A Cinematic Experience*. Unpaginated. I cannot help hearing echoes here of Richard Burton's promotional claims about 'liveness' and the 'miracles of Electronovision' in advance of the broadcast of his *Hamlet* 'theatrofilm' in 1964, about which see my chapter on The Wooster Group *Hamlet* in *Reenacting Shakespeare in the Shakespeare Aftermath: The Intermedial Turn & Turn to Embodiment* (New York: Palgrave Macmillan, 2019), 185–213.

8 See Kiarostomi, 'An Unfinished Cinema' (1995), https://www.sabzian.be/article/an-unfinished-cinema, accessed 17 December 2021. See also Rebecca Bushnell's chapter in this volume for more detailed discussions of liveness and interactivity in video gaming and VR experiences in particular.

9 As film reviewer Dan Fainaru notes, 'this is not a documentary and the [women] are in fact not watching a film but staring at a blank screen and only hearing the poem' on which the alleged film is based. What's more, 'Kiarostami shot the entire film in his living room using three chairs as his entire set', and 'the women's gestures, expressions, frowns and looks betray the same degree of embarrassment anyone experiences when they know they are being watched'. *Screendaily*, 29 August, 2008, https://www.screendaily.com/features/shirin/4040475.article, accessed 17 December 2021.

10 Monkman and Buchanan have made many inspired alterations in how and in what order *Macbeth* is scripted and performed. Most notably, they have cut the opening 'Double, double' witch scene, displacing it with the considerably more benign appearance of the robed and hooded woman accompanied by two children described in my next paragraph so that reproduction of the play now properly begins with the report of the Bloody Man/Captain. Similarly inspired reassignments of speeches (his letter to Lady Macbeth is read aloud in voice-over by Macbeth himself, supplemented by visual flashbacks to the actions it references) and compressed restructuring of entire scenes (notably 4.1, discussed later) reoccur throughout the film.

11 Judith Buchanan, 'The Legacy, the Silent Film and the All-Knowing Porter', *Website Essay*, http://www.macbeththefilm.co.uk/all-knowing-porter/, accessed 17 December 2021.

12 Auslander, 'Digital Liveness: A Historico-Philosophical Perspective', *PAJ* 102 (2012): 7.

13 Ibid., 9, emphases mine.

14 Doran generally confined his use of motion-capture technology to moments when his Ariel avatar was engaged in the character's various performances. The ethereal Ariel otherwise remained physically grounded in the more or less quotidian form of actor Mark Quartley. See Michael Paulson, 'At This "Tempest," Digital Wizardry Makes "Rough Magic"', https://www.nytimes.com/2017/01/04/theater/at-this-tempest-digital-wizardry-makes-rough-magic.html, accessed 17 December 2021. For a considerably more informed and comprehensive analysis of this production, see '"Tech-Enabled" Theatre at the RSC: Digital Performance and Gregory Doran's *Tempest* (RSC, 2016)', a chapter in Pascale Aebischer's *Shakespeare, Spectatorship and the Technologies of Performance* (Cambridge: Cambridge University Press, 2020), 108–48.

15 N. Katherine Hayles, *How We Think: Digital Media and Contemporary Technogenesis* (Chicago and London: University of Chicago Press, 2012), 183–4.

16 Henry McMahon, 'The Art of the Movies', *New York Times*, 6 June 1915.

17 Chris Banks, 'Something Mediocre This Way Comes', https://vulturehound.co.uk/2018/04/something-mediocre-this-way-comes-macbeth-film-review/, accessed 17 December 2021.

18 The quoted phrases are borrowed from Gemma Allred's and Benjamin Broadribb's case study of Big Telly's *Macbeth*, 'Present Fears are Worse Than Horrible Imaginings', 196. Thanks to Benjamin and Gemma for generously sharing their chapter in *Lockdown Shakespeare: New Evolutions in Performance and Adaptation* (Arden, 2022), 195–205, which they have edited along with Erin Sullivan.

19 Amy Borsuk, 'Review: *Macbeth*', *Big Telly Theatre*, 16 October 2020, http://exeuntmagazine.com/reviews/review-macbeth-big-telly-theatre-belfast-international-festival/, accessed 17 December 2021.

20 Pascale Aebsicher, *Viral Shakespeare* (Cambridge: Cambridge Univ. Press, 2022), 56.

21 Ibid., 61.

22 This information was supplied by producer and stage manager Crissy O'Donovan in an email exchange on 23 August 2021.

23 'An interview with Zoe Seaton, Big Telly Theatre Company', https://www.voicemag.uk/interview/7085/an-interview-with-zoe-seaton, accessed 17 December 2021.

24 Benjamin Broadribb, '"Peace! The Charm's Wound Up": Subverting Virtual Theatre in Big Telly's *Macbeth* and Hijinx Theatre's

Metamorphosis', https://medium.com/action-is-eloquence-re-thinking-shakespeare/peace-the-charms-wound-up-subverting-virtual-theatre-in-big-telly-s-macbeth-and-hijinx-15b01f5488d2, accessed 17 December 2021.

25 Auslander, 'Digital Liveness', 12.

26 As Erin Sullivan observes, 'while experiential aliveness at broadcasts is often enhanced by the liveness of shared time and place, one factor is not necessarily dependent on the other'. 'The Audience is Present', 62.

27 As Aebischer observes, 'Seaton's *Macbeth* emerged within this context as the dystopian counterpart to the utopian spirit of *The Tempest*, whose model of "Zoom performativity" had expressed a joyful belief in the ability of theatre to transport audiences and performers into a virtual community, and thereby to uplift and inspire optimism about our ability to overcome Covid-19 through the sheer power of our collective creativity. The marketing for *Macbeth*, by way of contrast, made the most of the seasonal obsession with witchcraft and suspicion of strangers at the door' (*Viral Shakespeare*, 73).

28 Benjamin Broadribb thoughtfully demurs from this reading, noting that 'Waving to Macbeth and raising a glass to his coronation made [compliant auditors] complicit in the deception of the central couple'. In '"Peace! The charm's wound up"'.

29 Gemma Allred and Benjamin Broadribb, 'Present Fears are Worse Than Horrible Imaginings', 196.

30 Herbert Blau, 'The Human Nature of the Bot: A Response to Philip Auslander', *PAJ* 24, no. 2 (2002): 22.

PART TWO

Performance

4

Liveness in VR and AR Shakespeare adaptations

Aneta Mancewicz

With the proliferation of onstage technologies, live broadcasting and online theatre, audiences' perceptions of liveness have radically changed. Recent advancements in mixed reality media, which incorporate virtual reality (VR) and augmented reality (AR), coupled with innovative forms of digital performance during the Covid-19 pandemic, have further revised theatrical forms of liveness, calling for new accounts of this concept. This chapter explores liveness as an audience experience in the context of applying VR and AR to performing Shakespeare. Because of its dramaturgical openness, imaginative language and cultural significance, Shakespeare's oeuvre has been frequently used as a litmus paper for experimentation with technology. The following discussion focuses on two adaptations of Shakespeare, in which I have been involved as an academic and artistic collaborator.

Recent debates on liveness have underlined the importance of the spectators' reception within distinctive affordances of the medium in which an experience takes place.[1] Building on these debates, this chapter closely examines audience feedback in VR and AR productions to advance the understanding of liveness in mixed reality. More specifically, it explores dramaturgical and technological challenges in CREW's *Hands-on-Hamlet* (2017) and Nexus Studios' *The Tempest* (2020). The creative choices and audience responses to these two adaptations foreground sociability and interactivity as crucial markers of liveness. The chapter shows that in VR and AR performances, spectators have a strong need for copresence and co-creation. They want to be emotionally and dramaturgically included in the work; they want to be acknowledged and given some degree of agency. What is particularly important, however, is that if a performance is to be recognized as live by the audience, sociability and interactivity cannot be merely built into it as design features, but they should also be actively experienced by the users. Liveness in VR and AR depends on the audience's ability of interaction with each other and with the digital world. It can be facilitated by a technical setup, but ultimately, it is a function of the audience's perception of interaction.

CREW's *Hands-on-Hamlet* and Nexus's *Tempest*: goals and challenges

The two projects examined here were delivered by companies that are recognized as leaders in digital innovation. CREW is a performance collective based in Brussels. Founded in 1991 by Eric Joris, the company has consistently experimented with digital technologies, including VR and AR. According to its website, CREW 'is a pioneer in the research on how technology influences us and enables us to switch in real-time between different worlds: our own, the cultural and the virtual'.[2] Over the last thirty years, the collective has closely collaborated with artists, scientists, tech developers and curators; it has also relied on links with renowned digital research centres and industry partners, including the long-term partnership with the Expertise Centre for Digital Media at the University of Hasselt. This has inspired not only innovative applications of different technologies, including sophisticated motion capture setups and artificial intelligence, but also a range of new performance formats, such as one-to-one performances, visual arts installations, performance lectures, mixed reality stage productions and, more recently, remote live theatre.

Nexus Studios also has an established track record of digital experimentation. An independent animation and immersive studio based in Los Angeles, London and Sydney, Nexus specializes in film and immersive projects. Since its founding in 2000, it has been collaborating with leading brands and organizations, including Google, Samsung, BBC and UNICEF. Innovative and highly acclaimed (a BAFTA winner as well as Oscar and Grammy nominee), Nexus focuses on novel ways of entertainment and storytelling. As the company explains on its website, 'We work with real-time tech to produce technically and creatively groundbreaking work, pushing technology to its limits.'[3] With *The Tempest* project, Nexus has sought to apply their world-class animation expertise in a theatrical context to learn more about the possibilities of mixed reality technologies for audience engagement.

The performances produced by these two companies are prototype versions, developed with public funding for research and arts practice. CREW relied on its structural funding from the Belgian government as well as individual grants secured by participating researchers and artists. Nexus Studios received funding from the Arts & Humanities Research Council through *StoryFutures*, a £12m project on the future of storytelling led by Royal Holloway, University of London, which brings together higher education institutions and creative businesses to develop collaborations and deliver innovative projects in the field of immersive technologies.

Each of the two adaptations was thus designed as a research and development project to test the possibilities of mixed reality in performance. In particular, the two performances were produced to address dramaturgical questions concerning the organization of audience experience in the context of VR and AR. To evaluate the efficacy of their aesthetic and technical solutions, both the teams were keen to gain feedback from the spectators early on in the process. The desire to gain audience input, in combination with a relatively modest budget, has put several constraints on the makers. The performances had to be short and easily accessible to considerable numbers of viewers. At the same time, the technological and logistical constraints have forced the two creative teams to develop original dramaturgical solutions.

CREW's version, which involved a VR experience, seemed particularly challenging in terms of reaching wide audiences. It was meant to be available for touring as well as sharing with multiple viewers. The two goals were at odds with each other. On the one hand, the company could not use multiple headsets, as transporting equipment is logistically complex and expensive. On the other hand, if CREW could rely only on a handful of headsets, the spectators would be able to experience the work one at a time, which in turn would limit the accessibility of the piece (and if it were to be commercially shown, its financial viability). Ultimately, the company chose to transport only a few headsets to foreign locations, which means that they had to shorten the duration of the experience to a few minutes per user. Given the complexity and intensity of VR, such exposure was still considered to be sufficient as a basis for audience feedback.

The dilemmas faced by CREW are well known to companies working with VR, given that headsets are not (yet) part of the mainstream market and that incorporating them into the dramaturgy of the performance poses artistic and logistical challenges. In its earlier live performance with VR, *Terra Nova* from 2011, CREW was successful in overcoming these challenges thanks to generous EU funding, but such a model is not sustainable on a long-term basis, even for big and well-established companies. What is needed for the theatrical breakthrough of VR is greater availability of headsets among general audiences combined with viable and meaningful solutions for integrating this technology in performance. CREW has sought to generate such solutions in subsequent iterations of their *Hamlet* project. This included two live performances at KVS theatre in Brussels: *Hamlet Encounters* (2018) and *Hamlet's Lunacy* (2019).[4] Each iteration has opened new dramaturgical possibilities, showcasing the potential of immersive and interactive technologies for theatre. More specifically, each of them has explored different configurations of liveness in VR performance, confirming the idea that the concept is a direct product of distinctive media setups and audience perceptions.

Similarly, Nexus made a production that was just ten minutes long to remain within the budget for digital development and appeal to a broad range of viewers. The adaptation was designed as an AR performance so that it could be available remotely to a broad range of users. Access to *The Tempest* did not depend on a headset but an iPhone or an iPad, which would enlarge the pool of potential participants. However, to ensure successful real-time transfer and transformation of digital data, the creative team requested the users to watch the work through an iPhone11, iPhone11 pro or a high-performing iPad (the latest two versions), which ultimately restricted audience numbers, as not many individuals had access to these advanced and costly devices.

As in the case of CREW's dilemmas with headsets, Nexus's challenges with personal devices show that the application of digital technology is about a fine balance between the sophistication of the work and the simplicity of audience access. In capturing a broad range of performers' movements and in allowing the users to co-create AR animation in real time, Nexus was able to strengthen the experience of liveness for the audience, but it had to accept that access to this experience was very much dependent on the high specification of devices available to the participants. Further work should be undertaken to explore the integration of motion capture in performance to understand better the opportunities and limitations of AR for the artists and to make this technology more accessible to the users.

Technological issues confronted by CREW and Nexus were part of a broader practical and theoretical exploration undertaken within the methodology of Practice as Research (PaR). In developing their Shakespeare adaptations, the two companies followed the model of PaR proposed by Robin Nelson in his *Practice as Research in the Arts* (2013).[5] PaR is based on the idea that research can be carried out *through* creative exploration. Consequently, each project based on a PaR model should begin with the articulation of what Nelson defines as 'research inquiry',[6] which is a central question guiding the intertwined processes of making and thinking. The notion of 'inquiry', as Nelson argues,[7] is to underline the open-ended nature of work, which might result in insights rather than firm conclusions. The inquiry is likely to be dynamic, which means that it can change during the rehearsal process, and it is often multilayered, which means that it can involve a range of different issues, from technical and dramaturgical questions to historical and philosophical ones. The following two sections discuss each adaptation as a PaR project individually, focusing on the design and experience of liveness.

CREW's *Hands-on-Hamlet*

In CREW's *Hands-on-Hamlet*, in which Nelson has been involved as an associate dramaturg, researcher and actor, the creative team spent a substantial amount of time identifying the main research inquiry. One of the key questions that emerged early in the process was 'How to act honourably in a conflicted world?' The notion of the 'conflicted world' referred to the seventeenth-century feeling of uncertainty and precarity. The feeling resulted from the paradigm shift in the period, which marked the transition from a medieval to a modern mindset. The process has been extensively theorized by different scholars, who have identified substantial changes in a range of fields throughout the seventeenth century. C.S. Lewis in *Discarded Image* (1964)[8] argued that in the Middle Ages the European culture developed a distinctive 'Model', a set of values and ideas that captured the medieval representation of the world and which influenced literature and the arts. The Model was abandoned by the end of the seventeenth century,[9] resulting in novel approaches to the production and reception of cultural imagery. The infamous Carl Schmitt, in turn, described the European transition from feudal and religious visions of society to a modern state.[10] He also argued that the Renaissance England turned away from land to sea and from attachments to Continental Europe to global expansion, as English trade companies began to impose colonial and imperial models of governance across the world.[11]

CREW's adaptations of *Hamlet* have embraced a range of these historical topics and perspectives to introduce audiences to the world of Shakespeare. As Nelson remarks, 'Besides conflicting ethico-legal issues of revenge killing and regicide at the centre of *Hamlet*, the project was concerned with the shift from a medieval conception of world order and the emergent modern world of renaissance humanism.'[12] These contexts were identified early on as crucial inspiration for Shakespeare, and they informed the development of CREW's adaptations. To bring a range of disparate topics together, the creative team sought to indicate analogies between scientific and philosophical issues. Thus, for instance, 'The move to a suncentric planetary model instigated by the Copernican revolution (and almost confirmed by Brahe) parallels a shift at the turn of the seventeenth century to an ethical approach to personal conscience as opposed to obeying rules notionally underwritten by God (as in *Hamlet* and the Elizabethan/Jacobean revenge tradition).'[13] The astronomical revolution together with the changing approaches to religion and monarchy are introduced in CREW's project as manifestations of the same paradigm shift and the ensuing turn towards scepticism and self-doubt. The historical conflicts depicted in the production are thus about the displacement of old truths and the resulting sense of disorientation, which, in turn, might serve as an analogy to contemporary shifts and insecurities, particularly in light of the team's reliance on immersive and interactive technologies. According to Nelson, the application of VR has been fundamental to articulating the links between the past and the present:

> The historical experience of such fundamental dislocations of bearings resonated . . . with today's post-truth culture and with the affordances of digital technologies for affective shifts. So the possibility of using time and spatial distance to bring the present into a new focus (as in Brechtian tactics) emerged, but augmented by the affordances of digital technologies.[14]

The exploration of historical and contemporary conflicts in CREW's production was enhanced by the application of VR, which enabled spatial and kinaesthetic experiences for the users. *Hands-on-Hamlet*, as an immersion set up in an almost bare room with a computer and a few chairs, allowed audiences to access two kinds of digital environments. The participants could walk around the castle, which was based on 3-D scans of a historical building, artfully re-drawn by Joris to emphasize its dilapidated and dreamy character. If they put their head into a spherical shape located in this environment, they could enter the actual CREW's studio filmed in 360 degrees during the rehearsals for this performance. Placing their head again in the sphere, they could return to the castle. The two environments were always available to the participants, who could freely move between them. In the castle, they encountered historically clad avatars (3-D scanned actors) delivering selected scenes from Shakespeare's tragedy, whereas in the studio they could observe the 360-degree video of the same actors in motion-capture suits recording the performance while they were being observed by the team of dramaturgs and technicians. The participants could thus choose between two different formats (animation and 360-degree video) and aesthetic conventions (fantastic and realistic), which would allow them to experience the virtual as distinct and complementary worlds. The combination of digitally produced and filmed material was particularly effective in that it juxtaposed imagined and real elements, but also questioned the nature of the real in the performance. According to Nele Wynants et al., 'The visual and spatial characteristics [of 360-degree video] are different from Virtual Reality (VR) where the user is immersed in a synthetic designed world.'[15] VR, in the sense of computer-generated animation, is about imaginary environments that are made to feel real for the users who can explore them at their own pace. By contrast, the 360-degree video, particularly in CREW's practice, is about actual physical locations that are being filmed with an omnidirectional camera and transformed into imaginary spaces, where the users have more limited opportunities for exploration. The combination of these two formats in *Hands-on-Hamlet*, together with the possibility of accessing the process of VR development alongside its product, has resulted in a highly disorienting experience for the users. Not only were they forced to negotiate two distinctive environments and forms of reality, but they were also invited to discover the development of motion-capture and 360-degree video.

Such a complex setup follows from another aspect of the research inquiry in CREW's production, which focused on '[t]he capacities of new technologies to afford distinctive new experiences of other worlds (in this instance the world of *Hamlet*)'.[16] *Hands-on-Hamlet* was created with a clear aim to address the challenge of guiding the participants through a VR immersion. As Chiel Kattenbelt, another associate dramaturg and researcher involved in this project, observes:

> A virtual world can easily be constructed as a world in different dimensions or as a configuration of different worlds. For the dramaturgy of a virtual world, it is important to give the experiencer a clear idea of how the different spaces relate to each other and how the plurality of the space translates into clear instructions for navigation. Uncertainty about this immediately leads to passivity or causes the navigation to demand so much attention or to become such a challenge that there is hardly any space to take in all that is offered and especially to be discovered. With regard to the latter, it is very important to respect the experiencer's own agency. This assumes, insofar as controllers are used, that the experiencer has a clear idea of how to use them or even better to play with them.[17]

Kattenbelt's commentary touches upon a fundamental problem of developing VR experiences, which is about creating dramaturgical links between different virtual environments as well as clear guidelines for their navigation. According to Nelson, VR can result in 'a radical re-definition of our senses'[18] through the process of 'extending the sensorium beyond regular perceptions of the world'.[19] This means that immersive technologies have a potential to reconfigure the user's experience of space, their own body and the bodies of others. The audience members can have an enhanced perception of their corporality and location, but they can also feel dislocated, disoriented and easily distracted.

Sensorial reconfiguration or 're-definition' has also critical implications for our understanding of liveness, as it became evident in the surveys completed by the audience members of *Hands-on-Hamlet*. CREW and its associates collected formal and informal feedback during several presentations of the work at international conferences. Here I will analyse the responses of audience members who experienced the installations at the European Shakespeare Research Association Conference in Gdańsk in July 2017 and at the International Federation for Theatre Research Conference in Belgrade in July 2018. Even though the surveys did not ask the participants about their age or education, the recruitment of respondents at international theatre conferences meant that they were a relatively homogeneous group, and so their answers reflect their advanced level of expertise in drama and theatre, as well as similarity of approaches.

In the surveys, several users underlined those aspects of *Hands-on-Hamlet* that traditionally have been associated with liveness, such as presence, intimacy, proximity and emotional involvement. The feeling of presence was mainly described as momentary and fleeting. For instance, one user explained it as something that only gradually developed during the performance: 'I think you can do what you want so at first I listened and observed then feel [sic] it like I was there'; another user noted, 'I could for a moment feel as if I was inside the play which was brilliant'. There was also an intriguing contrast in the responses between being inside the performance 'as a person' (being oneself) according to one user and '[m]oving into Hamlet in the Ophelia-Hamlet scene', as described by a different user, who also eloquently depicted the whole experience as '[u]nnerving – or perhaps re-nerving – making the nervous system aware of the physical space in a different way – vertiginous'. Similarly, audience members appreciated the experience of intimacy in this installation, which they linked with proximity. As one participant articulated it: 'The VR is working in terms of intimacy with characters. [It] [is] not so much about the technology that gets you involved but it is rather the physical proximity. I was an invited fellow, a passerby who had the chance to be part of an intense emotional moment in the life of the characters.' This idea was echoed by another user who observed, 'I felt like my identity was "me" but there was an access to an intimate moment even more private than in a film close-up.' Proximity was associated in these two commentaries with yet another concept related to liveness that is an emotional involvement. Importantly, both the users defined this involvement referring to 'moments' – 'an intense emotional *moment* in the life of the characters' and 'an intimate *moment* even more private than in a film close-up' (italics added) to accentuate the short-lived character of their emotional connection. The emphasis on the temporary and transitory nature of the users' experience is central to the idea of presence as the state of being fully engrossed in a particular situation, a state so intense that it can only be fleeting. The focus on temporariness underlines also the connections with other ephemeral concepts, such as intimacy, proximity and emotion, suggesting that these aspects of liveness are closely interrelated for the users.

At the same time, for many audience members, the notion of presence was inherently linked to the feeling of being a ghost. One participant perceptively remarked, 'The figure of the ghost is a wonderful "hook" for this kind of technology, and an appropriate guise for the audience to *inhabit* given that technology's affordance' (italics added). The impression was echoed by a user who noted, 'I felt like a ghost in Hamlet's castle which is quite relevant for a play which begins with a ghost', whereas another user remarked that witnessing the scene while feeling like the ghost was appropriate for the play's preoccupation with surveillance. The three commentaries praise the possibility for the users to become or 'inhabit' the ghost (in the sense of being able to observe closely while being invisible) as appropriate both for VR as a medium and for *Hamlet* as a play. The position of 'an unseen observer of a performance' in VR (as commended by yet another user) became thus an appropriate equivalent of watching a theatre play in a dark theatre auditorium.

The questionnaires were also insightful in terms of revealing the difficulties with staging theatre in VR. One participant captured this particularly clearly by claiming that 'the ability to defy gravity and float through space, or stand in the empty universe was very exciting, especially when using the remote to control my own movement. But it was also a lonely experience, being like a lost soul! Theatre is usually a social event and this was not'. The comment brings us to the core of liveness in this production. Despite the enhancement of presence, intimacy, proximity and emotional involvement in VR, the medium might not offer the feeling of theatrical liveness to the audience if there is no interaction with actors and other participants, or, at least, a feeling of copresence, or being with others. If the immersion focuses on an individual exploration of the virtual space, it will be perceived as a solitary experience, with the user isolated in the digital environment; such a mode of participation will not satisfy the expectation of theatre as 'a social event'. At the same time, the emphasis on presence, intimacy, proximity and emotional involvement means that the audience members in VR immersions might expect to have some degree of agency, as one participant explicitly noted:

> Being among actors but not able to join in was frustrating but shifting in to the bubble where I was 'onstage' and part of the performance watched by an audience was exciting. The difference between the 'live' actors and the avatars was disconcerting – with the 'live' actors I felt intrusive; with the avatars I felt as I was hidden/unseen. Pulling the actors close was fine but I wanted to pull them right and left! I felt I wanted to inhabit the actors.

The commentary indicates that in VR the users might expect to be able to activate or embody ('inhabit') other characters, as if in a computer game. It is important thus to establish clearly the conventions of the medium, decide how the users will be situated in the experience and then offer them appropriate instructions for their activity in the virtual environment.

Ultimately, the challenges of simulating the conditions of a live theatre performance in VR are also reflected in the difficulties of *Hands-on-Hamlet* users with labelling their experience. Asked if what they saw was 'theatre, film, a videogame, or something else', many responded that it was 'something innovative', 'something in between' or 'something else', with the word 'something' used as a placeholder for an experience that escaped conventional terminology. Several participants described *Hands-on-Hamlet* as a 'combination' or 'mixture', while others sought to introduce novel terminology, such as '[i]nteractive performance video' or '[a] live-theatre-production-video-experience' with a question mark at the end to indicate the respondent's hesitation. Some of these descriptions explicitly underlined the notion of liveness, as when an audience member noted that CREW's adaptation was '[d]efinitely something else but felt much more "*live*" than film' (italics added). The comparison with film as a well-established medium, combined with difficulties around defining this adaptation, suggests that *Hands-on-Hamlet* offered a radically new theatrical experience. In fact, some audience members explicitly addressed this novelty in their feedback, when they expressed concern that VR immersion is a challenging and unfamiliar form for adapting Shakespeare. One user noted, for instance, 'I think for an untrained participant, the newness of the experience and the desire to explore sometimes trumps engagement with the text and performance'. Similarly, another participant observed, 'I'm just wondering about the learning curve it takes to adapt to the VR world and finally begin to enjoy the storyline (though it is not exactly about that either!). I'm conflicted about this. I suppose the fascination is more about what the medium can do to a very well-known storyline'. These commentaries reveal the challenges of adopting VR as a medium for staging theatrical texts. In developing *Hands-on-Hamlet*, the team consciously grappled with these challenges, and it subsequently produced two other versions, in which VR experiences were fully integrated into a live theatre performance. What emerged clearly from CREW's early installation was that the opportunity of coming close to the characters or inhabiting them is highly attractive to the users, but it might also distract them from the performed scenes. Even more importantly, if the immersion does not allow the participants to become emotionally involved in the interactions between the characters or experience the characters and other spectators as co-present, the opportunity to create a sense of live theatrical moment will be lost. This suggests that future theatrical work in VR should focus on establishing moments of togetherness and emotional engagement for the audience. Similarly, in Nexus's *Tempest*, the participants have insisted on becoming part of the AR experience and forging a connection with both the actors and other audience members.

Nexus's *Tempest*

Nexus's *Tempest* was conceived during the first year of the Covid-19 pandemic. In this period, the UK government introduced lockdown measures, which brought strict restrictions on social interactions in an effort to curb and control the rapidly rising numbers of infections and hospitalizations. Theatres and other cultural venues were closed with no immediate prospect of reopening, forcing artists and arts managers to invent alternative forms of cultural experience that could be accessed online or in safe conditions of social distancing. Shortly before the lockdown, my colleague Rebecca McCutcheon and I developed a project for *StoryFutures* on VR and the experience of togetherness. The project grew from our research expertise and theatre-making experience; it was also designed to explicitly address some of the key questions about presence and sociability that emerged from CREW's *Hamlet* adaptations. In the call for collaborators, we wrote:

> VR is frequently described as solitary and disembodied practice. Such descriptions, however, do not take into account that VR experiences have a great potential for interpersonal interactions and reconfigurations of virtual and physical spaces. Working with social and spatial dimensions of VR foregrounds its ability to offer users multilayered modes of interaction within virtual and real worlds that enable complex and self-reflexive modes of experience.

With this call, we aimed to appeal to artists and developers interested in exploring entanglements of virtual and physical spaces. In particular, we were keen to investigate strategies that would enable audiences to experience moments of heightened sensorial awareness, in which their sense of location and perception would be altered and ultimately sharpened. At the same time, we wanted to revisit the notions of interactivity, togetherness and sociability through the interactions of the real and the virtual. The call resulted in a number of exciting proposals from theatre practitioners; ultimately, however, we decided to work with Nexus to gain an insight into technology from an industry perspective. Together with

Nexus, we quickly chose to work with AR as opposed to VR to make this project both feasible and accessible.

Given that our work with Nexus coincided with the national lockdown, the project gained unexpected urgency. Our research inquiry narrowed down to the following question: how might we create the feeling of togetherness for the audience in AR? The decision to stage a shared sense of space while relying on remote technology became embedded in the very process of making the work. The government's ban on social mixing made it necessary for the creative team to establish novel approaches to performance design, development and distribution. The rehearsals were delivered in a hybrid mode, with some team members being present physically in the studio and others participating online, while the final performance was produced by two actors in the studio with technicians, with other members of the team and the spectators connected remotely.

Having considered various historical and contemporary scripts, Nexus decided to stage *The Tempest*. In doing so, the company followed the rich tradition of *The Tempest* adaptations that have used immersive and interactive technologies. This includes productions with motion-captured Ariel directed by David Saltz (2000) and Gregory Doran (2016, RSC), but also Tender Claws' live immersive VR *The Tempest* (2020). At the same time, the creative team was inspired by avant-garde film versions of the play, including Derek Jarman's *The Tempest* (1979) and Peter Greenaway's *Prospero's Books* (1991). Identifying these forerunners was crucial in terms of establishing the originality of Nexus's project; it was a fundamental stage of PaR process, which Nelson defines as 'location in a lineage', and whose aim is to ensure that the practice produces novel ideas or insights.[20] The recurring use of motion capture in *The Tempests* produced between 2000 and 2020 testifies to the appeal of Shakespeare's play to theatre makers experimenting with technology. This appeal lies in Prospero's magical power and Ariel's ethereal presence, but also in the unique ability of these two protagonists to change the perception of other characters and the spectators alike. This means that *The Tempest* has an extraordinary potential to play with the audience's imagination: it invites us to enter a magical world in one instance, only to reveal its fictionality in the next one. At the same time, the play was chosen because of its thematic relevance for contemporary audiences. Its focus on the separation and solitude of Prospero and the shipwrecked party offered parallels with social isolation during the lockdown period. The play's emphasis on environment and the characters' desire to control nature resonated with the growing awareness of the climate crisis. Finally, the play's portrayal of Prospero's exploitation of Ariel and Caliban introduced the notion of racial inequality, which gained exceptional momentum in the context of George Floyd's murder in May 2020 and Black Lives Matter protests. Although Nexus's *Tempest* did not extensively address all these issues, given the funding limitations and a short development period, they formed an important cultural context for the company's creative process.

The Tempest was designed as a ten-minute AR experience, with actors performing live in a studio and with audience members accessing the performance remotely via their iPhones and iPads. The work from the beginning was conceived as a liberal adaptation: an exploration of the play's rich moods and settings rather than a plot summary. The choice of remote AR as a format has supported this approach: first, the creative team was able to completely re-imagine the characters and their environments through virtual avatars and sets; second, the team had to design innovative forms of transitions between the scenes. To address the unique possibilities and challenges of AR, the principles guiding the composition were borrowed from music as a more formalized and abstract medium than drama, with Matt Padden's soundtrack designed to strengthen the feeling of immersion for the audience.

A musical approach to composition has determined the organization of the script not only as an emotional experience but also as an encounter. In the final version, the adaptation featured five characters – Ariel, Caliban, Gonzalo, Miranda and Prospero – who were represented to the audience as five different avatars. The avatars were designed as fantastic and mythical creatures associated with specific elements of nature, with no markers of age, gender or race to allow for flexible casting. Tonderai Munyevu performed Ariel, Miranda and Gonzalo, whereas Flora Wellesley Wesley played Caliban and Prospero. Their performance explored movement and characterization in AR performance, where the use of avatars and motion capture both limit and liberate the performers. On the one hand, AR constrains the range of the performers' expression and hides their distinctive features; on the other, it allows them to take any shape or size.

At the same time, the swift transformations of the characters were accompanied by the changes in the virtual scenery to create multiple locations for the audience. Each of the characters delivered a monologue to the spectators, allowing them to become immersed in a distinctive situation and landscape. Each scene also represented an important moment from the text in which a character expressed a powerful emotion or idea. As such the project sought to underline the importance of the space, both in terms of the physical setting of the show, a room in which a spectator meets the avatars, and in terms of a metaphorical, imagined environment, in which real and virtual elements come together, allowing the audience to engage with performance and play. In Nexus's *Tempest* as an AR performance, individual homes of the users became at once the stage and the auditorium, with the performance being distributed across multiple locations. At the same time, the division of the script into five scenes was structured to facilitate the spectators' journey through a range of digital environments. These included a pool of water, trees, clouds and plants – all of this was expected to change the users' perception of their own surroundings.

In the course of the performance, the spectators' living rooms were thus transformed into unique versions of Prospero's magical island. They were unique because as the audience watched the adaptation in their living rooms, the AR elements of the performance were being calibrated and mapped onto their physical surroundings. Moreover, in some scenes the spectators were able to influence the process of digital transformation; for instance, in Gonzalo's monologue, they could plant seeds and watch different shrubs growing out of them. Similarly, in the RSC's *Dream*, streamed live in 2021 with elements of VR and real-time studio performance, the spectators were able to launch fireflies on the screen and grow virtual seeds, even if in this production, unlike in Nexus's *Tempest*, interactivity was limited to ticket-paying users. In both cases, the interactive possibilities were meant to allow the audience to make themselves visible in the digital world of the performance.[21]

In Nexus's *Tempest*, the integration of virtual elements with the physical space of the spectators, the build-up of digital imagery that complements the real-time actors' performance and the ability of the audience to influence the AR environment were all designed to create the impression of liveness for the users. However, audience surveys demonstrated that the principal strategy that supported the perception of liveness from the perspective of the participants was their ability to interact with the virtual world and co-create it, even if they were not able to view the input of others (unlike in the RSC's *Dream*). The responses to Nexus's *Tempest* articulated the desire for interactivity and impact, which was also expressed by the users of CREW's *Hands-on-Hamlet*.

Given the prototype nature of Nexus's adaptation, the audience survey was integrated into the delivery of the performance. The spectators were recruited explicitly to provide feedback, with the call-out form explaining the project as follows:

> Our prototype looks to explore live performance through the use of new technologies and the current restrictions around colocating in the times of Covid. We want to have a radical rethink about how theatre, sports and music can be reconfigured and enjoyed by a remote audience. Our prototype explores live theatre through a small curated performance of Shakespeare's 'The Tempest'. Using real time technology, we are able to stream a performance in Augmented Reality straight to your device. We're seeking people to help test our prototype and give feedback and insights on the performance and the application.

The description underlined the concept of liveness. The term 'live' was used twice, alongside the reference to 'real-time technology'. Moreover, right before the performance, audience members met virtually with Helen Broadbridge, the show's producer, who further foregrounded the concept of liveness by explaining that the actors would be performing in real time in the studio, with the AR performance being simultaneously streamed to the spectators.

Since the application required the users to have highly advanced devices (not older than two years), only six audience members participated in the testing and filled the surveys. In fact, one of the users explicitly noted in their response that the technological requirements were a barrier to participation: 'The tech needed in terms of new phones/iPads is challenging for ensuring you reach an inclusive/wide audience.' This also means that the spectators were a relatively homogeneous group. They were between 36 and 46 years old, and they all declared to 'regularly go to the theatre to watch live performances'. Four out of six claimed to have already used an AR application. Asked if they would be interested in seeing 'more experiences like this one' all ticked 'very much so' or 'yes' as their answer.

In their descriptive responses, the users uniformly praised two aspects of the performance: its interactivity and its location in their own space. Several of them linked the interactivity with a sense of agency and presence, as it is evidenced in the following commentaries. One participant, for instance, claimed to have liked '[i]nteractivity to enhance room and bring the elements into your space', noting that it 'enhances personal experience'. There was a similar response that read 'It was fun to interact with my environment and be part of the process', while another user noted that 'The set that was created made me feel very much in the action'. When commenting on the use of private space in this adaptation, the users commended the transformative potential of AR technology. One of them observed, 'I very much liked the fact that the interactive components operated on a familiar space and transformed it', and another echoed it by noting, 'I enjoyed the potential of integrating virtual elements with my surroundings'. The location of the performance in the users' homes was also appreciated as it allowed audience members to access '*live theatre* in a safe environment' (italics added), even though the same spectator argued that '[t]he amount of space needed to scan properly is unrealistic in a London home'.

Finally, many users liked the relationship with the avatars in real time, suggesting directly or indirectly that such relationship could be related to liveness. One of the spectators remarked, 'I enjoyed the interactive elements and the scale of the performers and the fact that the performers were performing *live*' (italics added). Another one appreciated the presence of the performers in the room: 'I also enjoyed the unexpected moments where the performer was behind me, although this was due to me moving around the space'. One user explicitly pointed out the potential of connecting performers with the participants in AR: 'I also liked the possibilities I anticipate to connect a virtual performer with their audience in different ways, making it clear the performer is a real person and is aware of you'. The focus on future development is highly appropriate given the exploratory nature of Nexus's *Tempest*; indeed, one spectator complained about 'the lack of expression and odd movements of the figures/floating', which indicates teething troubles that are typical of early experimentation with technology.

Here, however, comes a crucial twist. The responses – with their references to interactivity, spatial integration and connection with 'real' performers – would have suggested that the users of Nexus's *Tempest* have uniformly experienced this adaptation as live, especially after being prompted about the show's liveness by its producer. And yet, out of six audience members who filled the surveys only one gave a positive answer to the following question: 'Were you able to tell the performance was live?', while five others answered 'No'. This prompts a question about what these audience members mean by 'liveness' and what conditions would have to be met for them to experience this AR performance as live. The user who recognized the performance as live praised its 'interactivity' and 'the immersive experience (e.g. clouds, waves, plants)', as well as 'unexpected moments' of encountering the performer. Most important, the spectator highlighted that the interactive elements 'connected well with the narrative and did not feel like as isolated aspect'. A meaningful application of interactivity in performance might indeed be a crucial marker of liveness for audience members, particularly since this was the main area of complaints among four of out five users who did not see this *Tempest* as live. Their comments concerned three distinctive issues: the design of AR elements (including their relative crudeness and their complicated positioning in the space), the user experience (the range of actions available to the audience and uncertainty around their activation) and the inclusion of interaction in the narrative.

Both the user who commended the integration of interactivity in the performance and the users who discussed its challenges have thus revealed the fundamental role of audience involvement in creating the feeling of liveness. It also became clear that given the importance of interactive elements, they should be designed and applied in AR performance in a way that is visually attractive, accessible and meaningful to the spectators. What became particularly striking was that AR elements should be part of the story, and they should not distract the users from the performance's content. One respondent in particular suggested that to connect the narrative with technology, it would help to have 'all members sharing the same components and the live host reacting to them' while allowing for hand-free use of the phone in AR. The comment reveals the spectator's desire to have an experience that is equivalent to traditional theatre, with the simultaneity of audience experience, direct contact with the actor ('live host') and unrestrained (hand-free) access to the action. The desire testifies to the power of physically co-present live performance as a model for VR and AR, but equally to the difficulty of transcending this model to radically re-imagine mixed reality theatre.

Conclusion

When we examine liveness in the context of mixed reality performance, we realize not only that the term has been evolving but also that it is medium specific and audience dependent. The two adaptations analysed in this chapter demonstrate distinctive challenges and opportunities of VR and AR for engaging spectators on emotional and narrative levels. While VR is uniquely placed to enhance the feeling of proximity and presence in a virtual environment, its users might also feel isolated, inactive and even emotionally indifferent if they are not given enough opportunities to connect and interact. AR, in turn, has a potential to transform a physical environment and heighten the users' perception of their space, but it can also confuse them if the actions available to them are not sufficiently clear. In both VR and AR, appropriately designed interaction is fundamental to creating a sense of agency, emotional involvement and connection with others. As such, interactivity in mixed reality performance is strongly linked with the experience of liveness.

Ultimately, however, liveness depends not only on the strategies deployed by artists but also on the audience's perception. A performance might be explicitly designed and advertised as a live experience in VR or AR, but it will not be necessarily perceived as such if the users do not feel that there is a real-time connection with others, or if they are not able to influence the content of the work. Understanding more clearly how the sense of copresence and co-creation is experienced in mixed reality is thus crucial. It might serve not only as a theoretical contribution to research but also as a practical tool supporting future theatrical experimentation, particularly in the post-pandemic era of online communication and cultural participation.

Notes

1 Matthew Reason and Anja Mølle Lindelof, ed., *Experiencing Liveness in Contemporary Performance: Interdisciplinary Perspectives* (Abingdon and New York: Routledge, 2016); Pascale Aebischer, Susanne Greenhalgh, and Laurie E. Osborne, ed., *Shakespeare and the 'Live' Theatre Broadcast Experience* (London: The Arden Shakespeare, 2018), doi.org/10.5040/9781350030497.0008.

2 CREW, 'About CREW', https://crew.brussels/en/over-crew, accessed 23 December 2021.

3 Nexus Studios, 'About', https://nexusstudios.com/about/, accessed 23 December 2021.

4 For discussion of *Hamlet Encounters*, see Robin Nelson, 'Practice Research Process: Documentation and Publication', in *Practice as Research in the Arts (and Beyond): Principles, Processes, Contexts, Achievements*, 2nd edn. (Cham: Palgrave Macmillan, 2022), 85–91. For discussion of *Hamlet's Lunacy*, see Aneta Mancewicz, '*Hamlet's Lunacy*, CREW', in *Hamlet after Deconstruction* (Palgrave-Macmillan, forthcoming, 2022).

5 Robin Nelson, *Practice as Research in the Arts: Principles, Protocols, Pedagogies, Resistances* (Basingstoke and New York: Palgrave Macmillan, 2013).

6 Ibid., 30.

7 Ibid.

8 C. S. Lewis, *Discarded Image: An Introduction to Medieval and Renaissance Literature* (Cambridge: Cambridge University Press, 1964).

9 Ibid., 13.

10 Carl Schmitt, *Hamlet or Hecuba: The Irruption of Time into Play*, trans. Simona Draghici (Corvallis: Plutarch Press, 2006), 54–5.

11 Ibid., 55–6.

12 Nelson, *Practice as Research in the Arts (and Beyond)*, 89.

13 Ibid.

14 Ibid.

15 Nele Wynants, Kurt Vanhoutte, Philippe Bekaert, 'Being Inside the Image. Heightening the Sense of Presence in a Video Captured Environment through Artistic Means: the Case of CREW', in *PRESENCE 2008. Proceedings of the 11th Annual International*

Workshop on Presence. Padova 16–18 October 2008, ed. Anna Spagnolli and Luciano Gamberini (Padova: CLEUP, 2008), 157.

16 Nelson, *Practice as Research in the Arts (and Beyond)*, 90.

17 Chiel Kattenbelt, 'On Artistic Research, Intermediality and the "Hamlet Encounters" Project', in *Performing/Transforming. Transgressions and Hybridizations Across Texts, Media, Bodies*, ed. Floriana Puglisi (Torino: Otto, 2021), 33–4.

18 Nelson, *Practice as Research in the Arts (and Beyond)*, 90.

19 Robin Nelson, 'Crew's *Terra Nova*: Experiencing Modes of Immersion in Actual-Virtual Space', *Body, Space & Technology* 12 (2013): 9.

20 Nelson, *Practice as Research in the Arts*, 31.

21 For further discussion of interactivity in the RSC's *Dream*, see also Rebecca Bushnell's chapter in this book.

5

Alive in the (early) modern repertory

Elizabeth E. Tavares

In the late 1980s and early 1990s, scholars of early modern performance attuned their endeavours to how theatre was and is made. This has included explorations of the business of playing, theatre companies, and their personnel and training; the spaces of playing, performance venues, and their archaeology and reconstruction; and the materials of playing, such as props, costumes and cosmetics, and their makers. Deriving from this critical energy was an impulse to apply select historical practices (such as shared light) and materials (such as period costume) to new productions of early modern plays by William Shakespeare and his contemporaries. These experiments across the United States and the United Kingdom have practised an eclectic selection of period or 'original' practices in order to further economic goals constrained by a marketplace whose economics no longer closely align structurally or culturally with that of sixteenth- and seventeenth-century England. Applying only select practices rather than a systematic ecosystem of performance conditions has likewise limited the extent to which the observations and results garnered from these tests can be replicated and theorized.

An especial factor impeding experimentation with early modern theatre has to do with its most fundamental structural and economic feature: repertory scheduling. Playing companies of the late sixteenth and early seventeenth centuries produced up to six different plays a week, distributing new and revised parts among a stable group of players. This system, emphasizing a variety of plays rather than players, inverts the current Anglophone marketplace, whose typical practice it is to hire a new cast and production team for several-month runs of a single play. The early modern production system makes room for the unpredictability, accident, improvisation and other affordances of 'liveness' that come with little rehearsal and much variety. The current production system prioritizes ostensibly perfect delivery of a text and a specific artistic vision, duplicated with as little variation as possible up to eight days a week. Employing players trained within this second system in short-lived or one-off experiments can cause anxiety as it is sometimes interpreted as asking professionals to un-train themselves, adding further variables to the exploration.

It is hardly a novel observation to say that part of what it meant to be live in the early modern theatre was to be in collaboration, to be playing with others. While 'original practice' (OP) and other performance-based research projects readily attest to this collaboration in the making ready of a single play for performance, a crucial next evolution is the study of players sharing a discrete ecosystem of co-dependent practices over an extended period of time. As Stephen Purcell and Rob Conkie have observed, 'specifically Shakespearean projects [have] tended to focus entirely on modern practice', or what contemporary practitioners might gain from period practices, rather than considering those practices regardless of applied utility.[1] While both aims are valuable, the results they can sustain vary and are limited by their economic contexts. It is significant that two crucial projects that come close to employing a repertory schedule – the Read Not Dead Project, which stages readings of all the surviving plays by Shakespeare's contemporaries, and Edward's Boys, which performs the repertory of the boy companies by players of comparable age, both operate adjacent to a subsuming organization: Shakespeare's Globe in London and King Edward VI School in Stratford-upon-Avon, respectively.[2] (As late as 2016, no experiments approaching an early modern repertory schedule have been recorded.[3]) The eclectic nature of the selection of practices for which there is historical evidence and the inability to test these practices in a repertory context introduce variables that impact what happens in performance. What might a project design concerning early modern dramaturgy that identifies and traces a discrete practice or technique live in performance look like?

This chapter offers a case study of one company, the Original Practice Shakespeare Festival (OPSF) based in Portland, Oregon, which regularly employs a repertory schedule and dedicated company, and trains their cast in a fixed if eclectic selection of 'original practices' as standard practice. By charting a trend in their 2017 season with the prompter at its centre, I provide a snapshot from which one might derive the beginnings not necessarily of research questions but rather of research project designs for studying early modern drama in live performance – Shakespeare or his contemporaries, for then or now.

Practices

A key feature of medieval and early modern performance, the prompter 'ran' performances, argues Tiffany Stern and Simon Palfrey, by 'unit[ing] the actors with their separate parts, gestures, actions'.[4] The early modern prompter was responsible for text and action, directing players within the tiring house as well as 'those already on stage'.[5] Sixteenth- and seventeenth-century archives attest to the success of the prompter in offering 'ways in which separately prepared actors could be successfully brought together' and diminishing the 'need for over-much ensemble preparation before performance'.[6] In cataloguing several contemporary companies' experiments with 'First Folio techniques', Don Weingust observes two additional features of the prompter.[7] First, the job of the prompter 'would not have been to interfere with the progress of the play', such as correcting minor misspoken words, but rather to 'keep the play moving' and counteract any 'danger posed by a missed cue'.[8] The incorporation of a 'visible, aurally unmasked' prompter in performances by the Original Shakespeare Company (OSC) at Shakespeare's Globe in the late 1990s and early 2000s, and the later publication of Patrick Tucker's *Secrets of Acting Shakespeare: The Original Approach* (2002), would go on to have a significant, lasting impact on regional theatre companies. A rise in American universities sponsoring study-abroad trips to Shakespeare's Globe (London, UK) in the early 2000s particularly for undergraduate majors in English and Theatre, as well as the early popularity of the venue as a destination for professional development, quickly normalized the practice of using an onstage prompter to these one-time and occasional playgoer-practitioners. The practice was also carried out by former members of the influential New England Shakespeare Festival (1994–2006) helmed by Demitra Papadinis, which used an onstage prompter and employed a variation on techniques promoted by Tucker.[9]

While OP would continue to be debated at major institutions such as Shakespeare's Globe and the American Shakespeare Center (ASC, Staunton, Virginia), many smaller regional theatre companies and Shakespeare in the Park community groups formed in the early 2000s and detached from these debates retained this approach. This regional emphasis on OP might be understood as a further evolution from the 1980s and 1990s critical ferment Jeremy Lopez identifies across literary criticism related to the advent of New Historicism, as well as popular re-investment in a range of re-enactment modes, from 'reconstructed' theatre spaces to the now well-known Civil War monument building boom of the late twentieth century.[10] The 'pervasive pedagogical language used by original practice companies', offering school visits and kid-friendly programming to low-income communities (as does OPSF), is deeply entwined with larger cultural shifts in the United States to find new ways of monetizing scholarship.[11] Festivals like OPSF are an 'influential phenomenon', argues Paul Prescott, representing the 'first meaningful live encounter with the plays of William Shakespeare and, for some, the time they see live Shakespeare – or theatre of any kind'; 'for tens of thousands . . . it's what they *do* every summer'.[12] It can be argued that since their rise in the 1960s, North American Shakespeare festivals have advertised something akin to OP in their venue architecture, costuming, approach to dialect or other features that position the theatre-going experience as somehow more 'authentically' Shakespeare than other modern theatres.

Shakespeare's Globe and other international venues moved away from 'authenticity' as a central marketable feature throughout the early 2000s, relying instead on an axiology of the unexpected suggested by OP; 'OP' as a term Stephen Purcell argues 'recognizes that Globe practitioners hand-pick what is useful from historical performance in order to transform modern theatre practice'.[13] Smaller regional companies like OPSF, Back Room Shakespeare

Project (Chicago, Illinois), Shakespeare's Tavern (Atlanta, Georgia) and others have maintained this feature of their *institutional dramaturgy*, James Steichen's term for 'the practices through which an arts institution structures its patrons' experiences in the service of advancing its goals or articulating its identity'.[14] All of those features of the performance event beyond the recitation and enactment of a play's text, from pre-show speeches to Instagram marketing campaigns, work to 'stage an institution', positioning how playgoers should understand the personal value of attending and investing in a specific theatre company. US-based OP companies routinely rely on a simultaneous appeal of history instruction with what Purcell describes as 'a nostalgic image of a lost and better past' to cultivate returner audiences from low-income communities unable to access the more expensive or travel-dependent Shakespeare-oriented venues.[15] Weingust has similarly critiqued the 'selective nature of original practices as practised', suggesting endeavours like that of OPSF 'are more "performances of authenticity"' rather than '"authentic performances"'.[16] Large-scale projects with the potential infrastructure for repertory-scale explorations, such as the ASC, 'invoke historical authenticity as a means to an end' with 'strict adherence to the past in some respects and blithe disregard in others' as a marketing tool only: 'You'll come for the past, but you'll stay for the present'.[17] While the company has experimented with what they term the 'Actors' Renaissance' or 'Ren Run' season and a recent actor–manager pay-scale hierarchization, both still employ a dedicated pre-performance rehearsal period, most recently of a four-play rotating repertory not analogous with surviving schedules from the period. As Sarah Dustagheer outlines, early modern performance practices 'real or assumed . . . exposes the contradiction at the heart of much modern theatre between the intensely collaborative and the deeply hierarchical practices, as well as issues of interpretive power, singular or collaborative creative visions, artistic control and audience focus'.[18] Such choices are about 'sustaining the *conditions* in which performances of Shakespeare can thrive', observes Prescott, 'more to do with *organizational practices* than aesthetic choices'. Contemporary playgoers have been habituated to occasional theatre attendance through long runs of a single play. Occasional attendance habits do not support a repertory schedule designed to facilitate more regular, if not weekly or daily, attendance in order to be economically sustainable. Thus, study of the effects of repertory on early modern performance practices stands at odds with a theatre's survival in the current marketplace.

Teleprompter

Since 2009, indicative of an OPSF performance has been the Prompter. The figure emblematizing OPSF's institutional dramaturgy of instruction combined with nostalgia was that of the Prompter. The role presents a period practice unfamiliar to playgoers based on previous theatre-going experiences that is also framed by the comfort of the familiarity of Shakespeare, resonating with at least the federally recommended Common Core for high school instruction.[19] The Prompter performed a live historical re-enactment while externalizing the acceptability not only for error but also for an invitation to improvisation and the unexpected – what Conkie has described in Shakespeare's Globe as 'aleatoric' effects where the unexpected prompts new avenues for inquiry.[20] After nearly a decade of experimentation and refinement of the Prompter as a part of performance, in OPSF productions the 'role' took on a level of virtuosity beyond what early modern archives attest and thus developed into a unique, company-specific practice. In a typical OPSF performance, the Prompter dressed in a black-and-white striped sports referee jersey with a field whistle (see Figure 5.1). After introducing the production title with a brief historical survey of their practice – describing scrolls as Shakespeare's 'teleprompter' – the Prompter would take a seat in the lawn stage-left with a folding chair, table and prompt book. The OPSF Prompter's role is to serve as a 'safety net' for the players when they 'fell out' enough so that cues for the next speaking part were missed, as well as for the playgoers, interjecting as to keep them clear on the plot and characters' motives. Prompters provided missed lines, missed entrances and supplemented the soundscape. For example, in *Macbeth*, the Prompter rattled a sheet of tin for thunder, slapped their thighs to mimic war drums and rapped on the Prompter's table to replicate knocking for the Porter's gate.[21] They provided cover for the unexpected, especially in the case of Shakespeare in the Park performances so marked by a public, shared environment. Playing in rep across several city parks gave

FIGURE 5.1 Romeo and Juliet, *Willamette Park, 21 July 2017. From left: Kaia Maarja Hillier (Juliet), Jonah Leidigh (Paris), Alec Lugo (Nurse), Joel Patrick Durham (Tybalt), Isabella Buckner (Prompter), accompanied by musicians Rachel Saville and David Bellis-Squires. Courtesy of the author with permission from the company.*

OPSF opportunities to experiment with new spaces and practice the skill of appropriating the features of landscape and architecture. That the company primarily travelled to perform in non-dedicated spaces could be understood as an 'original practice' given that, according to Siobhan Keenan, touring was a regular practice of playing companies, predating and continuing alongside the advent of dedicated venues.[22] For example, Willamette Park is also the site of a busy boat launch in southeast Portland. On a noisy afternoon, Prompter Beth Yocam, referring to the loud honking and party music coming off the river during a performance of *The Comedy of Errors*, asked Antipholus of Syracuse (Shandi Muff), 'There's a lot of boat stuff going on right now. Antipholus, could you tell us how you got to this island?' The show-stopping laughter that erupted to Muff's reply, 'Boat', was only accessible by performers and playgoers being live to the opportunity the environment made available and evidenced playgoers' imaginations actively converting the hip-hop from a party speed-boat to merchant sailors singing as they pull in to Ephesus.

Improviser

A few weeks into the summer season, OPSF launched its central fundraising campaign for the year, WIL Fest, whose initials stand for the three major Portland metro parks in which the company performed: Willamette, Irving and Laurelhurst. The aim is to demonstrate the virtuosity their unmemorized approach sponsors in a repertory setting, ideally garnering larger audiences, donations and potential school clients for in-class workshops during the academic year. In July and August of 2017, the company performed fifteen different plays by Shakespeare over a three-week period, either at 2:00 p.m. or 7:00 p.m., and on some days both. Each year the company adds two new Shakespeare plays to their repertory to be introduced during the WIL Fest. There was no rehearsal with the exception of what the company calls 'batting practice', or a separate rehearsal time for any music, fight or dance choreography. In late spring, the company held 'play sessions' to practice moving with scrolls in hand and improv techniques. The sports metaphors are of a piece with the framework employed by Edward's Boys; Harry McCarthy has observed that the 'company's approach runs parallel to the operations of a rugby team'.[23] Otherwise, players were provided with just the text of their individual part for the performance that day, which they each were asked to individually print and mount on a dowel to create their own scroll, usually held in place with elastic hair ties. The players were invited to review their individual parts in advance as well as decide on and provide their own costumes based on a contemporary dress unless a specific need, such as armour or a friar's robes, were required. Without a rehearsal period, the company paid players by performance, typically US$75 per show, which was funded through community sponsors and donations gathered after passing the bucket. While players could treat the performances as professional, résumé-building work, the lack of a rehearsal period made the company ineligible for regional theatre accolades, the Drammy Awards.[24] Individual performances regularly employed doubling, with casts ranging from thirteen to seventeen members, including apprentices and interns, as well as one of three rotating stage managers. Company members participating in the WIL Fest performed in as many as eleven and as few as a single performance of the fifteen productions mounted between 21 July and 7 August.[25]

Well practiced as a company by the start of the WIL Fest, the Prompter's role had evolved from a 'safety net' into one that made creative opportunities out of unexpected interruptions to the action of the play, including regularly interrupting the action on purpose for such improvisations. Prompter interruptions were most frequently in the service of character development, suggesting the company's mindfulness of playgoers unfamiliar with Shakespeare. For example, prompting for a performance of *Romeo and Juliet*, Isabella Buckner made the most of a few extra seconds due to a slow entrance to ask: 'Hey Benvolio, what's your favourite band?' Noah Goldenberg (as Benvolio) replied, capitalizing on recent events: '3 Doors Down, until they played the inauguration'. The knowing laughter this produced in playgoers was commensurate with the larger scene in which Romeo, Mercutio and Benvolio prepare to infiltrate an elite party not unlike an inaugural ball. A challenge to creating the opportunity for such 'one-liners' seems in being keenly aware of the affective priorities of a particular moment in the world of the play; 'pitching' a player a brief open-ended question they can do something with; and possessing a honed awareness of pacing in order to take advantage of silences, delays and interruptions, the most frequent being passing planes flying in and out of Portland International Airport. During one such interruption of *Julius Caesar*, Joel Patrick Durham (as Prompter) asked Lissie Lewis (as Lucius), 'Why are you always so tired?', to which she immediately replied, 'Well, I have a new boyfriend'. Brutus's servant is routinely falling asleep in the Shakespeare text, which, while ultimately serving important dramaturgical goals later in the play, goes unexplained initially. Playing a male-identified Lucius, the improvisation not only inserted a quick moment of queer affirmation but also invented a reason for Lucius's hitherto unexplained sleep deprivation (see Figure 5.2). While the function of the Prompter was ostensibly that of safety net, in effect they did more work as a collaborator with the company and co-author of the Shakespeare hypotext.

The company comprised a rotating troupe of fifty-five members employing a policy to avoid casting players in the same role twice.

FIGURE 5.2 Julius Caesar, *Irving Park*, 22 July 2017. From left: Beth Yocam (Brutus), Lissie Lewis (Lucius), and Joel Patrick Durham (Prompter). Courtesy of the author with permission from the company.

There were and have since been certain exceptions for specialists needed for skills, such as Andrew Bray performing original live music as the many singing clowns, or accounting for race and gender equity, such as the regular performance of Jennifer Lanier, a local drag-king who identifies as multi-racial, in the title role of *Othello*. (Lanier would later become co-artistic director as part of the company's ongoing efforts to sponsor diversity and inclusion.) Players experimented with a wide range of parts that a lifelong career as a Shakespeare specialist at a major professional company may not necessarily afford. Female-identifying members frequently voiced the professional and personal importance of their being able to perform major roles that, in their experience, were rarely cross-gender cast, such as Macbeth or Benedick. The company benefited from developing a rapport, becoming familiar with one another's timing, movement preferences and improvisational habits regardless of part. Ivo van Hove, artistic director of International Theatre Amsterdam (ITA), has employed a similar practice since 2001 of contracting players for a season to work across all of ITA's productions in order to benefit from 'develop[ing] deep working relationships with one another, and with directors, over many years'.[26] As Helen Lewis contends, the trust cultivated in these regular collaborators enables van Hove to 'create boundary-pushing productions' that confront issues such as self-harm, paedophilia and anti-Semitism.[27] OPSF's use of the repertory system similarly habituated performers to one another rather than individual performers to their individual roles.

These structural features of casting made available opportunities for Prompters to cultivate 'running gags' or repeated jokes within a single performance, as well as across performances. For example, when prompting for *Merry Wives of Windsor*, Muff interjected in the very first scene to get a sense of how the wealthy Windsor husbands, Mr Page (Tom Witherspoon) and Mr Ford (Keith Cable), proposed to their wives. As characters with few lines and little opportunity for development, it was a crucial moment to introduce themselves and help playgoers differentiate between them and the two kinds of marriages they represent. While his wife (Shani Harris-Bagwell) was performed as devoted, Ford's proposal was less than romantic:

> FORD Wehavebeenseeingeachotherforawhilewouldyouliketo getmarried. There was a proposal. It was agreed to. It was a transaction. I don't know what you want!
> PROMPTER How long have you been married?
> FORD I don't know!

Mrs Page (Sarah Jane Fridlich) made clear in her own improvised aside that a happy marriage is one where you are at the 'top of the relationship food chain'. Later, the Prompter interjected to ask the same of Mr Page while speaking with Shallow (David C. Olson). Mr Page turned to Shallow, got on his knee and delivered a proposal so affecting it resulted in an impromptu make-out session. Asides about the quality of marriage proposals continued throughout the performance almost as if a parallel play or verbal footnotes. Any mention of love operated as an offer or cue from the context of the play on which players improvised, gradually increasing the stakes over time. The production's use of text to warrant choices related to but beyond merely presenting the words captures W.B. Worthen's model for critically approaching Shakespeare in performance:

> Theatre is not a vehicle for textual transmission. Stage performance uses writing not to communicate with words to an audience, but to create those problematic performativities of the stage, the entwining of the fictive in the actual, the drama in the performers' *doing*, that animates (our appetites for) acting. The words of 'the text' (itself a manifest fiction: no performance, of Shakespeare or otherwise, uses a single text) may be spoken, but in a crucial sense actors don't deliver 'words' to their offstage auditors: they *do* things with them, entreat, condescend, wound, instrumentalize the verbal text as one of many means to creating acts in the event of performance.[28]

OPSF's repertory casting; material stage technologies of part, scroll, and backstage plot; travelling schedule; and onstage prompter might seem at first glance to centre a preservation of a supposed authentic or original text. In effect, these practices make the text readily and immediately available to players from which to improvise verbally or non-verbally, to '*do* things with them'. Local reviews emphasize simultaneously the improv and the collaboration as notable features of the company, spending more time considering these over OP elements. A 2016 Oregon ArtsWatch piece concluded, 'Original Practice Shakespeare players have a great talent for improv', which 'allows the audience and cast to work together, and the words to stand, as they can, on their own'.[29] So while the Prompter was present ostensibly to keep the company on book, the majority of their time was spent taking the company off-book, and were rewarded.

Shepherd

The Prompter was also the cornerstone of the company's institutional dramaturgy: marketing themselves on programmes, flyers and social media with the tagline, 'Because Shakespeare should be a little dangerous!'[30] This was tied to both the unmemorized nature of performance, with parts in hand, and the Prompter that necessitated it. While the Prompter is text centred, using the prompt book to track the action of the play, the other text they negotiated – both for warrants to performance and to ward off interruptions that might bring the production to a halt – was the outdoor environment (see Figure 5.3). The performance took place in busy public parks with heavy traffic, from walkers, runners, cyclists, pets and boat-owners during an increasingly hot summer; on 3 August, during the last week of the WIL Fest, temperatures peaked at 104°F (40°C). Unlike indoor theatres in the region, such as Portland Center Stage and Artists Repertory Theatre, where cellphones and candy wrappers are carefully policed, interruptions of all kinds were routinely invited, specifically as a source of improv in order to get

FIGURE 5.3 Much Ado About Nothing, *Irving Park, 23 July 2017. Attempting to use the audience as a substitution for the arbour to hide behind and overhear the other men, Brian Burger (Benedick) borrowed hats from individual playgoers stacked high on his head as a disguise. Kerry Leek (Prompter) would later collect and redistribute them back to their owners. Courtesy of the author with permission from the company.*

passers-by to stay, watch and donate. For example, the performance of *Twelfth Night* was set upon by a great number of cyclists using the nearby path on the edge of the lawn. Approximately thirty stopped to watch a scene featuring Viola/Cesario (Kaia Maarja Hillier), crowding the concessions and startling the group. The Prompter (Durham), a cyclist himself, paused the action: 'Woah, so many bikes! Cesario, would you, in a poem, invite them to join our show?' Hillier walked through the playgoers, up to the cyclists, opened her arms and improvised a first stanza of a sestina that was part explanation of the performance and part invitation to sit, which a few did. Advertising was facilitated by the Prompter role in both advance marketing and during performances.

The afternoon performances in the middle of weekends typically had the greatest ambient volume, such as ongoing basketball games, commercial planes flying over to the nearby airport and frequent off-leash visitors, including dogs, cats and squirrels. When, in *Julius Caesar*, a servant re-enters in act two and Caesar (Brian Allard) asks 'What say the augurers?', he addressed the question to a group of dogs rather than the servant. During one flyover that was too loud to really continue the text as written, the Prompter (Kerry Leek) asked Dogberry (Cable), 'Dogberry, if you ran the TSA, what would that look like?', to which he replied:

> *(To tied-up Borachio and Conrade)* What is your destination? Jail? Good. *(Gestured as if to guide them through a metal detector.)* Now Verges, typically if they had anything to declare they would do so before proceeding. That they proceeded without declaring proves they are innocent.

As illustrated here, interruptions by airplanes, boats or other vehicles were typically addressed through object work or other kinds of miming to either continue the scene unspoken or reiterate an aspect of plot. Usually, when a plane was too loud to perform, the Prompter cried out, 'It's a plane! Everyone make an SOS real quick!' The players would shout, jump and improv anything else one might do to get the attention of rescue, which was especially effective for narratives set on an island, such as *The Tempest* (see Figure 5.4). Doing so on multiple occasions worked to conscript the real world into the fiction of the play rather than trying to rigidly demarcate a difference between them. Similarly, during *Romeo and Juliet*, loud

FIGURE 5.4 Much Ado About Nothing, *Irving Park, 23 July 2017*. From left: Sarah Jane Fridlich (Hero), Beth Yocam (Beatrice), Mara McCarthy (Margaret), and Kerry Leek (Prompter). Courtesy of the author with permission from the company.

police sirens passed during a scene between Friar Lawrence (Allard) and Romeo (Ken Yoshikawa). The Prompter (Buckner) asked, 'Romeo, why are the cops after you?', to which Romeo responded by silently jumping and disappearing into the tent that served as the company's mobile tiring house. To this the Friar remarked, 'Trespassing'. Later, a thirty-second industrial barge horn overtook the scene when Juliet (Hillier) is impatient to hear news of her love from the Nurse (Alec Lugo). While the Prompter did try to ask a redirecting question ('Hey Nurse, how did you meet your husband?'), it was not possible to really hear or give an answer. Instead, as the cross-dressing Nurse, Lugo held up his skirts to feign a hoop-sized fart. Several other players joined in to fan and waft around him as if trying to dispel a pungent and loud passing of wind.

Oregon ArtsWatch interpreted the tagline of 'dangerous' as an invitation to 'throw out all the decorum that your bluehaired grandma worked so diligently to foster in you'.[31] Despite

FIGURE 5.5 Much Ado About Nothing, *Irving Park, 23 July 2017. From left: Kerry Leek (Prompter), Sarah Jane Fridlich (Hero), and Mara McCarthy (Margaret). Courtesy of the author with permission from the company.*

this claim to danger, in the three weeks of performances not a single case of falling out occurred where the performance had to be brought to a halt or major prompter intervention needed (see Figure 5.5). Friction lay elsewhere. In the WIL Fest performance of *The Taming of the Shrew*, Brian Burger demonstrated how performer knowledge of a play could impact the Prompter's performance, and even be resisted by the company. Having played Petruchio in the Mission Theatre performance the preceding April, he cued for improvisation frequently so as to draw attention to and at times satirize the play's structural misogyny. For example, when stopping Gremio (Cable) to ask, 'Gremio, what's your opinion on women's suffrage?', Cable replied, 'I don't think anyone should have to suffer, except maybe for love'. In a similar moment, as Prompter he took advantage of a delayed entrance to ask Petruchio (Michael C. Jordan) to 'give us your thoughts on Title IX'. The reply, 'I'm not a softball coach; I don't care', began a trend for the improvisations that dismissed opportunities to engage with the play's sexism, although it could be argued that this was in the spirit of characterization warranted by the text. Despite Burger's good intentions to make explicit the sexual politics of the play, the other male-identifying cast members instead leaned into their characters in a move not typical of the general trend of cued improvisation during the 2017 WIL Fest. After Horatio (Lugo) had been beaten with his lute by Katherina (Jessica Hirschhorn), again the Prompter attempted to create an opportunity from a pause, asking 'Hortensio, what do you think of the recent transgender military news?' Lugo's sputtering reply, 'Why are we having this conversation?!' was commensurate with his character's need to nurse his physical wounds but not the broader trends of the company's reliance on pop culture and topical news. The distinction between Prompter and player blurred when Berger replied, 'Because I said so!' Rather than continue the engagement, Lugo found his next line as Hortensio and continued the scene anyway, dismissing the Prompter's direction. All three interruptions used a component of women's rights history to draw out the quality of the misogyny surrounding Katherina.

The final example is perhaps the most effectively nefarious where Hortensio (as Cambio) resists the direction of the Prompter, suggesting that he believed the rules of the game quite literally do not apply to him. None of the female-identified players or players in women's roles were provided similar cues to improv, so the disjunction between the male-identifying prompter and male-identified players produced the sense that only men were having conversations about and dictating the gender politics of the world of the play, which could be read as either satirizing the misogyny of the play or replicating it. It was a surprising contrast to the performance of the same play with the same company three months earlier that incorporated pink knit 'pussyhats', recently a feature of #MeToo political marches in Washington, D.C., and across the United States. That production had been prompted by Lauren Saville, a company member and professional therapist who used expressive arts therapy praxis to organize the playgoers' processing of the play both during and in a seventy-person talk-back afterwards.[32] The two performances in relatively close succession suggest the impact the Prompter role has in leveraging improv to divergent political positions.

One challenge *Shrew* poses to cuing has to do with the fact that improvisation is culturally habituated in the United States to serve humour as compared to other kinds of affective response. For example, when prompting for *The Tempest*, Lugo frequently cued to establish the island setting (aided by the nearby busy Willamette River) and character development. The company seemed primed to respond to opportunities to evolve their characters in context. This frequently was located in the body or in costumes that, in the speed of an improvised moment, relied on fat-shaming and possibly racially derogatory stereotypes. For example, Falstaff (Bellis-Squires) of *Merry Wives* was 'on the Atkins Diet, the South Beach Diet, and four or five others . . . I don't think you're supposed to do them all at once'. By contrast, in a performance of *The Comedy of Errors* improvisation is leveraged to the opposite effect. When Dromio of Syracuse (Buckner) described the kitchen maid as 'spherical, like a globe; I could find out countries in her', Antipholus of Syracuse (Muff) broke from character to directly address playgoers: 'Strap-in, folks, we have some serious fat-shaming coming up. Triggers'. The desire to inject humour into every serious or threatening moment of *The Tempest* came most often at the expense of Caliban, such as in a cued exchange that included players of colour:

> PROMPTER Can you guys do a fashion show and discuss the clothes you've found?
> CALIBAN These are clothes. I wear them like a man do.
> STEPHANO These are the latest in island fashion. I am the best model on this island!
> PROMPTER How about you, Trinculo?
> TRINCULO I was feeling pretty good until the others went and now I'm just sad.

The communal effects of improvisation are apparent here, where each player was provided an opportunity to clarify how their character's attitude was different from their immediate peers. The political risks of non-scripted performance (as opposed to technical risk, where the work of acting comes to a full stop) were similar to *Shrew*. Caliban was performed with incorrect grammar even in this extratextual moment, making him seem not only the least fashionable but the least articulate of the group. The intended rhetorical error of 'do' for 'does' was not an emulation of an indicative rhetorical pattern for the character warranted by the Shakespeare text but an entirely new strategy of derogatory portrayal of a piece with nineteenth- and twentieth-century US minstrelsy conventions, inserting a mode of contemporary rather than contemporaneous racism. There were a few occasions when players used improvisation to counteract the normalizing effects of repeating un-remarked racist portions of the text live in performance, such as when Benedick (Burger) gave the line, 'Then I am – dammit Shakespeare – a Jew!' Such interjections were more infrequent as compared to the inverse.

As these examples suggest, the company also experimented with casting. Having routinely cast female-identifying players in the role of men, and vice versa, this season was the first to incorporate an added sensitivity. Individual players were also asked to decide what gender they were going to present their character as, indicated to the company in a pre-show circle warm-up for each performance. Pronouns were to be amended live to follow suit; playgoers were not notified but left to discover this as part of the performance. For example, in a performance of *Henry IV, Part One*, Buckner played Hotspur and also chose to perform the role as a woman. (That same summer the Oregon Shakespeare Festival cast Alejandra Escalante as Hotspur and emphasized the homoerotics made available in scenes with her wife; Ashland, Oregon, is approximately a five-hour drive from Portland.) While male-identified players seemed unable to engage gender politics in moments of improvisation with *Shrew*, the opposite was true in this performance where Hotspur, his wife, Hal and the Prompter were all performed by female-identifying players. For example, interrupting the first scene in the play between King Henry IV and Hotspur, who was refusing to turn over hostages, the Prompter (Muff) asked Hotspur, 'What makes you so hot?':

> HOTSPUR Well, they told me I had to wear a dress for this.
> PROMPTER So, you went looking for a white pantsuit?
> HOTSPUR Exactly.

The moment draws attention to the 2016 US presidential election the previous year and the historical fact that became popularized in relation to the Hilary Clinton campaign: women senators were unable to wear pants on Capitol Hill until the 1990s.[33] Commenting on the costume underscored Hotspur's difficulty not only with obeying the authority of his king but with inequitable social codes generally. Further facilitating this interpretation of Hotspur as resisting both political and gendered social codes then and now was the maintaining of Lady Percy's (Sullivan Mackintosh) gender identity so that they were a same-sex couple. As Prompter, Muff recycled a cue for improvisation from earlier in the season by asking for engagement stories:

PROMPTER Lady, how did she propose?
LADY PERCY Over waffles, milkshakes –
PROMPTER Was there bacon?
LADY PERCY We were having waffles but not bacon. I'm a vegetarian. When I was drinking my milkshakes, well, there was a ring at the bottom. Points for creativity, but it was all sticky!
HOTSPUR She's missing the part where (*mimes*) I took it out of her hand, popped it in my mouth (*mimes rinsing in mouth*), and (*mimes putting it on Lady Percy's finger*) plop!

Aside from building out the backstory of the Percys, who have little stage time otherwise, the moment comically humanized the otherwise odd pairing of personalities. By dramatizing their proposal story as had been done for heterosexual couples in other performances during the festival, playgoers were given a chance to catch up on their dynamic as well as affirm queer identity in a season otherwise centring heteronormativity.

In these variations over an intensive repertory festival featuring three weeks of back-to-back performances, and some twice daily, prompting had the capacity to expand beyond its function as a safety net and into an engine for improvisation and co-composition. If the Prompter was attempting to establish a meta-commentary with which the rest of the company were not commensurate, or was more invested in providing opportunities for improvisation than the story, a performer was more likely to fall out. The Prompter as a performance technology first served players, keeping them on text and on entrance, before facilitating any innovations. The Prompter sutured figuratively the backstage world of the personnel and the tiring house with the world of the play, as well as provided 'bandages' live in performance, to do things with the text while waiting for a missed cue or entrance. As a final example, the unpredictability not of the many passing bicyclists or boat horns but the player's body threatened to derail a *Twelfth Night* prompted by Durham. Late in the play, Lewis as Sir Andrew Aguecheek entered having acquired an abrupt case of the hiccups:

> PROMPTER Wait, wait, wait. Do you actually have the hiccups?
> AGUECHEEK I literally just got the hiccups.
> PROMPTER Would you explain to our audience how you got them?

As Lewis turned her back to start speaking, Durham crept up slowly behind her, quickly grabbed her shoulders, and 'scared' the hiccups out of her. Because the Prompter never leaves their chair, it was unexpected and worked to cure the hiccups while also upending a sense of reliability in the Prompter. Aguecheek moved over to Sir Toby Belch (Yocam) to whimper at her friend, so that the Prompter replied, 'Do you not feel safe anymore? I'm sorry, I'll take care of you'. A mild non-verbal antagonism between the two continued for the rest of the performance, producing comic results. Durham recovered his credibility as Prompter when veteran Fridlich (Olivia) had a faulty stretch in her scroll that was missing the better part of a scene. For a moment she leaned over the Prompter's shoulder to read from the prompt book and then resorted to taking it with her to finish the scene. Meanwhile, Durham wound through her scroll, located a cue line for her to re-enter, and handed it off during a pause. So while the Prompter had a dual role as part 'shepherd' and part creative contributor, it would seem that within this practice one could not sacrifice the shepherd status for the merits of a comic payoff. The Prompter here was protecting the cohesion of the show by startling Lewis out of her hiccups, but interestingly still needed to regain their position of safety net and did so through improvisation.

Live in repertory

In this chapter I have tried to track some of the effects of one OP technique, an onstage prompter, that manifested over three weeks of performing Shakespeare plays within a repertory schedule. What can be drawn from these observations about prompters is limited given that this variable was used within an eclectic set of 'original practices', although uniquely using a repertory schedule and a group of professional players habituated to this system and to one another. It suggests the co-dependent nature of certain historical practices, which creates an additional challenge to testing their effects. As scholar-playwright Emma Whipday recently remarked:

> I also hope that work informed by (and itself feeding into) theatrical-historical research . . . will continue to develop; I worry when these kinds of experimental work that challenge models of directors' theatre [are] too easily characterized as staid or backwards looking, when in fact they can be at once historically informed and radical, in challenging the prevalent models of twenty-first century theatricality.[34]

And surprise they can when accounting for repertory, as there is much to be learned from the affordances of sequencing. In *Romeo and Juliet,* OPSF had to solve for the lack of a balcony. Yoshikawa (Romeo) came up with the solution to dress as Where's Waldo?™ and sit among the crowd while speaking 'upwards' to Juliet, who maintained her position of merely standing in the playing place, strongly implying the hierarchy of their separation without architectural levels. The next day Yoshikawa performed as Fenton, suitor to Anne Page in *Merry Wives*, which summoned memories of him from the previous evening and attached them to this new romantic persona. Both Romeo and Fenton are young men desperate for their loves and blocked by mothers who have specific economic motivations about who the lady should marry. Rather than seek counsel from a friar or friends like Romeo, Fenton instead seeks help from the Host, played by Allard, who also played Friar Lawrence, another lover-boy's aide, the previous night.

Yoshikawa as both Romeo and Fenton suggests two models of what it might look like to be a romantic suitor. As Fenton, he came up with an ingenious repurposing of his part scroll to help narrate the complex abduction plan to the Host. Yoshikawa employed an old table-reading exercise, literally drawing out each of the steps in his plan to abscond with Anne on the back of another scroll using the same dowel strategy (see Figure 5.6). Timing the unrolling to match his thirty-six-line speech from act four, the innovation made a difficult text clear in addition to furthering his earlier claim that while her 'father's wealth was the first motive that I woo'd', it is now 'the very riches of [her]self' that was his aim. Both Romeo and Nym (also played by Yoshikawa in the run)

FIGURE 5.6 Merry Wives of Windsor, *Irving Park*, 22 July 2017. From left: Brian Allard (Host) and Ken Yoshikawa (Fenton). Courtesy of the author with permission from the company.

can be suspected of ulterior motives, the former perhaps aware of Juliet as sole inheritor of her father's wealth and the later having recommended to 'deal with poison'. That Romeo and Fenton were performed by the same player in close succession underscores these juxtapositions, implications of typecasting and historically situated lines of business. Both characters go for the marry-now-apologize-later tactic. Fenton does not attempt to secure his love alone, however, but works with his community, the opposite of Romeo's approach. The juxtaposition summoned questions live in real time, including: What kind of lover are you? What kind of lover do you have? What kind of lover do you want, or want to be? To get at the sorts of exciting opportunities that recycling in repertory affords, perhaps part of asking what the work of live performance might suggest means first performing more systematic work of asking.

Appendix

Original Practice Shakespeare Festival 2017 WIL Fest performances.

Date	2017-07-21	2017-07-22	2017-07-22	2017-07-23	2017-07-23	2017-07-28	2017-07-29
Time	7:00 PM	2:00 PM	7:00 PM	2:00 PM	7:00 PM	7:00 PM	2:00 PM
Location	Willamette Park	Irving Park	Irving Park	Irving Park	Irving Park	Irving Park	Willamette Park
Title	*Romeo and Juliet*	*Merry Wives of Windsor*	*Julius Caesar*	*Much Ado About Nothing*	*Tempest*	*Macbeth*	*Taming of the Shrew*
Total Cast	14	17	16	14	16	13	16
Allard, Brian (11)	Friar Lawrence	Host	Julius Caesar, Cinna the Poet	Borachio	Prospero	King Duncan, Porter, Doctor	Lord, Vincentio
Andersen, Amanda (2)					Antonio		
Ashenbrenner, Kelsea (6)							Nicholas
Bachrach, Hailey (4)							
Bellis-Squires, David (7)	Sampson, Musician, Friar John	Falstaff	Casca, Dardanius			Prompter	
Bray, Andrew						Witch, Angus	
Brown, Stan (5)		Sir Hugh Evans					
Buckner, Isabella (8)	Prompter		Caius Cassius		Stephano	Malcolm	
Burger, Brian (7)				Benedick			Prompter
Butler, Bryn (1)					Miranda		

ALIVE IN THE (EARLY) MODERN REPERTORY 135

2017-07-29	2017-07-30	2017-07-30	2017-08-04	2017-08-05	2017-08-05	2017-08-06	2017-08-06
7:00 PM	2:00 PM	7:00 PM	7:00 PM	2:00 PM	7:00 PM	2:00 PM	7:00 PM
Willamette Park	Willamette Park	Willamette Park	Laurelhurst Park	Laurelhurst Park	Laurelhurst Park	Laurelhurst Park	Laurelhurst Park
Comedy of Errors	*Twelfth Night*	*Henry IV, Part 1*	*Richard III*	*As You Like It*	*Hamlet*	*All's Well That Ends Well*	*Midsummer Night's Dream*
13	14	15	17	14	14	13	15
	Antonio	Henry IV, Glendower	Buckingham			Reynaldo, Interpreter	
		Prince John, Francis, Sheriff					
Officer, Balthazar, Messenger	Sailor	Traveler, Lady Mortimer		Audrey, Amiens, Le Beau		Gentleman 1, Lord 2	
			Rivers, Cardinal, Scrivener	Jacques	Ophelia		Snug, Moth
			Sir Stanley	Touchstone	Prompter		
		Blunt, Peto		Corin, Hymen, Clown 2, Page	Bernardo, Player, Messenger, Gravedigger	Lafeu	
Dromio of Syracuse		Hotspur	Richard III				Titania, Hyppolita
	Orsino	Falstaff	Henry VI, Rotherham, Henry VII			Parolles	Bottom

Date	2017-07-21	2017-07-22	2017-07-22	2017-07-23	2017-07-23	2017-07-28	2017-07-29
Time	7:00 PM	2:00 PM	7:00 PM	2:00 PM	7:00 PM	7:00 PM	2:00 PM
Location	Willamette Park	Irving Park	Irving Park	Irving Park	Irving Park	Irving Park	Willamette Park
Title	*Romeo and Juliet*	*Merry Wives of Windsor*	*Julius Caesar*	*Much Ado About Nothing*	*Tempest*	*Macbeth*	*Taming of the Shrew*
Total Cast	14	17	16	14	16	13	16
Cable, Keith (7)		Mr Ford		Messenger, Dogberry		Seyton	Gremio, Nathaniel
Davis, Jefferson (2)							
Dixon, Elise (3)			Trebonius, Varro		Boatswain, Francisco		
Driesler, Amy (4)	Prince, Peter		Cobler, Portia, Octavius				
Durham, Joel Patrick (8)	Tybalt		Prompter		Trinculo	Macduff	
Fridlich, Sarah Jane (7)		Mrs Page		Hero			
Goldenberg, Noah (5)	Benvolio						
Harris-Bagwell, Shani (4)		Mrs Ford	Calpurnia, Lepidus			Banquo, Siward	
Haynes, Megan (4)		Fairy			Mariner, Spirit		
Hershberger, Tara (1)							
Hillier, Kaia (5)	Juliet		Mark Antony		Ariel	Witch, Murderer, Lady Macduff	

2017-07-29	2017-07-30	2017-07-30	2017-08-04	2017-08-05	2017-08-05	2017-08-06	2017-08-06
7:00 PM	2:00 PM	7:00 PM	7:00 PM	2:00 PM	7:00 PM	2:00 PM	7:00 PM
Willamette Park	Willamette Park	Willamette Park	Laurelhurst Park	Laurelhurst Park	Laurelhurst Park	Laurelhurst Park	Laurelhurst Park
Comedy of Errors	*Twelfth Night*	*Henry IV, Part 1*	*Richard III*	*As You Like It*	*Hamlet*	*All's Well That Ends Well*	*Midsummer Night's Dream*
13	14	15	17	14	14	13	15
			Hastings, Messenger	Oliver	Polonius		
					Ghost, Player, Sailor, Fortinbras	Gentleman 2, Lord 1	
							Helena
Antipholus of Ephesus							Quince
	Prompter	Poins, Douglas			Hamlet		Oberon, Theseus
Luciana	Olivia		Elizabeth	Rosalind		Helena	
	Feste		Ratcliffe		Laertes		Prompter
Adriana							
		Bardolph	Guard, Messenger, Oxford				
Solinus							
	Viola						

Date	2017-07-21	2017-07-22	2017-07-22	2017-07-23	2017-07-23	2017-07-28	2017-07-29
Time	7:00 PM	2:00 PM	7:00 PM	2:00 PM	7:00 PM	7:00 PM	2:00 PM
Location	Willamette Park	Irving Park	Irving Park	Irving Park	Irving Park	Irving Park	Willamette Park
Title	*Romeo and Juliet*	*Merry Wives of Windsor*	*Julius Caesar*	*Much Ado About Nothing*	*Tempest*	*Macbeth*	*Taming of the Shrew*
Total Cast	14	17	16	14	16	13	16
Hirschhorn, Jessica (4)							Katherina
Hoback, Nik (5)				Don Pedro	Ferdinand		
Jordan, Michael C. (3)							Petruchio
Kane, Colin (2)							
Kirkpatrick, Erin (1)							
Landmann, Emilie (3)							Sly, Pedant
Leek, Kerry (6)		Pistol, Caius		Prompter	Caliban	Ross	Tranio
Leidigh, Noah (9)	Abraham, Paris	Fairy		Verges			Servant, Curtis
Lewis, Lissie (6)			Lucius		Sebastian		Biondello, Philip
Lipsey, Mkki (4)					Gonzalo		
Lugo, Alec (7)	Nurse, Montague	Slender		Balthasar, Watch	Prompter		Hortensio
Mackintosh, Sullivan (5)			Marullus, Metellus Cymber, Pindarus				Grumio, Widow
McCarthy, Mara (2)			Cinna, Lucillius	Margaret			

2017-07-29	2017-07-30	2017-07-30	2017-08-04	2017-08-05	2017-08-05	2017-08-06	2017-08-06
7:00 PM	2:00 PM	7:00 PM	7:00 PM	2:00 PM	7:00 PM	2:00 PM	7:00 PM
Willamette Park	Willamette Park	Willamette Park	Laurelhurst Park	Laurelhurst Park	Laurelhurst Park	Laurelhurst Park	Laurelhurst Park
Comedy of Errors	*Twelfth Night*	*Henry IV, Part 1*	*Richard III*	*As You Like It*	*Hamlet*	*All's Well That Ends Well*	*Midsummer Night's Dream*
13	14	15	17	14	14	13	15
		Mistress Quickly				Diana, Lord 3	Starveling, Cobweb
		Henry V			Rosencrantz, Servant	Bertram	
					Claudius	King of France, Soldier 2	
			Prompter				Flute, Peaseblossom
	Sailor						
Angelo	Maria						
				Adam			
		Mortimer, Vernon	Brakenbury, Prince Edward	Silvius, Clown 2	Voltemand, Priest		Lysander
Aemilia, Merchant	Aguecheek		Margaret, Ely				
Aegeon, Doctor Pinch		Northumberland, Traveler	Duchess of York, Blunt				
				Orlando		Prompter	
Dromio of Ephesus		Westmoreland, Lady Percy	Catesby				

Date	2017-07-21	2017-07-22	2017-07-22	2017-07-23	2017-07-23	2017-07-28	2017-07-29
Time	7:00 PM	2:00 PM	7:00 PM	2:00 PM	7:00 PM	7:00 PM	2:00 PM
Location	Willamette Park	Irving Park	Irving Park	Irving Park	Irving Park	Irving Park	Willamette Park
Title	*Romeo and Juliet*	*Merry Wives of Windsor*	*Julius Caesar*	*Much Ado About Nothing*	*Tempest*	*Macbeth*	*Taming of the Shrew*
Total Cast	14	17	16	14	16	13	16
Mounsey, Tom (1)						Macbeth	
Muff, Shandi (9)	Lady Capulet	Prompter		Don John, Watch, Sexton		Lady Macbeth	
Neeko, Jurnee (7)		Anne Page, Rugby	Commoner, Plebian, Soldier		Shipmaster, Adrian	Fleance, Young Macduff	
Olson, David C. (2)		Shallow		Leonato			
Passolt, Barbara (2)							
Ruckman, Megan (2)		Mistress Quickly					
Saville, Lauren (6)	Mercutio		Decius Brutus	Claudia, Watch		Witch, Murderer, Gentlewoman	Bianca, Gregory
Shier, Madeline (1)							
Streeter, Michael (2)	Lord Capulet		Soothsayer, Messala				
Van Buecken, Beth (3)							
Whiteside, Emma (9)	Gregory, Apothecary, Watch	Bardolph, Simple, Robert	Flavius, Artemidorus, Titinius	Conrade, Priest	Mariner, Spirit	Donalbain, Young Siward	Host
Witherspoon, Tom (5)		Mr Page			Alonso		Baptista, Tailor
Yocam, Beth (7)			Marcus Brutus	Beatrice			
Yoshikawa, Ken (7)	Romeo	Fenton, Nym, John					Lucentio

ALIVE IN THE (EARLY) MODERN REPERTORY 141

2017-07-29	2017-07-30	2017-07-30	2017-08-04	2017-08-05	2017-08-05	2017-08-06	2017-08-06
7:00 PM	2:00 PM	7:00 PM	7:00 PM	2:00 PM	7:00 PM	2:00 PM	7:00 PM
Willamette Park	Willamette Park	Willamette Park	Laurelhurst Park	Laurelhurst Park	Laurelhurst Park	Laurelhurst Park	Laurelhurst Park
Comedy of Errors	*Twelfth Night*	*Henry IV, Part 1*	*Richard III*	*As You Like It*	*Hamlet*	*All's Well That Ends Well*	*Midsummer Night's Dream*
13	14	15	17	14	14	13	15
Antipholus of Syracuse		Prompter		Duke Frederick, Phoebe	Horatio		Puck
Merchant, Cortezan	Sailor, Officer, Priest						Hermia
		Worcester					Egeus
					Marcellus, Player, Gravedigger, Osric		
			Lady Anne, Murderer				
				Celia			
			Guard, Priest, Norfolk	Duke Senior		Widow	
	Curio, Fabian						Demetrius
	Malvolio						Snout, Mustardseed
Prompter	Belch			Prompter	Gertrude	Countess, Mariana	
			Clarence, Mayor	Charles	Guildenstern, Servant	Clown, Soldier 1	

Notes

1 Stephen Purcell, 'Practice-as-Research and Original Practices', *Shakespeare Bulletin* 35, no. 3 (2017): 428.

2 For a survey of the first twelve years of the important Read Not Dead Project along with its repertory schedule, see James Wallace, '"That Scull Had a Tongue in It, and Could Sing Once": Staging Shakespeare's Contemporaries', in *Shakespeare's Globe: A Theatrical Experiment*, ed. Christie Carson and Farah Karim-Cooper (Cambridge: Cambridge University Press, 2008), 147–54, 243–52. For an ethnography of the working practices and processual knowledge cultivated by the Edward's Boys repertory, see Harry R. McCarthy, *Performing Early Modern Drama Beyond Shakespeare: Edward's Boys* (Cambridge: Cambridge University Press, 2020).

3 Don Weingust, 'Original Practices', in *The Cambridge Guide to the Worlds of Shakespeare*, ed. Bruce R. Smith and Katherine Rowe (Cambridge: Cambridge University Press, 2016), 1476–77; Don Weingust, 'Authentic Performances or Performances of Authenticity? Original Practices and the Repertory Schedule', *Shakespeare* 10, no. 4 (2014): 403.

4 Tiffany Stern and Simon Palfrey, *Shakespeare in Parts* (Oxford: Oxford University Press, 2007), 73.

5 Ibid., 74.

6 Ibid.

7 Don Weingust, *Acting from Shakespeare's First Folio: Theory, Text and Performance* (New York: Routledge, 2006), 98.

8 Ibid.

9 For a summary of practices variously adopted by these companies, see Don Weingust, 'Rehearsal and Acting Practice', in *A Companion to Renaissance Drama*, ed. Arthur F. Kinney and Thomas Warren Hopper (Hoboken: Wiley Blackwell, 2017), 250–67.

10 Jeremy Lopez, 'A Partial Theory of Original Practice', *Shakespeare Survey* 61 (2008): 304.

11 Ibid., 306–7.

12 Paul Prescott, 'The Event: Festival Shakespeare', in *The Arden Research Handbook of Shakespeare and Contemporary Performance*, ed. Peter Kirwan and Kathryn Prince (London: Bloomsbury, 2021), 47.

13 Ibid., *Shakespeare in the Theatre: Mark Rylance at the Globe* (London: Bloomsbury, 2017), 24.

14 Ibid., 27.
15 Ibid., 24.
16 Weingust, 'Authentic Performances or Performances of Authenticity?', 405.
17 Paul Menzer, *Shakespeare in the Theatre: The American Shakespeare Center* (London: Bloomsbury, 2017), 219–20.
18 Sarah Dustagheer, 'Original Practices: Old Ways and New Directions', in *The Arden Research Handbook of Shakespeare and Contemporary Performance*, ed. Peter Kirwan and Kathryn Prince (London: Bloomsbury, 2021), 62.
19 Peggy O'Brien, *Declaration on Common Core State Standards*, Folger Shakespeare Library, 28 January 2015, https://www.folger.edu/sites/default/files/CCSS1.28.15.pdf.
20 Rob Conkie, *The Globe Theatre Project: Shakespeare and Authenticity* (New York: Edwin Mellen Press, 2006), 121.
21 See Appendix 5.i for a complete list of dates, times, locations and cast list for each of the performances discussed here.
22 Siobhan Keenan, *Travelling Players in Shakespeare's England* (London: Palgrave Macmillan, 2002), 2–3.
23 McCarthy, *Performing Early Modern Drama Beyond Shakespeare*, 57.
24 The distinction between amateur and professional company is complex; see Michael Dobson, *Shakespeare and Amateur Performance: A Cultural History* (Cambridge: Cambridge University Press, 2011).
25 The mode number of performances for an individual company member was two, with the average being four to five performances. Forty-eight of the fifty-five company members who serve as performers participated in the 2017 WIL Fest. Early afternoon performances typically limited scheduling for those whose other employment conflicted.
26 Helen Lewis, 'Broadway's Dirty Secret: Ivo van Hove's Success Shows How Much American Commercial Theater Relies on European State Funding', *The Atlantic*, 6 November 2019, https://www.theatlantic.com/international/archive/2019/11/ivo-van-hove-and-broadways-secret-reliance-state-funding/601219/.
27 Ibid.
28 W. B. Worthen, 'Intoxicating Rhythms: Or, Shakespeare, Literary Drama, and Performance (Studies)', *Shakespeare Quarterly* 62, no. 3 (2011): 333.

29 Christa McIntyre, 'Stormy Weather: A "Tempest" Erupts', *Oregon ArtsWatch*, 5 July 2016, https://archive.orartswatch.org/stormy-weather-a-tempest-erupts/.
30 As of this writing, the tagline remains prominent on the company webpage, https://www.opsfest.org.
31 McIntyre, 'Stormy Weather'.
32 Elizabeth E. Tavares, 'Review of *The Taming of the Shrew* (Original Practice Shakespeare Festival 2017)', *Scene: The Journal of the Internet Shakespeare Editions* 1, no. 2 (2017): 66–72.
33 Juliet Linderman, 'A Look at Women's Advances over the Years in Congress', *PBS NewsHour*, 4 November 2017, https://www.pbs.org/newshour/politics/a-look-at-womens-advances-over-the-years-in-congress.
34 C. K. Ash and Nora J. Williams, curators, "Hot Take: Emma Whipday (Playwright, Director and Academic)', in *The Arden Research Handbook of Shakespeare and Contemporary Performance*, ed. Peter Kirwan and Kathryn Prince (London: Bloomsbury, 2021), 263–4. For details of Whipday's performance-based research, see Jensen Freyja Cox, et al. 'The Disobedient Child: A Tudor Interlude in Performance', *Shakespeare* 16, no. 1 (2020): 60–7; and with Lucy Munro, 'Making Early Modern "Verbatim Theatre", or, "Keep the Widow Waking"', in *Loss and the Literary Culture of Shakespeare's Time*, ed. Roslyn L. Knutson et al. (Cham: Palgrave Macmillan, 2020), 233–49.

6

Contemporary Turkish Shakespeares

New breath to old lives

Murat Öğütcü

Turkey has a long tradition of reading, translating and staging William Shakespeare's plays as part of the country's Westernization process. Ranging from faithful productions to free adaptations, Shakespeare has become one of the most important non-Turkish authors and an indispensable part of the educational curricula and theatre repertory.[1] Recent Turkish productions and adaptations of Shakespeare have given new life to his plays by localizing and interpreting their content through culturally specific resonances amid the changing notions of live performances during the Covid-19 pandemic.

This can be seen especially via three commercially successful recent Turkish adaptations of Shakespeare. Serhat Yiğit's *İkinci Katil* (Second Murderer) (2017) is an urban intellectual retelling of Shakespeare's *Macbeth*. The simultaneous presence of the source text and the adaptation enables the urban Turkish audience to scrutinize the tragedies of ordinary people and associate some of these with their own real-life problems. Likewise, the documentary about the performance process of staging *Kraliçe Lear* (Queen Lear) (2019) shows how an all-female, rural, travelling theatre company deals with gender inequalities. Their backstories give Shakespeare new significance for the lives of the performers and their sceptical audiences. Similarly, Ayhan Hülagu's performance of Shakespeare's *Hamlet* as *Dream of Hamlet* (2020–21) uses the traditional Turkish shadow theatre to exemplify how Western tragic and Eastern comic forms of dramatic performances can conflate.

These adaptations also shed new light onto how to conceptualize live theatre amid Covid-19 restrictions. The pre-pandemic productions of live theatre in *İkinci Katil* and the documentary of *Kraliçe Lear* generate remembrances of live theatre productions amid restrictions on live performances in Turkey.[2] The online airing of *Dream of Hamlet* in the United States tries to compensate for the loss of live performances. The play exemplifies how such restrictions in the United States have enabled Turkish audiences to view the play online despite geographical restrictions. Accordingly, this essay will illustrate how the live medium of theatre is reconfigured in the pandemic period as a palimpsestic recollection of personal, literary and cultural remembrances that transfigure temporal and spatial immediacy to a personal one.

İkinci Katil

Shakespearean productions have usually been perceived as urban dramatic entertainments in Turkey, as an extension of the Westernization process that has aimed to raise intellectual literacy.[3] Therefore, it is not surprising that *İkinci Katil*'s emphasis on urban life has been well received by its urban audiences in the State Theatre stages in Ankara and other major cities.[4] Yiğit's *İkinci Katil* premiered in 2017, sold out for the rest of its performances until 2018, and was revived in the summer season in 2019, becoming one of the most acclaimed adaptations of Shakespeare in Turkey. Having received many awards in Turkey, the play is marked by its emphasis on the lives of minor characters and their personal traumas created by social injustice.[5] Its title *İkinci Katil*, the Turkish words for 'second murderer', alludes to how the play portrays how the murderers from Shakespeare's *Macbeth* become murderers because of socio-economic necessities before their fatal ends. The play centres on the life of an innkeeper, not present in Shakespeare's play, who is caught up in Macbeth's machinations of homicide. The encoding and decoding of associations between the source and the adaptation are, of course, impulsive and idiosyncratic on a personal level, but the simultaneous presence of the adapted text and the source text in the live performances of Yiğit's play enable a fluidity of associations in the meaning-making process. By telling the story of how Warden, the host of a tavern near Inverness castle, and his wife, Mary, struggle economically and domestically before becoming murderers, the play transforms the source text's focus on royal life to that of commoners.

This transformation is achieved not just discursively through the play text, but also through the director Barış Erdenk's stagecraft. By constructing the stage as a pyramidal structure, source text characters like Macbeth, Lady Macbeth and Banquo are confined to the throne at the top from which they overlook and control the main action below them as a panoptical presence. Thereby, the play creates a material dialogue between the source text and Yiğit's adaptation.[6] The geometry of this dynamic triangular form of power and class relationships in higher social strata is contrasted with the flatness of the remaining rectangular props, such as tables and the bed, which hint at the static lives of the lower middle-class characters.

The problems in the play are represented by the rotten appearance of the scenic devises and the use of rope pieces in the background, which look like cobwebs. Representing the complex network of relations among the characters and how social and domestic problems are left unresolved, they hint at possible fatal consequences.[7] The concentration of these rope pieces on the throne underscores the state's central position in this corruption, extending to its subjects (Figure 6.1).[8]

Moving from socio-political to private matters, Yiğit's adaptation presents the actions of the normally typecast lower- to middle-class murderers of Shakespeare's play and a relatable story for its urban audiences. By pushing the main and noble characters of the source text into the background, the play 'looks at the ordinary man's tragedy' usually 'hidden' through 'social' definitions of 'ethics' and 'tragedy' that make us 'empathise' only with one's 'betters' rather than one's 'equals'.[9]

The movement into the private sphere is also shown via the play's initial scenes which proceed from the source text to the main story

FIGURE 6.1 *Macbeth (background), Mary (left), Warden (right), Kerem Kantarcı,* İkinci Katil, *2017, Behance.net, https://www.behance.net/gallery /57411513/KNC-KATL-ANKARA-STATE-THEATER*

of the adaptation. The abbreviated version of the witches' encounter with Macbeth and Banquo parallels how the disguised witches cause trouble for Warden, who is threatened by a guest for protecting the incognito witches.[10] When the scene moves to how Warden and Mary retire to their bedroom, we see even more private issues. Interestingly, rope pieces around the throne are haphazardly used in the bedroom's background to hint at domestic problems like their childlessness and economic struggles. Building upon Macbeth and Lady Macbeth's own possible and hotly debated childlessness, the explicit rendition of fertility problems recalls some of the Turkish audiences about similar problems they possibly have.[11] There is a relative low fertility rate in urban areas in Turkey, worsened later by the fear generated by the co-existence of medical treatments of Covid-19 patients and those who want to get an IVF treatment.[12] Therefore, Mary and Warden's childlessness would be recognized during and after live performances and remembered amid restrictions on theatres in Turkey by individuals or families of those who have been going through that painful process of hope and hopelessness.

Vacillating between optimism and pessimism and struggling to cover their costs, Warden and Mary receive the news that Macbeth will buy all their wine to be used in the festivities to host Duncan. The dramatic irony does not arise about what happens to Duncan, but with the consequences of Warden's benevolence and hospitality shown towards the witches. The tavern is stormed by soldiers of a mysterious and discontented guest, who turns out to be Lord Lowrey, a greedy nephew of Banquo not found in the source text.[13] Ordered to pay a heavy fine for insulting Lowrey and overrun by the might of his forces, Warden and Mary are left devastated. Musing on whether they will use the money they receive from Macbeth to pay that fine, their desires, ambitions and empty hopes for a better future life are desperately set against socio-economic realities.

Their worries have profound impacts on the course of their lives and other disenfranchised people. For instance, the backstory of the First Murderer in *Macbeth*, here a character called Evan, shows the fatal consequences of his desperation after he gambled away his possessions to Lord Lowrey in a game with loaded dice. Considering the high amount of lower- and middle-class people in debt in Turkey and news about people being tricked by Ponzi schemes, Evan's disappointments recall similar economic conditions during the 2017–18 season and its revival in mid-2019.[14] Remembering the play during the Covid-19 period, along with the pandemic's effects on the economy, might further audience empathy towards Evan's misanthropy.[15] Like many recent Turkish plays reflective of the correlation of economic distress and rise in crime rates, Evan's frustration with social inequality, demise into alcoholism and becoming a murderer represent how socio-economically marginalized people can become violent.[16]

Machiavellian but insecure powerholders like Macbeth try to use these forms of desperation to secure their hold on power by instrumentalizing social polarization. *İkinci Katil*'s Macbeth not only provides backstories for the murderers' otherwise flattened characterization,[17] but also shows how powerholders can manipulate the people through populist rhetoric to inflict violence. Before Macbeth eventually hires Warden and Evan to murder Banquo, Warden's questioning of Banquo's fabricated involvement in Duncan's murder is counteracted by Macbeth's emphases on the well-being of the state. Macbeth does not only devise a sense of belonging by telling Warden and Evan he reaches out for them because he trusts his people more than his court, but his words also create a fear against being excluded by hinting at treason if they do not follow his orders.

This fear of social exclusion is fuelled by Warden's wife, Mary, who mimics Lady Macbeth by inciting her husband to go after his aspirations. Threatening to commit suicide and using her femininity, Mary persuades Warden to murder Banquo and Fleance.[18] Yet, like Macbeth's anxiety about Fleance's escape, Warden's insecurities are extended in his restless sleep haunted by nightmares after he has murdered Banquo.[19] Seeing the witches in his dream, Warden, just like Macbeth, is temporarily reassured of his future happiness.[20]

Mary's encounter with a tavern frequenter, Marlow, who has figured out the connection between Duncan and Banquo's murders and the involvement of Warden, however, necessitates her to kill Marlow and become another murderer. Trying to rub Marlow's blood, alluding to the 'Out, damned spot' scene, Mary's regrets are shown as an extension of Lady Macbeth's guilty conscience.[21] Seen above the stage, Lady Macbeth simultaneously tries to clean her hands as she sits on the throne.

The psychological effects on Mary and Lady Macbeth, their downfall and how the mysteries surrounding the murder cases are unravelled in the adaptation recall, for the Turkish audience, daily daytime popular reality shows. Similar to the play, the investigations of murder cases on Turkish TV show how the culprits' suppressed guilty consciences gradually resurface through their own behaviours.[22] Particularly, having metaphorically murdered sleep like Lady Macbeth and Macbeth, Warden and Mary are sleepless and haunted by their crimes in nightmares, as seen in Mary's nightmare.[23] Splitting the dialogue of Lady Macbeth's sleepwalking scene from Shakespeare's play among Lady Macbeth who sits on the throne, Mary sleeping in her bedroom and Mary in her dream where she is literally in water that cannot clean her of her sins, *İkinci Katil* presents the physical and psychological downfall of its female characters. It interrogates notions of the here and now in this multisensory scene. The splash of water and the frantic and confessional diegesis of past crimes make the audience question notions about the past, present and future by showing that these are not demarcated straight lines but spaces that palimpsestically overlap each other. When Lady Macbeth cuts her wrists and commits suicide, all voices that unharmoniously repeat Lady

Macbeth's sleepwalking monologue overlap and end with 'What's done cannot be undone' in *İkinci Katil*.[24] In the externalization of the guilty consciences of these women, Yiğit creates a voyeuristic space for the hidden lives of the murderers' psychologies. Towards the end of the play, Evan is murdered and Mary dies in the arms of Warden. While Warden tries to comfort her by talking about their imagined prosperous lives with their unborn children, Warden is still metaphorically imprisoned by his anticipation of future happiness as a promised condition. Eventually, Warden is murdered, too, by Macbeth's henchman, Doyle.

Despite leaving most of its audiences desperate about the possibilities of change, none of the audiences would have known that they would miss such an experience when the Covid-19 pandemic forced the closure of theatres. As digital copies are only available for researchers who can visit the State Theatre's archive in Ankara, the general audience is only able to remember the bits and pieces about their shared experience. While this puts limitations on re-experiencing the play as live performance, it fosters an active act of remembrance whose ellipses and anachronisms are filled with personal experiences which, thus, enrich the play's cultural transference.

Kraliçe Lear

Moving from an urban to a rural context, Pelin Esmer's documentary about the performance process of staging *King Lear* as *Kraliçe Lear* (2019), interspersed with interviews with its actors, shows how Shakespeare's plays can be domesticated and democratized.[25] As an all-female and rural travelling theatre, the Arslanköy Theatre Company's free performances aim to dissuade rural people from their general disbelief at the necessity of dramatic entertainment. The geographical distance between urban and rural places in Turkey has created a gulf between these places regarding economic, health and education opportunities.[26] This has triggered large-scale internal migration, which has worsened that gulf.[27] It has also necessitated rural people to work harder in agriculture, which prevents creating the time and money to spend on artistic entertainments. Therefore, performing a play from Shakespeare, whose foreignness and status as highbrow urban entertainment create a gap between the text and rural audiences, is very daring. The interview-like backstories of the rural performers and rural audiences prior to and following the performance of Shakespeare's play create a hindsight for the documentary audience regarding live performance. Laying bare gender inequalities and problems about the public presence of women, still considered as a shameful act in villages, *Kraliçe Lear* is a documentary by and for rural women's emancipation. Thereby, the backstories also open new insights on the immediacy of Shakespeare for the lives of these rural people, lives which have been hitherto hidden from the perspective of urban practitioners and audiences. Re-watching the documentary after Covid-19 on Turkish TV, and within lockdown measures, like long hours of curfews and travel restrictions, created a sense of nostalgia.

The documentary starts almost like how the witches meet in *Macbeth*, though with more positive overtones.[28] The darkness, sound of waves and female laughter create a multisensory experience of the rural female players' informal but democratic and constructive rehearsal process at the seaside.[29] The actual rehearsal within the ruins of the Anemurium ancient amphitheatre in Mersin blurs the now and the then and creates a visual palimpsest. The performers in their *shalvars*, traditional pants worn by men and women alike, and the violin that plays Turkish folk ballads like 'Kadifeden Kesesi' in the interims represent the now, whereas the marble *orchestra* where the main action takes place and the *koilon*'s (seating area's) broken steps remind us of times bygone.

However, despite these idyllic pictures, the performers' anxieties about their success and their family members, who they left behind, are shown in sporadic close-ups in pre-, mid- and post-performance sequences. This adds a humane and realistic side to the documentation of their experiences. The village's pristine landscape with old biofriendly houses, the sounds of animals and the small talk about rural life create a kinaesthetic experience of everyday village life. These images were especially liberating amid the lockdown measures that forced people to stay in their houses when *Kraliçe Lear* aired on TV.

Notwithstanding these peaceful images, the obstacles regarding the performers' interaction with rural audiences are seen in the theatre company's director's efforts to connect the everyday life and festive life by incorporating the villagers into the play. For instance, the director recruits an angry and sceptical villager to play one of Lear's daughters by convincing him that theatre can reflect his anger at the lack of care for the farmers in Turkey.[30] The scene shows the function of theatre to present problems and alchemize social discontent into harmony.

Yet, as the documentary explicitly addresses, the disinterested-to-hostile attitudes towards theatre are ingrained problems. Even though the very presence of Arslanköy Theatre Company proves the possibility that rural people can perform and appreciate theatre, the villagers cannot associate the performers with rural life. The villagers are astonished when they hear that the performers also look after crops and herd cattle. The villagers have created a glass ceiling and placed the rural performers above themselves and think they cannot achieve what the performers have achieved.

Despite these handicaps, the theatre company's efforts to make sense of the play for themselves and the rural audiences they are playing are noteworthy. The director uses the surrounding habitat to decorate the costume of Lear by putting green leaves around her and cutting a withered branch to symbolize Lear's abandonment. Visualizing the heath scenes with the withered branch, the theatre company appropriates the folk ballad 'Kendim Ettim Kendim Buldum', by Neşet Ertaş, which refers to how people wither like a rose because of their errors, to domesticate the play's content to be more legible and meaningful for the theatre sceptic rural audience.[31] Yet, rather than merely decorative, the emphasis on how problems emerge because of one's own fault is important to underscore Lear's confrontation with his errors of judgement.

On the actual evening of the performance, this confrontation is also seen in a flash-forward, which adds more depth to the performance itself set against the rural performers' unseen lives. As a voice-over contemplation, Fatma Fatih remembers sitting on a balcony in front of Mersin's urban silhouette, where she is dreaming about having a small house of her own. The rural performer's experience of hardship and her dream to be able to live in the city are contrasted with the intended urban audience's view of village life as a beautiful pasture. Comparing herself with Shakespeare's Lear, who loses his belongings and health, the performer muses on the haves and have-nots along with the importance of health, which has become our major concern since Covid-19. Further thinking on how she might not be able to support her own daughters materially but will always be there for them contrasts with the lack of reciprocity in Lear's behaviour and treatment.³² The subsequent scene about the actual performance night indicates how the performer's identification with the text is helpful to establish a sincere relationship with a hostile audience.

With the flourish sound and the entry of Lear onto the stage, the audience's preliminary reservation about theatre seems to be transformed into enjoyment, especially by making Shakespeare accessible by domesticizing the play with folk drama elements. Rural costumes, the angry male villager's cross-dressing and guest performance as Goneril, and his kissing of Lear's hand as sign of the veneration of elders in Turkey all create a carnivalesque environment the rural audiences are familiar with.³³ The inversion of gender and status roles creates comedy and releases fears associated with the patriarchal pressure put on these people. The play's conclusion with a jig-like performance of the folk ballad 'Kesik Çayır' (The Lawn That Is Cut) forms the *komos* (revelry) that creates harmony and a positive attitude towards drama (Figure 6.2).

Before another performance is documented, we get a glimpse at the performers' backstories, their hardships and their families' support. For instance, the lines of Behiye Yanık, the performer of

FIGURE 6.2 *From left to right: Fatma Fatih (standing), Ümmü Kurt, the angry villager, Cennet Güneş, Zeynep Fatih (from left to right), Pelin Esmer,* Kraliçe Lear, *2019, Pelinesmer.com, http://pelinesmer.com/portfolio/kralice-lear-basin-odasi/*

Cordelia, who wishes only 'good health' to Lear and does not want any 'worldly belongings' from him/her, have deep resonances with the performer's life, and broadly for the audiences regarding the many illness-related deaths following Covid-19.[34] Caring for her chronically ill and almost bed-bound husband, the performer's happiness of having a husband who acknowledges her love contrasts with Lear's lack of insight. With other examples from the lives of other performers, we see a panorama of gender relations in rural Turkey that underscores the performers' multifaceted lives that have been imperceptible even by their rural audiences. Discussing didactically how drama has enabled them to surpass daily restrictions of community pressure and rural conservatism, the documentary's eyewitness-like documentation of the performers' lives makes their lives recognized and not lost.

But the Sisyphean cycle of trying to persuade the rural population to see, enjoy and learn from their play is more empathetically shown when almost all villagers they encounter in another village find excuses not to attend the play. Two teenage girls who secretly try to help the performers give hope, whereas two women in their early 30s with children illustrate the destined role of girls as child bearers.

To ease relations, the presentation of a documentary from 2005, titled *Oyun* (Game/Play), before the performance of *King Lear* is used to prove the performers' rural backgrounds to create a shared basis between the performers and audiences. Also directed by Pelin Esmer, *Oyun* refers to the theatre company's origins, how a high school performance was influential on them to start their theatrical careers, and the initial antagonism of Behiye Yanık's husband as examples of the obstacles they faced. Along with Fatma Fatih's diegetic chorus-like storytelling, which gives further information to the two young girls from earlier, the scenes from *Oyun* complement the performers' overall aim to persuade rural audiences of the necessity to instrumentalize Shakespeare and the theatres for the self-esteem and the public presence of women in rural Turkey. The scenes act as non-linear remembrances of the hardships the performers have faced like those which they want to challenge in their rural audiences. The screening of the documentary-within-a-documentary seemed to be effective to establish the audience's empathy towards the performers by provoking comic and tragic catharses.

When yet another fragment of the performance of *King Lear* is presented, we see how regional overtones are used to make the play more understandable for the rural audiences. The singing of Suat Sayın's 'Sevemez Kimse Seni', a Turkish classical song about a person's protestation that nobody could love the addressee more than him/her, complements Lear's quest to find who loves him/her best. The audience's singing along with the song creates a mutual experience almost akin to early modern English plays where songs would trigger possible audience involvement.[35]

Despite the performers' commitment, the next venue shows how the company must repeatedly work hard to convince rural authorities and people of the benefits of drama. The mukhtar of the next village actively tries to prevent the performance and dissuade people from attending them.[36] The mukhtar's version of Lear's absolutism, supported by the disinterested male population, however, is challenged by the performers' derisive laughter and the female population's relative support.[37] Fatma Fatih's confrontation with the mukhtar shows both the resistance against patriarchal figures and their shaky grounds, which silences the mukhtar. But the mukhtar's mindset is repeated when they visit a local family. Behiye Yanık mentions that she might have problems that the villagers might not see, and that performing drama can heal such problems by making one forget about them. These experiences are easily understood by the documentary audience who knows the backstory of her ill husband, which illustrates theatre's therapeutic potentials. Yet, lacking such foreknowledge, the rural women, with learned helplessness, and the men in this village do not see such a connection. Their mindset associates public life as a domain reserved for the male population and considers the public appearance of women on their own without male guardians as shameful acts, which is among the chief reasons for the hostile attitude towards the theatres in rural parts of Turkey.

However, when with a flash-forward the scene moves from the anagnorisis of Lear's confrontation with Goneril and Regan's real selves to Fatma Fatih's terrace, we see how the content affects the performers and the audience on several levels. Fatma Fatih's concerns about old people, her will to be happy with all her children and not to be dependent on them, make the performer think upon being afraid of her own old age and becoming like Lear. Moving back to the performance night, Lear bewails the truth of his/her daughter's words, wishes to be blind and deaf and feels as if being hit by a bullet in his/her chest, which is followed by a sad song on being shot and left alone in nights to wander. These do not just refer to Gloucester's blindness, Lear's wandering in the heath or Lear's manner of death, but also create catharsis for the performer, who remembers the scene and cries in the flash-forward.[38] An old widow with whom the performers had spoken earlier is also crying, possibly seeing herself on the stage. This scene possibly triggered catharsis in the documentary audience, too, as Covid-19 has left mostly old people dead or permanently ill in Turkey.[39]

Moving to a nomad village at the top of the Taurus Mountain belt, the performers are welcomed by female nomads. But the need to persuade the husbands to use vehicles used for farming to attend the play shows once again how patriarchal pragmatism becomes an obstacle for rural people's appreciation of the arts. Fatma Fatih's small talk with a very supportive girl about herding, however, creates common ground between them and reveals Fatma Fatih's own childhood trauma. In the pre-show, the scene about how her father prevented her from becoming a teacher and forced her to herd goats shows how patriarchal restrictions still haunt people although they have become self-confident adults thanks to drama.

When the scene moves to the end of the performance of *King Lear*, the full revelation of the altered resolution shows how poetic justice is instrumentalized for didactic means.[40] Having domesticated the play's conflict hilariously, Regan (Zeynep Fatih) pretended earlier to go on a holiday and Goneril (Cennet Güneş) excused herself with a hairdresser appointment not to host Lear after the distribution of his/her goods.[41] Cordelia's eventual reward with all of Lear's belongings for her true love is, therefore, balanced with the dramatic irony at the expense of his/her other daughters. Goneril and Regan do not get anything because Lear did not transfer his/her goods via the land registry office, necessary to formalize property transference in Turkey. The final poetic justice is a wishful thinking aimed at audience appreciation that ends the Arslanköy Theatre Company's adaptation in comedy and harmony. The nomadic people's storm of applause and their enthusiasm show how the performers have been successful in bringing arts and Shakespeare to rural people in Turkey. The documentary ends with a flashback to a jig-like dance on a boat during their first rehearsal at the ancient ruins, a scene that creates coherent closure for the multisensory and palimpsestic experience of the performance process. *Kraliçe Lear* enables communication between rural and urban audiences and generates a retrospective and recorded vision at live performances in the pre- and mid-Covid-19 periods.

Karagöz *Hamlet*

The online streaming of *Dream of Hamlet* shows the metatheatrical adaptation process of the tragic *Hamlet* into comic Turkish shadow theatre form and exemplifies the efforts to compensate and recreate live performances during Covid-19. *Dream of Hamlet*'s apparent handicap in the recreation of live performance through digital media derives from its creation of a material and discursive duality of alienation through the shadow theatre screen and the digital screen. Projecting semi-transparent and partly movable coloured leather pieces in the form of certain literary and racial stereotypes onto a screen, the 700-year-old Turkish shadow theatre, also called Karagöz, is based on formulaic tropes of content adjusted by the puppeteer, the *Hayalbaz* (dreamer), and his helpers to topical socio-political issues. While Hacivat is a high-pitched-voiced, witty and urbane character, Karagöz is his deep-voiced, naïve, boorish, and angry counterpart. Based on this duo's adventures, the shows combined wordplay, farce and social criticism.[42] Performed daily and on special occasions like weddings or religious festivities, traditional shadow theatre became an important social event to create comic catharsis in the Ottoman period.[43] But shadow theatre lost its importance with the introduction of Western forms of theatre and technological advancements in the late nineteenth century and is performed today mostly on special occasions.[44] Written by Hüseyin Sorgun, the *Dream of Hamlet*'s attempt to combine Shakespeare and Turkish shadow theatre bears the age-long tradition of both dramatic forms and the burden to revive widespread interest of modern audiences in shadow theatre.[45]

Performed in English by Ayhan Hülagu, the *Dream of Hamlet* invites audience involvement and reaction akin to early modern English performances. The screen creates a transparent barrier between the hidden performer and the audience and illustrates how the medium determines our understanding of live performances. This barrier is furthered through the necessity to screen the play on a digital platform because of Covid-19 restrictions in the United States, which enables Turkish audiences who know English to see the play despite the geographical distance.[46] Blurring the binaries of liveness and the digital, the double-detachment created through the shadow screen seen through the digital screen becomes paradoxically a shared space for geographically detached audiences on both spectrums of the English-speaking and Turkish-speaking dramatic entertainment forms. Thus, this duality enables the re-appreciation of Shakespeare's well-known *Hamlet* in a traditional Turkish dramatic form. Beside referring to socio-economic concerns that both the US and the Turkish audience can acknowledge, the play promotes the not widely known Turkish shadow theatre form to a wider international audience.

The *Dream of Hamlet* starts with the depiction of a dark brown, hence rotten, skull that bears a golden crown at the centre of the shadow screen.[47] In this rather Western-styled pre-prologue, the skull not only represents the memento mori tradition, but also the disintegration and corruption of Old Hamlet's body natural and Denmark's body politic.[48] The appearance of a crow, which in a very Cookie Monster manner begins to munch on the decaying skull, does not just create dark humour about the natural cycle of life. Its unsuccessful attempts to eat away the crown also show the eventual uselessness of social distinctions at the face of death.

In the prologue proper, Hacivat appears and reflects his happiness to be in the United States with a rhythmic *semai*, an improvisational song.[49] Referring to the American Dream trope, the puppeteer builds upon several notions of the concept of dream as a space for limitless creativity and felicity.[50] Establishing a familiar basis for the interaction between the Turkish forms of puppeteering and the US audience, the somewhat outdated notion of the United States as a land of unlimited opportunities seems at first to flatten the presence of social, racial, gender-based and healthcare problems.[51] It also reflects how the majority of the Turkish youth envisions the United States as a utopic place to overcome restrictions posed by economic recession, unemployment and nepotism.[52] Likening the world's transiency to the shadow screen, and noting how oblivion has taken over the worldly glory of kings and kingdoms, Hacivat extends his optimism by asking to '[g]ive a helping hand to the desolate' and 'love everyone from [the] heart' to point out the show's didactic function. He continues with an emphasis on social harmony through 'brotherhood', 'love and camaraderie' against 'sorrow' and loneliness.[53]

Apart from being a comic relief marked by physical humour and close audience interaction, the dialogue part after Karagöz's entrance also contains social criticism. Frustrated with the economic problems he has experienced, Karagöz tells Hacivat that despite having worked in numerous jobs, he is still unemployed.[54] Contrary to Hacivat's optimism about the American Dream, Karagöz seems to be more realistic and points out that 'Dreams do not satisfy [his] tummy'.[55] While Karagöz's eagerness to 'do any kind of work' refers to a formulaic play where Karagöz unsuccessfully tries his luck in several trades, it also has resonances with the US and the Turkish audiences. It reminds the US audience of the poor conditions of unskilled workers who migrate to earn their living because of economic or political turmoil in their home countries.[56] It also alludes to problems of unemployment and the high proportion of workers who earn either below or around the minimum wage in Turkey.[57] Thereby, Karagöz refers to the shared experience of the US and Turkish audiences.

As part of finding an occupation and establishing the Karagöz Theatre Company, Hacivat and Karagöz state they are going to adapt *Hamlet*. Yet the brevity of the time spent off-stage to prepare for the play hints at the adaptation's looseness and the upcoming comedy created through the duo's clumsy performance. When it is revealed that Karagöz is to perform the role of Hamlet, it creates in him an over-enthusiasm akin to Bottom in *A Midsummer Night's Dream*.[58]

The actual play starts with showing the skull from earlier, a vague silhouette of Old Hamlet's ghost, and Gertrude's laughter.[59] Just like Ophelia later in the play, Gertrude is portrayed as a man in woman's clothing, which refers to the early modern English convention of using male players to perform female characters on the stage.[60] Gertrude looks like a mixture of the courtesan character *Kanlı Nigar*, with her red gown, and the generic woman character *Zenne*, who has a fan in her hand, almost in the vein of the representation of early modern Venetian courtesans, and the character's beard is used to create laughter as part of misogynistic, farcical and politically incorrect humour.[61] Claudius' green robe is almost in the Ottoman fashion and, together with Gertrude's European looks, reflects the resonances of performing Shakespeare and traditional

FIGURE 6.3 *Ghost and Karagöz Hamlet (left). Ophelia and Laertes (right), Ayhan Hülagu,* Dream of Hamlet, *Karagöz Theatre Company, 2021.*

Turkish theatre. Explicitly joking about their relationship as former in-laws and present spouses, their sinister and overjoyed laughter builds upon the audiences' knowledge of *Hamlet* (Figure 6.3).

Additions and redactions that built upon that foreknowledge, however, are used in a contrastive way to build the tragi-comic characterization and plot of the adaptation. For instance, after the couple exits, a clock strikes and solemn Christian hymns are heard, when a crucifix appears, followed by the sound of exaggerated crying.[62] *Hamlet Efendi*, a.k.a. Karagöz as Hamlet, cries his heart out, which complements the tragic tone created with the Christian funeral objects and solemn liturgy. Yet his exaggerated manner, like in blowing his nose or his constant breaking of character, contrasts with his attempts to appear as a tragic actor. He rather becomes a clumsy comic actor akin to those in the recent re-production of *Der Bestrafte Brudermord* (Fratricide Punished), an eighteenth-century comical reinterpretation of *Hamlet* as a German puppet theatre version marked for its exaggeration and farcical elements.[63]

Following his appearance and explanation of his backstory, the Ghost's encounter with the Danish soldiers and Horatio underscore shadow theatre as a comic form.[64] Putting Horatio, Marcellus and Francisco as a single puppet, with each character attached to each other, is an economic measure to have a better grip on several characters at once, which enables the puppeteer to foreground their shared experience of terror when they see the Ghost. The trio's coordinated movement creates humour, especially when they sneeze because of the cold in Denmark, consecutively fall asleep, are woken by each other's snoring, shake together when they get afraid of the Ghost and exit the stage without turning their backs; again almost in the vein of the knee-shaking characters in *Der Bestrafte Brudermord*.[65]

When the Ghost and the trio disappear, the sound of kissing is heard off-stage, and Hamlet and Ophelia appear.[66] Neither the Quartos nor the Folio editions explicitly show the relationship between Hamlet and Ophelia.[67] Yet, depicting Ophelia's passionate love life in contrast with her later meek characterization creates comedy at the expense of the hypocritical double-life similarly forced as a way out for women to avoid violence within patriarchal restrictions in Turkey.[68] Like in *Hamlet*, these patriarchal forces are represented by Polonius and Laertes, portrayed as a *Tuzsuz Deli Bekir* (Saltless Mad Bekir) character famous for being a choleric young man.[69]

The need for dissembling is further illustrated when Gertrude and Claudius try to cover up their lustful laughter by using solemn voices in their public speeches to win over their subjects. But their hypocrisy is laid bare through the puppeteer's inclusion of oriental music when Claudius refers to how they 'mourn for [Old Hamlet] deep in [their] hearts', after which they begin to perform a belly dance.[70] Composing himself and trying to control the crowd he is talking to, Claudius uses populist rhetoric about a possible Norwegian invasion and wins over the crowd despite their inappropriate behaviour.[71]

While the play vacillates between comedy and seriousness, most of the remaining parts of Hamlet's words stick faithfully to the text, which shows how traditional shadow theatre's comic form is also capable of rendering tragic storylines. Despite Karagöz's problems with sticking to his role, he can render Hamlet's cynicism when he talks to Claudius and deeply contemplate on matters of life and death in his first soliloquy.[72]

Hamlet's encounter with the Ghost follows that seriousness by conflating the Ghost's narration of Old Hamlet's death and the play-within-the-play through a dumb show.[73] The shadow of the puppeteer's arm that pours poison into the Ghost's ear represents not only the murderer, but also underlines the actual murder's shadowy nature. When the Ghost warns Hamlet to '[w]ake up, from this terrible dream', it conceptually refers to the dream that combines shadow theatre with Shakespeare as a concept of unreality or false reality like in *A Midsummer Night's Dream*.[74]

Karagöz's rendition of how Hamlet tries to cope with grief about his murdered father and his mother's relation with his uncle furthers the capacity of shadow theatre as a serious dramatic form. Alone, Hamlet shouts for his father in anguish.[75] While the repetition of his climbing up and falling down the frame creates a funny choreography, his heavy drinking to cope with his depression shows how the vacillation between comedy and tragedy reflects that between sanity and madness. Watched alongside the increasing amount of stress disorders following the death or illness of close circles both in Turkey and the United States, Karagöz Hamlet's behaviours confronted the US and Turkish audiences with these disorders.[76] This is furthered when Karagöz delivers the 'to be or not to be' soliloquy and it seems both the actor and character are really mad, almost suffering early phases of the Hamlet syndrome.[77]

To help Karagöz get out of his role, the puppeteer begins to play with him, retelling the famous soliloquy, caressing Hamlet's head and soothing him. When Karagöz scratches his head and for a last time climbs up the frame of the screen, he falls down with his real clothes, which literally illustrates his getting out of his role. He says that the play's remaining parts will be performed in a rush after ensuring the audience knows what happens at the end, excusing omissions with the audience's foreknowledge.

After Karagöz's recovery from his nervous breakdown, the play goes on with Hamlet being spied by Rosencrantz and Guildenstern, depicted as Siamese twins who look like a motley fool, and Hamlet's preparations for the play-within-the-play.[78] When Hamlet announces the staging of 'The Murder of Gonzago', it becomes part of a great feast similar to Ottoman public festivities illustrated in miniatures that include acrobatic rope dancing, monocycles and animal shows.[79] Hamlet, who leaves his role as an internal spectator, climbs a unicycle and acts as if he is pouring poison on a performer, which makes Claudius get so angry that he finally reveals his real self when his head changes to that of a devil. Almost in a psychomachic rendition, Karagöz Hamlet beats the devilish Claudius and strangles him with the rope used to dance in the acrobatics. The chosen murder weapon references the Ottoman custom of strangling as a form of executing people with royal blood, and nods to the strength of the arts to criticize and challenge flawed politics.[80] In lieu of a traditional shadow theatre epilogue, the play ends with a cross for each character, placing the skull with golden crown into the centre, and the crow's reappearance which gnawed at the skull earlier.[81]

Apart from these social and philosophical observations, the *Dream of Hamlet*'s digital nature allows commentaries on what liveness constitutes. Being able to rewatch the play through screening services allows the audience to pause and focus on some unnoticed elements, such as details in costumes. Thereby, the digital screening substitutes first the act of personal remembrance and then live performances as straight synchronic experience. Ultimately, it problematizes remembrance as a thought-upon and discontinuous experience and liveness as a continuous experience of associations.

Conclusion

Contemporary Turkish Shakespeares provide new culturally specific resonances of Shakespeare's plays through regional overtones and retrospective meaning-making processes before and during the Covid-19 pandemic. They illustrate how live theatre is a palimpsestic recollection of personal, literary and cultural remembrances that transfigure temporal and spatial immediacy to a personal one. Conscious of their stagecraft and dramaturgy, *İkinci Katil*'s scrutiny of the tragedies of ordinary urban people, *Kraliçe Lear*'s documentation of rural performance and reception and *Dream of Hamlet*'s liminal presentation in traditional Turkish shadow theatre underscore how the appreciation of Shakespeare is closely connected to the lives and daily concerns of their audiences.[82]

Notes

1 All quotations from Shakespeare's works are from *The Arden Shakespeare Complete Works*, rev. edn. (London: Arden, 2001).

2 From 16 March 2020 to 23 June 2020, no live theatre was permissible. Although restrictions were relaxed by allowing vaccinated, masked and small-scale gatherings, tight regulations and lack of funding forced many theatre companies not to open their stages well until mid-2021 and beyond.

3 Ayşegül Yüksel, *William Shakespeare: Yüzyılların Sahne Büyücüsü* (İstanbul: Habitus, 2017), 278–86.

4 In Turkey, the urban spaces consist of working-, middle- and upper-class members of the society. Most theatregoers consist of middle- and upper-class people who have the time and money to spend on dramatic entertainments. The State Theatre's subsidized general admission fee for its stages in the bigger cities is also among the factors why theatre-going is perceived as an urban activity.

5 A. Deniz Bozer, '*İkinci Katil*: "Kral Neyse Tebaası da Odur"', *Yeni Tiyatro Dergisi* 99 (2017): 25–32; 'Sanat Kurumu Geleneksel Sanat Ödülleri Töreni', *Tiyatro Online*, 21 March 2019, https://tiyatronline.com/sanat-kurumu-geleneksel-sanat-odulleri-toreni-25-mart-2019-da--9785, accessed 15 February 2022. Murat Öğütcü, '*İkinci Katil* [*The Second Murderer*]: A Turkish Adaptation of Shakespeare's Scottish Play, *Macbeth*', *English Studies* 102, no. 8 (2021): 1086–104.

6 Öğütcü, '*İkinci Katil*', 1088–9.

7 Ibid., 1088, 1095.

8 Ibid., 1089.

9 Barış Erdenk, the director, from the Turkish programme notes to this production. Translations are mine.

10 *Mac* 1.3.30–78.

11 Margaret Omberg, 'Macbeth's Barren Sceptre', *Studia Neophilologica* 68, no. 1 (1996): 39–47. V. Calef, 'Lady Macbeth and Infanticide or "How Many Children had Lady Macbeth Murdered?"', *JAPA* 17, no. 2 (1969): 528–48. Daphna Oren-Magidor, and Catherine Rider, 'Introduction: Infertility in Medieval and Early Modern Medicine', *Social History of Medicine* 29, no. 2 (2016): 211–23.

12 Tezcan Ekizler, 'Anne Baba Adayları için "Tüp Bebek Tedavisi" Önlemlerle Başladı', *Anadolu Ajansı*, 22 June 2020, https://www.aa.com.tr/tr/saglik/anne-baba-adaylari-icin-tup-bebek-tedavisi-onlemlerle-basladi/1885543, accessed 15 February 2022. Özel HRS Ankara Kadın Hastanesi, 'Covid 19 Hasta Kabul Edemiyoruz', *Facebook*, 6 April 2020, https://fb.watch/7T1tURrMvh/, accessed 15 February 2022.

13 *Mac* 2.3.62–116.

14 For Ponzi schemes, see S. Keskin, 'İnsanların Dolandırıcılara Kanma Nedenlerinin Analizi: Çiftlik Bank Örneği', *Ahi Evran Üniversitesi İİBF Dergisi* 2, no. 2 (2018): 53–62.

15 G. Çetin, and Y. Balcı, 'Covid-19 Pandemi Sürecinin Türkiye'de İstihdama Etkileri ve Kamu Açısından Alınması Gereken Tedbirler', *İTÜ SB Dergisi* 19, no. 37 (2020): 40–58.

16 Hatice Şaşmaz, 'Türk Oyun Yazarlığında Ekonomik Koşulların Yarattığı Şiddetin Temsili', *IBAD SBD* 10 (2021): 264–91.
17 *Mac* 3.1.73–141.
18 Ibid., 1.7.1–80.
19 Ibid., 3.3.1–22.
20 Ibid., 4.1.48–135.
21 Ibid., 5.1.33.
22 Ö. U. Küçükcan, 'Medya Sarkacı: Kurgu İle Gerçeklik Arasında Suç', *TDA* 123 (2019): 11–34.
23 *Mac* 2.2.1–73, 3.2.4–56.
24 Ibid., 5.1.30–65, 5.5.16. Öğütcü, '*İkinci Katil*', 1100–101.
25 All references are to my personal notes taken from the documentary's airing at TRT 2 on 12 August 2020 and are my translations.
26 N. Ertürk, and B. Aydın, 'Türkiye'de Yaşam Memnuniyeti Endeksi Çerçevesinde Bölgesel Karşılaştırmalar', *Politik Ekonomik Kuram* 1, no. 2 (2017): 118–42.
27 Serdar Sağlam, 'Türkiye'de İç Göç Olgusu ve Kentleşme', *HÜTAD* 5 (2006): 33–44.
28 *Mac* 1.1.1–12.
29 The performers are Fatma Fatih (Lear), Behiye Yanık (Cordelia), Cennet Güneş (Goneril), Zeynep Fatih (Regan) and Ümmü Kurt (substitute player).
30 Ertürk and Aydın, 'Türkiye'de', 118–42.
31 *KL* 2.2.453–75, 3.1.1–50, 3.2.1–78, 3.4.1–180.
32 Ibid., 1.1.35–309, 1.4.180–344, 2.2.316–475.
33 Metin And, *Dionisos ve Anadolu Köylüsü* (İstanbul: Elif, 1962), 5–22. Nurhan Karadağ, *Köy Seyirlik Oyunları* (Ankara: İş Bankası, 1978), 9–11.
34 *KL* 4.7.1–84.
35 David Lindley, 'Musical Community in Early Modern Theatre', in *Community-making in early Stuart Theatres: Stage and Audience*, ed. Anthony W. Johnson, Roger D. Sell, and Hellen Wilcox (London: Routledge, 2018), 164.
36 A mukhtar is the elected neighbourhood representative who acts as the head of the smallest unit of local authority in Turkey.
37 *KL* 1.1.35–309.
38 Ibid., 3.7.1–96, 3.2.1–78, 5.3.304–9.

39 For instance, the Health Ministry's 2020 report shows that more than 72 per cent of Covid-19-related deaths were about people at the age of sixty-five and over. Sağlık Bakanlığı, *Covid-19 Haftalık Durum Raporu 12/10/2020 – 18/10/2020 Türkiye* (Ankara: Sağlık Bakanlığı, 2020), 6.

40 *KL* 1.1.35–309.

41 Ibid., 1.4.180–344, 2.2.316–475.

42 Ahmet Refik Sevengil, *Türk Tiyatrosu Tarihi*, vol. 1 (Ankara: Milli Eğitim, 1969), 56–9.

43 Ibid., 39–41. Özdemir Nutku, *Zaman İçinde Zaman* (İstanbul: Opus, 2014), 189.

44 Nutku, *Zaman*, 201–5. Ünver Oral, *Canlı Karagöz* (İstanbul: Kitabevi, 2015), 5–7, 58–71.

45 All references are to my personal notes taken from the play's online streaming on 27 March 2021 and an unpublished script provided by the Karagöz Theater Company. References are to this English translation of Sorgun's text and are cited by page numbers.

46 Chad R. Wells, and Alison P. Galvani, 'The Interplay between Covid-19 Restrictions and Vaccination', *The Lancet Infectious Diseases* 21, no. 8 (2021): 1053–4.

47 Hüseyin Sorgun, 'Dream of Hamlet' (unpublished manuscript, 2020), PDF file, 3.

48 *Ham* 1.4.90. Rose Marie San Juan, 'The Turn of the Skull: Andreas Vesalius and the Early Modern Memento Mori', *Art History* 35, no. 5 (2012): 958–75.

49 And, *Drama*, 151.

50 Sorgun, 'Dream', 4.

51 Sylvester J. Schieber and Steven Nyce, 'Healthcare USA: A Cancer on the American Dream', *Council for Affordable Health Coverage and Willis Towers Watson*, 26 August 2018, 5–83, http://dx.doi.org/10.2139/ssrn.3410449, accessed 15 February 2022; R. L. Abreu, et al., '"What American Dream is This?": The Effect of Trump's Presidency on Immigrant Latinx Transgender People', *Journal of Counseling Psychology* (2021), advance online publication, https://doi.org/10.1037/cou0000541, accessed 15 February 2022.

52 Aysu Köksal, *Mutluluk Ekonomisi ve Beyin Göçü: Türkiye Örneği* (Aydın, Turkey: Aydın Adnan Menderes Üniversitesi, 2021), 48, 70.

53 Sorgun, 'Dream', 4–5.

54 Ibid., 5.

55 Ibid., 6.
56 Susan Martin, B. Lindsay Lowell, and Micah Bump, 'Skilled Immigration to America: U.S. Admission Policies in the 21st Century', in *Skilled Immigration Today*, ed. Jagdish Bhagwati and Gordon Hanson (Oxford: Oxford University Press, 2009), 131–52.
57 Levent Gökdemir, and İsa Bucak, 'Neo-Liberal Politikalar Ekseninde Türkiye'de Emek Piyasasinin Değişimi: İstihdam ve Asgari Ücret', in *İktisadi Teori ve Gelişmelere Gelenekçi ve Yenilikçi Yaklaşımlar*, ed. Şahin Karabulut (Ankara: Gazi, 2021), 263–77.
58 Sorgun, 'Dream', 6. *MND* 1.2.17–69.
59 Sorgun, 'Dream', 6–7.
60 Pamela A. Brown, 'Jesting Rights: Women Players in the Manuscript Jestbook of Sir Nicholas Le Strange', in *Women Players in England, 1500–1660: Beyond the All-Male Stage*, ed. Pamela A. Brown, and Peter Parolin (London: Routledge, 2019), 305–14.
61 And, *Geleneksel*, 292–3. Margaret F. Rosenthal, 'Fashions of Friendship in an Early Modern Illustrated Album Amicorum: British Library, MS Egerton 1191', *The Journal of Medieval and Early Modern Studies* 39, no. 3 (2009): 619–41.
62 Sorgun, 'Dream', 7.
63 Hidden Room Theatre, 'Der Bestrafte Brudermord, or Hamlet Prince of Denmark', *Vimeo Video*, 10:17–25, https://vimeo.com/showcase/6953699/video/403556442, accessed 15 February 2022. Anon., 'Der Bestrafte Brudermord', in *Early Modern German Shakespeare: Hamlet and Romeo and Juliet*, ed. Kareen Seidler, and Lukas Erne (London: Arden, 2020), 123–99, 1.5.7–8.
64 Sorgun, 'Dream', 7–8. *Ham* 1.1.1–166.
65 Anon., 'Der Bestrafte Brudermord', 123–99, 1.5.7–8. Sorgun, 'Dream', 7–8, 12–13.
66 Sorgun, 'Dream', 8–9.
67 Paul Werstine, 'The Textual Mystery of Hamlet', *Shakespeare Quarterly* 39, no. 1 (1988): 1–26.
68 Seda Topgül, and Emre Kol, '6284 Sayılı Ailenin Korunması', *JIMEP* 9, no. 2 (2021): 146–58.
69 *Ham* 1.3.1–50, 1.3.87–135. Sorgun, 'Dream', 11–12. Nutku, *Zaman*, 198. Frederic B. Tromly, *Fathers and Sons in Shakespeare: The Debt Never Promised* (Toronto: University of Toronto Press, 2010), 152–80.
70 Sorgun, 'Dream', 9–10. The belly dance motif has been omitted from the play in recent productions.

71 *Ham* 1.2.1–39.
72 Ibid., 1.2.64–120, 1.2.129–59.
73 Sorgun, 'Dream', 12. *Ham* 1.5.1–112, 3.2.128–257.
74 Sorgun, 'Dream', 12–13. *MND* 4.1.191–217, 5.1.409–15. Patricia C. Miller, *Dreams in Late Antiquity: Studies in the Imagination of a Culture* (Princeton, NJ: Princeton University Press, 1998), 96.
75 Sorgun, 'Dream', 16.
76 Güler Boyraz, and Dominique N. Legros, 'Coronavirus Disease (Covid-19) and Traumatic Stress: Probable Risk Factors and Correlates of Posttraumatic Stress Disorder', *Journal of Loss and Trauma* 25, no. 6–7 (2020): 503–22. Serdar Aykut, and Sezen Soner Aykut, 'Kovid-19 Pandemisi ve Travma Sonrası Stres Bozukluğu Temelinde Sosyal Hizmetin Önemi', *Toplumsal Politika Dergisi* 1, no. 1 (2020): 56–66.
77 *Ham* 3.1.55–87. Jeffrey R. Wilson, and Henry F. Fradella, 'The Hamlet Syndrome', *Law, Culture, and the Humanities* 16, no. 1 (2016): 82–102.
78 Sorgun, 'Dream', 15–16.
79 *Ham* 3.2.128–257. Nutku, *Zaman*, 35–65. Aziz Altı, 'Osmanlı Devleti'nde Yırtıcı ve Yabani Hayvanlar İçin İhdas Edilmiş Bir Kurum: Arslanhane', *KARE* 10 (2020): 120–39.
80 Edhem Eldem, *Death in Istanbul: Death and its Rituals in Ottoman-Islamic Culture* (İstanbul: Ottoman Bank, 2005), 182–94. For reasons unknown, this example of onstage violence has been abandoned in the play in recent productions.
81 Similarly, in more recent productions, the skull has been replaced by a *Vakvak* tree, a mythological tree associated with death in Turkish folklore.
82 My project 'Turkish Shakespeares' tries to document these experiences by introducing texts, productions and research to a broader international audience. More on https://turkishshakespeares.wordpress.com/, accessed 15 February 2022.

PART THREE

Premonition

7

Death draws down our curtain

Liveness beyond life in early modern Persianate Islam

Kenneth Molloy

In his magisterial Persian hagiographical compendium *Nafaḥāt al-Uns* ('Wafts of Intimacy'), the renowned Timurid-period *ṣūfī* writer ʿAbd al-Raḥmān Jāmī (d. 898 Ḥijrī/1492 Christian Era) tells of a funeral for an unnamed person from the *awliyāʾ Allāh*, 'the friends of God', the so-called 'saints' of Islam. 'One of the grandees of the jurists' sits over the grave reciting *taqlīn* – literally 'instruction', a reminder of basic doctrine to ready the audient dead for his imminent interrogation by God's representatives. Suddenly, from amid the assembled mourners, the *ṣūfī* teacher Najm al-Dīn ʿAbdullāh ibn Muḥammad al-Isfahānī (d. 711/1311)[1] bursts into laughter. A student asks why, and, after reproving the question, Najm al-Dīn answers: 'When the taqlīn-reciter (*mulaqqin*) began taqlīn, the companion of the grave said, "are you not astonished at a dead person who performs taqlīn to a live one?"'[2]

This vignette distils a complex challenge to the schematization of liveness vis-à-vis life that currently holds sway in theories of performance. Even the ordinary act that backgrounds the extraordinary matter of the narrative, *taqlīn*, presumes that one who is not living remains live, sensible to mortuary performance and receptive to the advice spoken before his grave, an idea generally well beyond the scope of now-hegemonic approaches to this theoretical terrain. Yet as striking a variance with today's theatre and performance studies orthodoxy as the practice of *taqlīn* itself implies, for the interred friend of God this practice is a customary piety that calls for radical inversion. The *walī* does not only hear, but speaks in response. His remark abstracts completely the meaning of death and life from the phenomenal world as the student and the *mulaqqin* perceive it, while maintaining life's axiological priority. The essence of life is that of a state superior to death, and so the friend must be live and the jurist must be dead, regardless of the one's inert body and unbeating heart and of the other's breathing and walking about. The friend is of course not confused – he is well aware of the dissonance between the appearance that encloses the masses and the reality that opens to the exceptional few, hence his private joke with Najm al-Dīn in the thick of his own funeral. From the perspective of Najm al-Dīn's student, which twenty-first-century performance-theoretical reckonings of liveness broadly share, he, his teacher and the *mulaqqin* are live together in the bounded time and space of the friend's burial and their experience thereof, but Najm al-Dīn and the friend in fact stand apart, on a stage more proximate to the real, and such proximity is a more accurate measure of who is live and who is dead, insofar as the former is superior and opposite to the latter, than is the apparent disposition of the body. Encapsulated here is the tension between liveness as life – the animacy whose *anima* is the breath – and liveness as presence – the animacy whose *anima* is the soul. If liveness subsists in empirically observed bodily processes, for example, respiration as the circulation of air, then the inhabitants of the graves cannot be live, but if liveness subsists in non-empirically unveiled extra-bodily processes, for example, respiration as the circulation of spirit, then the inhabitants of the graves may be more live than those who walk over them.

'Liveness', as a substantivization of 'live', signifies an attribute of certain experiences as well as of certain experiencing subjects. Formulated another way, for experiencing subjects such as you the reader or I the writer, 'liveness' implicates two conceptually distinct yet deeply entangled experiences, one an inter-relative experience of shared space and time – the liveness of live performance – and the other an intra-relative experience of being alive – the liveness of a live body, the liveness that is life. This epistemic knot is woven into the seam of the contemporary theoretical discourse of liveness as an element of theatre or performance, such that liveness and life seem to become more tightly twisted together with every effort to extricate them. The incoherencies and contradictions that vex the theory of liveness as a quality of experience are the ineluctable consequence of paradigmatic assumptions regarding life as a quality of we-who-experience. The effect of these assumptions to control and ossify the contours of a discursive field cannot be overstated, for the quality of life that these premises define is the ultimate qualification to discourse. Without this quality, one can produce no live statement nor live act but belongs to the past, to the record, to the grave.

The deep structure of the performance theory of liveness is an ontology of life, and the deep structure of this ontology is a theology. The readiest example of the mystic vitalism that prevails in the theory of performance is the opening sentence of Peggy Phelan's widely discussed and debated 1993 essay 'The Ontology of Performance: Representation without Reproduction', which avers, 'Performance's only life is in the present';[3] that is, not 'performance only exists in the present', nor 'performance's only being is in the present', nor any phrase other than this forceful but opaque predication of life. 'Life' inscribes the ontological dialectic between representation and presence – between what appears and what is – within the theological distinction between the creativity of the created and the creativity of the uncreated. 'Life' names the difference between the artwork and the artist, and thus between the artist and the artist's own maker. The life-theology that hides in 'The Ontology of Performance' flashes into visibility when Phelan engages an early modern work of Christian art, Caravaggio's *Incredulità di San Tommaso*, in her later 'Whole Wounds: Bodies at the Vanishing Point'.[4] Arguing that the figure of Christ 'stands in for God' in the same way that the vanishing point of a perspective painting 'stands in for the illusionary convergence of parallel lines',[5] Phelan characterizes the early modern by 'a theatrical order of things … based on transformation and substitution'. The 'theatrical technology' of perspective is, she writes, 'crucial to the invention of a theatrical epistemology … The "as if", the illusionary indicative that theatre animates, allows for the construction of depth'.[6] In familiar poststructuralist fashion, Phelan's framework gives a strongly negative valence to 'God' but keeps the contours of the Christianate.

> Within the arc of resemblance and mimesis that perspective inaugurates, the stand-in stands in for a real that, like God and the Other, forever eludes us. The point is not so much to 'find' the Other, but rather to play the drama in such a way that the stand-ins come to reveal that *the kernel of the drama of the Other is that the Other is always a stand-in*. In this sense, Thomas is Christ's God at least as much as Christ is Thomas' ... in the two figures we confront the two incompatible propositions that perspective gives us: that we are framed, arrested in an illusion, a theatre of substantiation, and that the authenticity of our most intimate theatre can only become truly real through the agency of a stand-in.[7]

Phelan rejects the orthodox Christology of Jesus' godhood, reading Christ as God's 'stand-in' or 'decoy', but retains the principle of this stand-in's identity with the real. When Phelan writes that 'looking at and touching painting' may 'truly save us from death' because, 'unlike God, painting has a body we can touch',[8] she affirms a Christianate theo-logic of life delivered by embodiment, of reality as corporeality. Phelan's thesis in 'The Ontology of Performance' that 'performance implicates the real through the presence of living bodies' embeds this theology.

A fascinatingly lucid dialogue can be traced between Phelan's theory and a passage adduced by Khwāja Muḥammad Pārsā (d. 822/1420) in his *Faṣl al-khitāb li waṣl al-aḥbāb fī al-taṣawwuf* ('The Decisive Speech for the Union of Lovers in Ṣūfism'), a greatly influential doctrinal summa of the Khwājagan-Naqshbandī ṣūfī order to which the aforementioned Jāmī also belonged. Pārsā quotes from the *Maqṣad al-asnā fī sharh asmā' Allah al-ḥusnā* of Abū Ḥāmid Muḥammad al-Ghazālī (d. 505/1111) on the fallacious notion of the *ḥulūl* – 'setting-in' or 'inherence' – of the real in bodies:

> There is a difference between our saying 'it is it' and our saying 'it is as if it is it.' It is just as the poet sometimes says 'it is as if I am who I desire' and sometimes says 'I am who I desire.' This is a slippery foothold. He who has not a solid footing in the

intellectualities, perhaps for him one of the two is not different from the other, so he looks at the perfection of his essence, and it is adorned with what shines in it from the revelation of the real (*al-ḥaqq*) – transcendent – so he thinks that he is the real, and he is mistaken. The Christians make a mistake when they see this in the essence of ʿĪsā (Jesus); they see the dawning of the light of Allah – exalted – has shined in him, and they mistake it, like he who sees a star in a mirror or in water, and thinks that the star is in the mirror and in the water, so he extends his hand to grab it, but he is unable.[9]

The assumption here of *trompe l'oeil* and 'as if' as cosmological principles belies Phelan's association of Western Christian perspective painting with 'theatrical epistemology'. The Ghazālīan ontological architecture may be characterized as 'screenal', in that its basic element is the medial surface combining functions of hiding and showing, like the mirror or curtain. Translation is fluid between this 'screenality' and theatricality as conceptualized by Phelan, yet their common semiotics of veils, lenses and spectres is the mortar of different edifices. One posits the scrim of illusion as a mediation of reality, making 'as if' not contrafactual but perhaps 'praeterfactual', in the way that the image of an object in the mirror, though not identical with the object, is a reflection of the same light whereby vision perceives the object. The other, jaded by the simulation of depth, suspects that the depth itself is a disguise for the reality that is the surface; as Phelan writes in 'Whole Wounds':

> Skin lacks the depth, the interiority we want it to give us. If skin would give us this depth we might actually have proof that we do have such interiority, that the precarious feelings, dreams, phantasms, inner speech that we call subjectivity is real, that it can be embodied, enclosed in skin's own form. But this is precisely what skin, as a surface covering, cannot offer us ... Perspective itself, the transformation of a flat surface into an illusionary deep space, fosters our desire for skin to have depth.[10]

Early modern Muslim thinkers like Pārsā and Jāmī, adapting the ideas of such past luminaries as al-Ghazālī, understood the relationship of the body and the real through a screenal dialectic of apparent exterior – *ẓāhir* – and hidden interior – *bāṭin*. The above-referenced extended quotation of al-Ghazālī in *Faṣl al-khitab* includes al-Ghazālī's own quotation of an allegory attributed to the revered early *ṣūfī* master Abū Yazīd (Bāyazīd) Bisṭāmī (d. 261/874): 'I shed my self (*nafs*) as the snake (*al-hayya*) sheds its skin, then I look and lo, I am he'.[11] Bisṭāmī renders the *nafs* – subjectivity or the soulish self – not as a deep recess but as another skin; the veil of 'I' is torn away as 'he' shows himself as the one real existent. Of course, al-Ghazālī assures his reader that Bisṭāmī does not actually mean to declare himself God, explicating this remark by reference to the mechanics of *al-qalb*, the heart, a crucial anchor for Islamic discourses of life and liveness as the interface of reality and embodiment.

> When naught sets in the heart but the majesty of Allah and his beauty, such that it becomes immersed in him, it becomes as if he is him, not that he is him really … The heart is devoid of images in itself, and of aspects, save the aspect of reception of meanings and aspects and images and realities, so, what sets in the heart, it is as if taken unto it, not taken unto it really. He who does not know of the glass and the wine, when he sees a glass and in it is wine, does not perceive the difference of the two, and he confuses what is in the glass with the glass. Thus sometimes he says, 'there is no wine', and sometimes he says, 'there is no glass.'[12]

The heart operates in the subjunctive, as a screen, at once a partition and a medium between the body and the real. The eminent early modern Herati preacher Ḥusayn Wāʿiẓ Kāshifī (d. 910 H/1504 CE), a *Naqshbandī* affiliate like Jāmī and Pārsā, stands out for his explicit analogy of the interaction among the heart, the body and the real to the interaction among the components of theatre, on the basis of the screenality that defines both. This analogy appears in a section on puppet-play (*luʿbat-bāzī*) from Kāshifī's *Futūwatnāma-yi sulṭānī* ('The Sultanic Book of Young-Manliness'). Naming the two hallmarks of the puppet-player as the *khayma* – the tent, the theatre of the daytime puppet show – and the *paysh-band* – the curtain, the theatre of the night-time shadow play – Kāshifī explains the cosmological element to which each is an 'indication' (*ishārat*) or sign. The tent makes reference 'to the human body, which is at all times and in every moment the puppet of another; words and actions proceed from this tent, but in the tent there is but one who is the root of these differentia'.[13] The curtain indicates:

> The heart (*dil*) of the progeny of Adam, which is a cabinet of the wondrous and strange, and at all times another hand, another string gives movement to its qualities and states, and in this respect it is called [in Arabic] *qalb*, which is that which turns. A great one has said, 'Seek the one that turns.' [The Prophet said,] 'The heart of the believer is between two of the fingers of the Most Merciful; he turns it as he wills.' So when the maestro observes that, until he moves a puppet from the top of the box, it does not move, he should also comprehend this meaning: that until the end of the heart's string, which is between the two fingers of ordainment, finds movement, the heart has no power of movement. Hence he knows what it means that the heart is the thing seen in divine sight.
>
> The flickering in the royal tent-enclosure is the heart.
> Indeed, the divine seeing-place (*naẓar-gāh*) is the heart.[14]

The term *naẓar-gāh* that appears in the concluding couplet translates directly as 'seeing-place', in close parallel to the Greek *théatron*. These lines complete the recursion of the theatre of the heart within the theatre of the body that Kāshifī's analogy implies. The heart is at once as a thing hidden – the candle that glows through the fabric walls of the king's pavilion – and a thing shown – the spectacle of God's action upon unseen strings. The heart is the place where a performance of hiding is seen.

The importance that *ṣūfī* cosmology gives to the heart, the quintessential organ and synecdoche of the human being, furnishes an especially sharp point of contrast with the influential concept of the 'body without organs', originated by the eminent theorist of the theatrical avant-garde Antonin Artaud, discussed by Jacques Derrida, and famously taken up by Gilles Deleuze. Deleuze's account in his 1969 *Logique du sens* presents the Artaudian, 'schizophrenic' body as that for which there is no surface, 'nothing but depth', in apparent opposition to Phelan's meditation on the body as depthless, though these opposite approaches coincide in the conclusion that 'everything is body (*corps*) and bodily (*coporel*)'.[15] The juxtaposition recalls al-Ghazālī's heuristic of the confused person who sometimes says that there is no wine and sometimes that there is no glass; indeed, Deleuze writes, 'As there is no surface, the interior and the exterior, the container and the contained, have no more a precise limit, and they sink into a universal depth or turn in the circle of a present that contracts more and more as it is increasingly filled up'.[16] Derrida, in his essay on Artaud 'La Parole Soufflée', analogizes the figure of God to the theatre's '*souffleur*' – the prompter, literally the 'blower', 'breather' or, poetically, the 'spiriter' – who, in the very act of 'in-spiriting' words, 'spirits away' those words from the speaker's ownership: 'If my word (*parole*) is not my breath (*souffle*), if my letter is not my word, this is because already my breath was no longer my body, because my body was no longer my gesture, because my gesture was no longer my life'.[17] Deleuze likewise recognizes breath as a motive of the Artaudian body, which 'does all by insufflation, inspiration, evaporation, fluidic transmission'.[18] Breath is no less essential to the emphatically organic body theorized by early modern *Naqshbandī* ṣūfīs. In the *Naqshbandī* theory too, God also resembles the '*souffleur*'; however, the exchange that transpires as breath is not a furtive theft but a subtle return. Breath becomes a 'live performance' *par excellence*, a performance of life in the presence of the real.

Fakhr al-Dīn Ṣafī ʿAlī (d. 939/1533), son of the aforementioned Ḥusayn Wāʿiẓ Kāshifī, systematically explores *Naqshbandī* theories of breath as performance in his hagio-historiography of the order, *Rashaḥāt ʿayn al-ḥayāt* ('Droplets from the Font of Life'). In a section profiling ʿAbd al-Khāliq Ghujdawānī (d. 575/1179), known for codifying the path's eight maxims (*kalamāt qudsiyya*), Ṣafī explains the first of these principles: *hūsh dar dam*, or 'sensitivity to breathing'.

> Sensitivity to breathing – it is that every breath (*nafas*) that comes out from within must be in presence (*huḍūr*) and attention and not go unheeded. Ḥaḍrat[19] Mawlanā Saʿd al-Dīn Kāshgarī said that sensitivity to breathing means the circulation from breath to breath must be so that it is not in heedlessness but is in presence, and not a breath is taken empty or heedless of the Real (*haqq*), exalted. Ḥaḍrat said, in this path, the observation and guardianship of the breath are viewed to be urgent. This means it must be that all breaths are respired in the grace of presence and attention, and if such-and-such person does not guard the

breath, they say he has lost his breath, meaning he has lost the way and the path.[20]

The Persian *dam* – which I have rendered as 'breathing' – with its connotation of the measure of time, and the Arabic loan *nafas* – which I have rendered as 'breath' – with its etymological association with the *nafs* or soulish self, here combine through the nexus of *ḥuḍūr*, 'presence'. Ṣafī corroborates the words of Sa'd al-Dīn Kashgārī (d. 860/1465) with a statement by the eponym of the Naqshbandiyya, the great Khwāja Bahā' al-Dīn Naqshband (d. 718 H/1318 CE), emphasizing the temporality of *ḥuḍūr* that is transparent in the English 'present': 'The structural work in this path should be in the breath, such that engagement is turned to the most urgent exigency of the standing time (*zamān-i ḥāl*, i.e. the present) from remembering the past and contemplating the future'.[21] A quatrain on the theme follows:

> Oh you refuse of the sea, on the shore of the font.
> In the sea is release and on the shore disgrace.
>
> Take a clear look at the wave of being.
> Be attentive to the sea between breaths.[22]

Through the allegorical trope of the subject as a residue strained from the ocean of the real, the verse theorizes circulation of breath as an ontological heuristic, wherein differentiation – the interval of non-breathing that encloses each repetition of this quintessential performance of life – supplies an opening to *syncope* in its multiple senses of contraction together, rhythmic displacement and loss of personal consciousness. Ṣafī next draws from a *Risāla fawātiḥ al-jamāl* of Najm al-Dīn Kubrā (d. 618/1221), presumably meaning his *Fawā'iḥ al-jamāl wa-fawātiḥ al-jalāl* ('Perfumes of Beauty and Openings of Majesty'). Kubrā understands the act of breathing as *dhikr* ('remembrance'), referring to the practice of repeating Islamic formulae – for example, '*lā ilaha illallāh*', 'no god is there but God' – either audibly by the tongue or, as the Naqshbandiyya favoured, silently by the heart. For Kubrā, breath is both the performance and the theatre of *dhikr*, of remembrance as presence, an act of before-being and state of being-before-being.

> A dhikr that is aflow in animate souls (*nufūs*) is their necessary breaths (*anfās*), because in the rising and falling of breath, the

letter *hā'*, which is indication to the hidden ipseity (*huwiyya*) of the Real – transcendent – is said, whether they will or they will not – the same letter *hā'* that is in the blessed name of Allah. And the *'alif lām* is for definiteness, and the gemination of the *lām* is for stress on that definiteness, so it must be that the sensitive seeker in the linkage is attentive to the real – transcendent – in this aspect, such that at the moment of utterance (*taluffuz*), by this noble letter the ipseity of the essence of the real – transcendent – is his reference (*malḥūz*), and in the going-out and coming-in of breath he attends that he is established in godly presence, such that he reaches the place where without effort he observes this linkage always present to his heart, and by effort he cannot make this linkage remote from his heart.[23]

Appended is a verse by Jāmī:

> Behold (*hā'*), the hidden ipseity is found, oh letter-knower
>   And your breaths were on that letter based.
> Pay attention to that letter in hope and fear.
>   I have said the magnificent letter, if you take watch.[24]

Involuntary breathing repeats the name of Allah's ipseity – *huwiyya*, literally 'it-ness' – and Kubrā exhorts the seeker not to change the act of his tongue but to synchronize this act with a perceptual act of the heart. The paronomasia of Jāmī's first hemistich doubles the screenal relationship between dhikr and breath theorized by Kubrā: the same act of 'taking watch' locates the noble *hā'* disguised in the sound of breathing and in Jāmī's imperative to 'behold', an act that does not transform or convert but unveils. As Kubrā makes explicit the necessity of respiration to life, Jāmī gestures at that other necessity towards which each mortal breath counts down with hope and fear.

The place of death in the Naqshbandī theory of liveness finds elaboration in what may be the most well-known work of Ṣafī father, Kashifī, *Rawḍat al-Shuhadā'* ('Garden of the Martyrs'), a collection of hagiographical–martyrological narratives focused on the Ahl al-Bayt, the family of Prophet Muḥammad. Under the Safavids, who conquered Greater Iran from the Timurids at the turn of the sixteenth Christian century, public reading from the *Rawḍat al-Shuhadā'* became an institution of the new regime's mass-scale programme of Shīʿification, Kāshifī's own Sunnism notwithstanding.[25] These performances, associated with Muharram observances and commemoration of the tragic self-sacrifice of the Prophet's grandson Ḥusayn ibn ʿAlī, bore a crucial influence upon the development of the mode of Islamic historical re-enactment known as *taʿziyeh*, in which theatre and performance studies has shown some interest. The *Rawḍat*'s account of the death of the Prophet's beloved daughter Fāṭima, sick with heartbreak after her father's own passing less than a year before, and her final farewell to her husband ʿAlī ibn Abī Ṭālib, gives the temporality of counted breath outlined by Ṣafī another dimension:

> When the amīr [ʿAlī] heard from Fāṭima talk of parting, the water of grief poured out from his eyes, and he said, 'Oh Fāṭima, I am not yet recovered from the burn of your father's parting, my wound from his passing has not faded. Now the time of your departure too has arrived and laid another burn upon that one.'
>   Every breath, time lays the burn of my grief in the gut (*jigar*),
>   One burn has not healed, another burn it lays
>   Every burn it brings a little toward the better,
>   That burn it clears and another burn it makes.
>   Fāṭima said, 'Oh ʿAlī, you had patience in that misery, and in this *taʿziyeh* too bring forth resilience, and do not be absent at the time when my breath is numbered, the appointment of appearance in the house of tranquility'.[26]

The verse that channels ʿAlī's pain here, like the one paired with Kubrā's theory of breath in *Ṣafī*, is from Jāmī, and similarly pivots on the chronometric equation of the breathing process with another process: in one, *dhikr*; in the other, affective cautery. In juxtaposition, the respective uses of Jāmī by the senior and junior Kāshifī complete a syllogism that binds breath *qua* remembrance to breath *qua* burning. Remembrance *qua* burning, the presence of God to the heart as the burn of time upon the gut,[27] aptly glosses the word *taʿziyeh* as Fāṭima applies it to her husband's condition. While theatre history often reads *taʿziyeh* as a generic classification, in the vein of 'passion play', the term in fact encompasses this meaning within a far more expansive semiosis; a better analogy would be to the word 'passion'. To understand *taʿziyeh* as a performance of the heart, through reference to early modern Islamic paradigms of performance such as the *Naqshbandī* theory of *dhikr*, rather than to Eurocentric theatrological frameworks or taxonomies of social drama, is not only crucial to a performance historiography properly inclusive of the intellectual history of Islam, but makes possible an alternative concept of what the perceptual locus or 'seeing-place' of theatre may be. Both Ṣafī in his *Rashaḥāt* and Jāmī in his *Nafaḥāt* transmit an explanation of the technique of *tawajjuh* – 'regarding' or 'turning to' – from Khwāja ʿAbdullah Imāmī Isfahānī, a contemporary and companion of ʿAlāʾ al-Dīn ʿAṭṭār:

> The way of *tawajjuh* of the superior group and their cultivation of interior linkage is that, whenever it is they want to perform this engagement, first they bring forth in imagination (*khayāl*) the form of the person with whom they have found this linkage, until such time that the impression of his warmth and distinct quality is produced. Afterwards, they do not reject that imagination, but take care of it, and, with eye and ear and all faculties, by that imagination they turn toward the heart, which is a figuration of the comprehensive human reality, of which the totality of entities from high to low is the parcellation. Albeit unsubject to inherence in bodies, a linkage nevertheless exists between it and this pinecone-shaped piece of flesh, so *tawajjuh* should be performed toward this pinecone-shaped piece of flesh, and the eye and cogitation and imagination and all faculties should commit to it and be present to it and sink into the heart. We have no doubt that in this state the quality of hiddenness (*ghayb*) and seeing without self (*bī khud*) will emerge.[28]

The stages of *tawajjuh* are nested cosmoi: world – creation in its fullest but still finite scope – human – the synecdoche of the world – and the heart – the synecdoche of the human. Through imagination, which is by no means illusory but as much a perceptual power as hearing or vision, the subordination of these stages is looped. The practitioner forms the image of his master and sets it within the cardiac tissue, and thereby perceives the real that can only be perceived by non-perception of the self. The key is that the 'comprehensive human reality', of which the heart is the figuration or index, is the 'appearance (*maẓhār*) of the convergence of the essence and attributes of the real', which, Khwāja ʿAbdullah, like al-Ghazālī before him, is at pains to clarify, does not describe God's incarnation in the human body, but is an appearance 'as the form is in the mirror'.²⁹

Kāshifī's narrative of ʿAlī's death in Rawḍat al-Shuhadāʾ plays out across the recursive stages of world, human and heart. After calling the dawn prayer at Kufa's great mosque, ʿAlī is performing a supererogatory prayer when he is stabbed during prostration by ʿAbd al-Raḥmān ibn Muljam (d. 40/661). Ibn Muljam's tongue confesses against his will, and he is arrested by the people of Kufa.

> He [ʿAlī] said, 'What led you to make my children orphans, and break down the pillars of my household? Wasn't I kind to you?' He [Ibn Muljam] said, 'Yes, but what happened happened. "The command of Allah is an ordainment preordained (Q 33:38)."' The amīr said, '...... If I live, whatever my judgment requires of him, I will exact. If I pass, do not give more than one blow to him, who has not given me more than one blow.' Then they lay the amīr down on a rug, and one end of the rug Ḥasan took up, and the other end Ḥusayn, and they carried him out of the mosque. Dawn was breathing, and the world was bright. The amīr said, 'Face me to the east', which they did. The amīr said, '"by the dawn when it draws breath (*tanaffasa*) (Q:81:18) ..." Oh dawn, by the God by whose edict you came forth and by whose direction you draw breath, on the day of raising up I will ask you to witness, and, as you are truthful, you must give honest witness that from the day I first performed the prayer with the Messenger of God until today you have never found me sleeping and I have never found you unarrived.'³⁰

The Qurʾānic image of dawn as breath supports the correspondence between ʿAlī and the worldly sphere at the time when, in Fāṭima's earlier words, his own breaths are numbered. ʿAlī's apostrophe contracts its scope from that of universal history – beginning with God's first assignation of primeval morning, ending with his judgement on the last day – to that of a lifetime – beginning with ʿAlī's first prayer behind Muḥammad, ending with his prayer now at the threshold of death – to that of each single day – beginning with one dawn, ending with the next. In this process, a reciprocity comes about between the reckoning of time by cosmic cycles and the reckoning of time by the rhythmic habitus of the body; just as ʿAlī has always attended the dawn, the dawn has always attended ʿAlī. As an interpolated quatrain comments:

> Alas, the peace of the heart and the repose of the soul has gone
> The shah of the age and the exemplar of the world's creation has gone
>
> Grief is the encirclement of the center of the cosmos to every end
> For the noble center of the encirclement that core has gone.[31]

In the system of *tawajjuh* described by Khwāja ʿAbdullāh, the initiate's imagination of his master models the 'comprehensive human reality' as an appearance of the real. ʿAlī's own master is the individual most proximate to this reality, Muḥammad himself. Qāsim-i Anwār (d. 837 H/1433 CE), a profoundly influential if controversial Heratī *ṣūfī* master, whose poetry receives frequent quotation in the *Rawḍat* and to whom Kāshifī dedicated his occult treatise *Asrār-i Qāsimī*, takes a theoretical approach to the *Rawḍat*'s thematic terrain in a cosmological treatise styled as a question-and-answer (*suʾāl wa jawāb*) dialogue. Qāsim's interlocutor poses a question on the doctrine, mentioned by Khwāja ʿAbdullāh, of the cosmos outside the human as a parcellation or diffusion of what is comprehended or sublimated in the human: 'why was there a delay in the inception of Adam, who is the comprehensive being, after the inception of the cosmos?' Qāsim replies, in language reminiscent of Khwāja ʿAbdullāh's own, 'All entities in the cosmos, small and great, are one slave, and Adam is the inner (*bāṭin*) heart of that slave, so the exterior form (*ṣūrat ẓāhir*) must exist that the heart may be guarded in inception. The cosmos of form is the shell, in the sea of his ordainment, and Adam is the pearl of that shell'.[32] The questioner follows up, 'why was Adam prior to Muḥammad, and why was there a postponement of his mission among the prophets?' Qāsim's answer recurses the allegory of 'shell' and 'pearl' that illustrates the relationship between human and cosmos and between body and heart to illustrate the relationship between the first man and the seal of the prophets:

> Muḥammad, peace be upon him, with respect to meaning (*maʿnā*) and spirituality (*rūḥāniyya*), is prior to Adam and others – 'the first of what Allah created is my spirit (*rūḥ*)' – but with respect to form (*ṣūrat*), his subsequence is because Adam is the shell of the being of Aḥmad, and the seal is the pearl of that shell. . . .

Muḥammad, peace be upon him, is the appearance (*maẓhar*) of the essence of truth, and Adam is the appearance of the attributes and names of the exalted creator; as concerns pretemporality (*qidam*), there is preference for interior (*bāṭin*) essence over exterior (*ẓāhir*) attributes, but as concerns temporality (*ḥudūth*), there is progression from outer attributes to inner essence.³³

The intertwist of compound, looping *mises en abyme* is truly vertiginous: the human as pearl in the shell of the cosmos in the sea of the real, Muḥammad as pearl in the shell of Adam, the human as the cosmos of the heart, Muḥammad as the heart of Adam, the attributes of the real as exterior (*ẓahir*) to the essence of the real, Muḥammad as appearance, or exteriorization (*maẓhar*), of the interior and Adam as exteriorization of the exterior. A particularly salient term amid this constellation is *rūḥ*, which connotes a kind of breath that relates to the breath of *nafas* or *dam* as body relates to heart, that is, breath as *spiritus*. Qāsim explores Muḥammad's identification of his *rūḥ* as the first creation of Allah more deeply in reply to a later question, one that seems, by its succinctness, almost exasperated with Qāsim's tangle of heuristics: 'what was the first thing that the real, exalted, made appear (*ẓahir kard*)?' Qāsim meets this challenge not with a simplification, but, conversely, by elaborating the epistemic perspectivism of his screenal ontology:

> In the opinion of the *'urafā'* ('sages'), it is the spirit (*rūḥ*) of Muḥammad, peace be upon him – 'the first of what Allah created was my spirit' – and in the opinion of the *hukamā'* ('philosophers') it is intellect (*'aql*) – 'the first of what Allah created was the intellect, the light, the pen, and the spirit.' These four are all one substance. Regarding life (*ḥayāt*), the essence of the substance is called spirit, and this meaning relates to the word of the mighty lord, 'I breathed into him from my spirit (Q 15:29).' Regarding the acquisition of knowledge (*'ilm*) and insight (*ma'rifat*) of this substance, it is called spirit, regarding the meaning that it is the root of entities. Because of its being the inscription of elements written on the tablet of nothingness, it is reckoned the pen, and regarding that the reality of this substance is unmixed light and there is not a drop of darkness or temporality in it, it is given the name light.³⁴

Qāsim establishes *rūḥ* as Allah's first creation through two independent proofs based on two independent definitions, each associated with a different intellectual tendency and produced through a different methodology – one by reference to the *Qurʾān*, the other evidently by analogy between respiration and the circling back to the prime substance of the entities that proceed therefrom. However, his analysis of the second, 'philosophical' viewpoint supposes the impossibility of apprehending reality from any one positionality, or even by multiple sightlines. The spirit of Muḥammad, the primordial human meaning in contrast to Adam's primordial human form, is not only the invisible, elusive *élan vital* of which the breath is a reflection, but also the archetypal archival instrument – the pen that brings what it records to be from nothing – and the absolute visibility of unmixed light. Qāsim does not explain why he forgoes any focused treatment of *ʿaql*, to which term he gives seeming precedence among the four listed in the philosophers' favoured tradition, despite reading these as predicates of one subject, but the reason may be that, within Qāsim's conception of an *ʿaqlī* framework, the meanings of the spirit, pen and light cannot be attributed to the reality of the originary substance absent the intellective processes of calling, reckoning and naming in which *ʿaql* is fundamentally implicated. A notable curiosity is that Qāsim distinguishes the *ʿurafāʾ* view on spirit not only from that regarding *ʿilm* – generally connoting ratiocinative knowledge – but also from that regarding *maʿrifat* – bestowed insight or 'gnosis', formed on the same Arabic root as *ʿurafāʾ* – and identifies this view instead as one that regards life.

Kashīfī shows ʿAlī, in the aftermath of Ibn Muljam's attack, recounting to his anguished sons a vision he received of Muḥammad. The screenality of Qāsim's cosmo-anthropology and the dramaturgy of *Naqshbandī* techniques of *dhikr* and *tawajjuh* hang heavily over this reunion with the Prophet across the borderline of life:

> He said, '... On this night I saw Ḥaḍrat Muṣṭafā[35] – blessings of Allah and peace be upon him – in a dream, with his blessed sleeve he wiped dust from my face, and he said "Oh ʿAlī, you have achieved that which was upon you." This dream, the sign in it is that the veil (*niqāb*) of the body will be raised from the face of my spirit (*ruḥ*), so it may be bright in the vision of the holy ones.'
>
> The screen (*hijāb*) of the face of my soul is the dust of my body
> A sweet breath (*dam*), when I cast off the curtain from this face.[36]

Through ʿAlī's interpretation of his dream and the quoted verse from the poet Ḥāfiẓ (d. 791/1389), Kāshifī conveys the soul's ontological priority to the body by making the soul a dream-double of the body, a hidden body beneath the smothering dust of the apparent body. Muḥammad's intimate wiping of the dust to reveal ʿAlī's face in the imaginal space of the dream signifies the wiping away of his face, of the veil of the self between the heart and the recognition of the real. Ṣafī, Kāshifī's own heir, relays a dream experienced by Khwāja Muḥammad Yaḥyā (d. 906/1500), the son of the *Naqshbandī* teacher whose sessions first inspired Ṣafī to compose the *Rashaḥāt*, Khwāja ʿUbaydullah Ṭashkandī (d. 895 H/1489 CE). Desiring to make pilgrimage to the Ḥijāz, Khwāja Muḥammad Yaḥyā requests permission from his father, who asks his reason for going. Khwāja Muḥammad Yaḥyā answers, 'This *ḥadīth*[37] impels me: that Ḥaḍrat Prophet, blessings of Allah upon him and peace, said, "who visits me dead, it is as he visits me alive"'. Khwāja ʿUbaydullah instructs his son to wait three days for an answer.

> On the third night, I saw in a dream that Ḥaḍrat Prophet, blessings of Allah be upon him and peace, appeared. I fell at the feet of the Ḥaḍrat. He said, 'Seek out your father so we may have fellowship.' I ran and woke up that Ḥaḍrat, and he came in a hurry. Ḥaḍrat Prophet sat him at his right hand and I sat before him. I bowed my head and closed my eyes. After a moment I raised my head and looked and saw Ḥaḍrat Prophet double, and that Ḥaḍrat [Khwāja ʿUbaydullah] was not visible, and though I looked hard, between that Ḥaḍrat and him was no difference in any respect, and it became unclear who was the Ḥaḍrat and who was he.[38]

As in ʿAlī's vision, the dreamed body is closer to the real than the body that sleeps. Khwāja Muḥammad Yaḥyā's epiphany brings forth an esoteric meaning from the *ḥadīth* that ignited his desire to travel: the equivalence, through the *Naqshbandī* initiatic chain, between presence with his father and presence at the Prophet's sepulchre. In his dream, again as in ʿAlī's, the mask of the phenomenal world is removed. Ṣafī attests that, after Khwāja ʿUbaydullah's death, Khwāja Muḥammad Yaḥyā would kneel for hours in *murāqaba*, a meditative vigil, before his father's grave, 'his joints kept from extraneous movements'.[39] Khwāja ʿUbaydullah's own teaching on the proper technique for communication with the inhabitants of the graves, which Ṣafī transmits in the *Rashaḥāt*, follows the principles of other *Naqshbandī* practices. To ensure that the unveiling (*kashf*) from the grave is genuine, masters utilize the mimetic property of the heart:

> Their way of visiting the grave is, when they reach the grave of a dear one, to make themselves empty of all relations and qualities, and sit watchful, so that what relation appears, they become through that relation knowledgeable of the state of the owner of the grave. . . . The appearance of this meaning is by means of the perfect polish and clarity that their enlightened interior obtains; their mirror of reality is pure and clear of the etchings of existence.[40]

The breath of the body's life is a screen over the breath that is spirit, and a medium for its performance. ʿAlī's dream encounter with Muḥammad portends that he has reached the end of this performance – a part of a grander architecture of destiny, as the words of Allah verify even from the mouth of the killer Ibn Muljam. After ʿAlī's death and burial, his son Ḥasan, the inheritor of the imamate and of the political loyalty of his father's followers, must carry out the punishment of the assassin. When brought before Ḥasan, Ibn Muljam makes a bid for his release.

> Ibn Muljam came forward, 'Oh Ḥasan, what will be will be and what will pass will pass, what use now is lamentation and sighing and moaning? Do not kill me until I kill the governor of Shām, who was your father's enemy and now is your enemy—' Ḥasan did not allow him another word but drew his sword and plunged the sword into his breast, pulled him towards him and struck a blow on his neck. His head fell ten steps away. So the people took him out of the mosque, wrapped him in a sheet, and set fire to him to burn him. The princes (Ḥasan and Ḥusayn) became engaged in *taʿziyeh* and the people came and spoke taʿziyeh unto the Ahl-i Bayt.[41]

The overture that Ḥasan dramatically rejects is heavily portentous, for the governor of Shām, whom Ibn Muljam offers to kill, is Muʿāwiya ibn Abī Sufyan (d. 60/680), the first caliph of the Umayyad dynasty that would, according to the *Rawḍat* and other

'Alid accounts, treacherously engineer the usurpation and murder of Ḥasan and, later, of his brother. Ibn Muljam's reprisal of the argument he made by his Qur'ānic quotation to 'Alī, portraying himself as an agent of ineluctable divine ordinance, deepens the tragic irony of Ḥasan's resolute obedience to his father's instructions as he reciprocates Ibn Muljam's single blow with another that reverberates through time. The sword-stroke that decapitates Ibn Muljam obliterates his identity, leaving only the screenal corpse as a medium of projection; when the severed head hits the ground, it becomes the head of Ḥusayn, which, by the cosmological script that Ḥasan's actions drive onward, the army of Mu'āwiya's heir Yazid will take from his body at Karbalā'. The *ta'ziyeh* that Ḥasan, Ḥusayn, and the people of Kufa enact as the body burns does involve the past, insofar as it expresses grief for 'Alī, but it does not re-enact the past. Rather, this *ta'ziyeh* enacts the future: Ḥasan and Ḥusayn join in the mourning of their own deaths yet to come. An appended verse represents this *ta'ziyeh*, bridging the cosmic theatre to the microcosmic theatre of the heart:

> This tragedy has caused the eye of the sun
>   by hot tears to stain the skirt of heaven with blood.
> But by the rule of providence, thus the soul is taken.
>   The return (*marji'*) of the heart is naught but '*innā ilayhi al-rāji'ūn*'.[42]

The very daylight petitioned by 'Alī is visually and affectively transformed by his death; like the breath and the heart, it is both scene and actor. The heart, indeed, is the stage whereupon the pain of loss resolves as well as the agent of that resolution, for by the special linkage of this 'pinecone-shaped piece of flesh', per Khwāja 'Abdullah, with 'it' that is 'unsubject to inherence in bodies', the heart directs itself towards to its source. The final hemistich distils this meaning by reference to the Qur'ānic formula '*innā lillahi wa innā ilayhi rāji'ūn* (Q 2:156', 'we are for Allah and to him we are returning', oft-repeated by and to those whom death bereaves. The *marji'* of the heart is not only its return to God, but its remembrance of this return with every breath.

The work required for a history of theatre that sufficiently engages the intellectual history of Islam is extensive and difficult.

Not only must prevailing concepts of 'theatre' and 'performance' be thoroughly reassessed, but this reassessment will not be complete without interrogating profound epistemic prejudices that disguise themselves as common sense or lie ensconced in dense layers of theoretical orthodoxy. We are fortunate that sophisticated pre- and early modern Islamic discourses of mimesis, embodiment, presence and liveness exist in such profusion to provide the groundwork for this daunting task, but theatre historians cannot benefit from this material if we do not take the first step away from the precepts of a theatre history that constitutionally cannot acknowledge that this material even exists. Among the most trenchant examples of the status quo that has for decades reproduced itself, and, if the necessary effort is not made, will continue to reproduce itself, are the words of Peter Brook to a *Parabola* interviewer in 1979, which pertain to *ta'ziyeh*.

> The ancient theater clearly was, and the theater must always be, a religious action ... I have seen this in the Persian *Ta'zieh* [sic], which is probably the most living form of mystery play that still exists ... It is Shi'ite [sic], only the Shi'ites have dared break away from the great Islamic tradition of not representing anything ... In fact, at a certain season of the year in every single village there is the equivalent of the medieval plays of Europe ... I have seen in a remote Iranian village one of the strongest things I have ever seen in theater ... when he [Ḥusayn] was martyred the theater form became a form of truth – there was no difference between past and present. An event that was told as a remembered happening in history, six hundred years ago, actually became a reality at that moment. Nobody could draw the line between different orders of reality. It was an incarnation: at that particular moment he was being martyred again in front of those villagers.[43]

Here echoes the Christianate life-theology and body-ontology of the Euro-American theatrical avant-garde and the performance theory it generates: the practice of *ta'ziyeh* as historical re-enactment, which did not take shape until the seventeenth Christian century, becomes a 'living form' of a medieval European 'mystery play', the climax of which is, naturally, 'an incarnation'. The perfunctory rehearsal of that the most inveterate cliché, 'the great Islamic tradition of not representing anything', banishes from possibility al-Ghazālī's ontological 'as if', the art of *tawajjuh*, and the studied reflection of the grave-inhabitant's state in the mirrored heart of the master, clearing the way for the supervention of Brook's own ideas. The anti-historical effect of this self-validating methodology is well illustrated by the placement 'six hundred years ago' of Ḥusayn's death in the first century Ḥ/seventh century CE. Ultimately, Brook conflates the object of the performance he observes with his own artistic object: as his mission is to revitalize the spiritually moribund occidental theatre, so must the object of taʿziyeh to bring Ḥusayn back to life. Yet is Ḥusayn 'dead', as Peter Brook, Jacques Derrida or Antonin Artaud understand what it is to be dead? Does he require a return to life, or is he in a state of liveness? A verse that Kāshifī interpolates amid his narrative of the fateful battle of Karbalāʾ poignantly takes up this question:

> The death of the leaf falls when there is ease in it
> Death furnishes uncovered the kernel from the skin.
>
> Death draws down our veil in front
> So we pass from the branch unto its root.
>
> Death draws souls unto souls
> Draws songbirds the way of the garden.[44]

Notes

1 A student of the prominent Alexandria-based master of the *Shādhilī ṣūfī* order Abū al-ʿAbbās al-Mursī (d. 686/1287).
2 Abd al-Raḥmān Jāmī, *Nafaḥāt al-uns min ḥaẓarāt al-quds* (Tehran: Intishārāt Sakhn, 2015), 360. Translation from Persian, my own.
3 Peggy Phelan, *Unmarked: The Politics of Performance* (London: Taylor & Francis Group, 1993), 146.
4 Peggy Phelan, *Mourning Sex: Performing Public Memories* (New York: Routledge, 1997), 23–43.
5 Ibid., 25.
6 Ibid., 27.
7 Ibid., 33.

8 Ibid., 35.
9 Khwāja Muḥammad Pārsā, *Faṣl al-khitāb li waṣl al-aḥbāb fī al-taṣawwuf* (Tehran: Markaz-i Nashr-i Dānishgāhī, 2002), 99. Translation from Arabic my own.
10 Phelan, *Mourning Sex*, 41–2.
11 Pārsā, *Faṣl al-khitāb*, 99.
12 Ibid.
13 Ḥusayn Wā'iẓ Kāshifī, *Futūwatnāma-yi sulṭanī* (Tehran: Intishātāt-i Bunyād-i Farhang-i Īrān, 1971), 342. Translation from Persian my own.
14 Ibid.
15 Gilles Deleuze, *Logique du sens* (Paris: Éditions de Minuit, 1969), 106. Translation from French my own.
16 Ibid., 107.
17 Jacques Derrida, *L'écriture et la différence* (Paris: Éditions du Seul, 1979), 267. Translation from French my own.
18 Ibid., 108.
19 Lit. 'presence', a standard honorific.
20 'Alī ibn Ḥusayn Kāshifī Ṣafī, *Rashaḥāt 'ayn al-ḥayāt* (Tehran: Bunyād-i Nīkūkārī-i Nūriyānī, 1977), 38–9. Translation from Persian my own.
21 Ibid., 39.
22 Ibid.
23 Ibid., 39–40.
24 Ibid., 40.
25 See Babak Rahimi, *Theater State and the Formation of Early Modern Public Sphere in Iran: Studies on Safavid Muharram Rituals, 1590–1641 CE* (Leiden: Brill, 2012), 215; Said Amir Arjomand, *Authority and Political Culture In Shi'ism* (Albany: State University of New York Press, 1988), 74.
26 Ḥusayn Vā'iẓ Kāshifī, *Rawḍat al-shuhadā'* (Tehran: Ṣadā-yi Mu'āṣir, 2012), 310. Translation from Persian my own.
27 *Jigar* is most precisely translated as 'liver', but in contemporary English this word lacks the connotation of a seat of emotion.
28 Jāmī, *Nafaḥāt al-uns*, 261, Ṣafī, *Rashaḥāt*, 169.
29 Ṣafī, *Rashaḥāt*, 170–1.
30 Kāshifī, *Rawḍat*, 353–4.

31 Ibid., 352.
32 Anwār, Qāsim-i, *Kulliyāt-i Qāsim-i Anwār*, ed. Sa'īd Nafīsī (Tehran: Kitābkhāna-yi Sinā'ī, 1958), 389. Translation from Persian my own.
33 Ibid.
34 Ibid., 391.
35 Lit. 'the chosen', a standard epithet of Muḥammad.
36 Kāshifī, *Rawḍat*, 22.
37 A tradition from the Prophet.
38 Ṣafī, *Rashaḥāt*, 586.
39 Ibid., 581.
40 Ibid., 469.
41 Kāshifī, *Rawḍat*, 360.
42 Ibid.
43 'Leaning on the Moment: A Conversation with Peter Brook', *Parabola: The Magazine of Myth and Tradition* 4, no. 2 (1979): 47–59.
44 Kāshifī, *Rawḍat*, 485.

8

Signs of liveness

The blazing star in Renaissance drama

Gina M. Di Salvo

Stars sometimes dropped from the heavens in early modern theatre. In extant playbooks from the period, a curious stage direction leaves traces of liveness. Typically italicized or off to the side in the margins, phrases such as '*Heere the blazing Starre*' and '*A blasing star appeares*' animate a theatrical past of live performance and live fire.[1] The blazing star is an uncommon but well-documented dramatic device that drew from popular understanding of natural philosophy and astrology. Following the Great Comet of 1577, the late Elizabethan period experienced a notable uptick in references to comets. Treatises, almanacs and astrological literature considered the comet as an ominous sign, and a number of plays cite them as metaphors. For example, in the anonymous *Taming of A Shrew*, a husband who obeys his wife is described as 'Worse than a blasing star, or snow at midsommer/ Earthquakes or any thing vnseasnable'; in *All's Well That Ends Well* by William Shakespeare, the 'blazing star' is invoked as a rare and disruptive occurrence; and in *The School of Complaint* by James Shirley, a woman's '[r]esplendent' face is 'like a blazing Starre/We mortals wonder at'.[2] Yet, when it materialized as a pyrotechnic device, the blazing star developed into a technology of judgement. Two clusters of noncanonical plays between c.1589 and 1622 feature the blazing star as a pyrotechnic and plot device. It functions epistemically as an outward sign of a supernatural world, but it is not an efficacious sign, like a sacrament. Rather, I argue, its primary function in/as theatre is to confirm otherwise undetectable phenomena already at work. Through a close comparison of how and why blazing stars appear in eight early modern plays, I excavate the theatrical evolution of the blazing star from a marker of historical time – the 1577 comet – to a sign that responds to questions regarding fate or justice. As a species born of live theatre, the blazing star takes on a dramatic life of its own. These plays frequently instruct and, more importantly, rely on audiences to interpolate the meaning of the device. In its eventual form, the blazing star acts as a sorting device that adjudicates the question of right revenge.

Great comets and prognostication

In 1577, the Great Comet appeared. John Dee, the natural philosopher, noted the appearance of the comet on 22 November. Shortly after, 'Elizabeth I called on Dee to sooth her anxious courtiers', who feared the comet as a forewarning sign.[3] Dee, however, was not summoned by the Queen to dissuade the court from 'superstitions'. The court astrologer was there 'to interpret the comet's potentially eschatological message'.[4] As in ancient and medieval thought on the matter, early moderns understood the blazing star as an interpretable sign. Frequently, theologians and scientists interpreted the blazing star to prognosticate destruction. While this sort of reaction to astronomical events strikes us as 'superstitious', that is not how they saw it. Naturally, their world was subject to supernatural phenomena – from god and the devil to angels and witchcraft.

The widely held understanding of superstition at the turn of the seventeenth century involved much more than belief in blazing signs of destruction. As Mary Floyd-Wilson clarifies, 'superstition implied the risky assumption that one could engage with spirits or magic and avoid interacting with the devil'.[5] The issue at stake was not that belief in supernatural phenomena was irrational, but that certain types of interacting with supernatural phenomena were idolatrous and damning. For example, John Foxe, the Protestant polemicist and martyrologist, condemns Roman Catholic intercessory practices and hagiographic miracles as superstitious, but he allows for the interpretation of astronomical signs. He reports on ominous signs in the night sky in 1109 CE in earnest: 'ij full Moones appearyng together, one in the East thother in the West (on maundy thursday) with a blasing starre in the same yeare', which is then succeeded by an earthquake, pestilence and flooding.[6] That the comet could portend unfortunate things to come is not superstitious to the rational, reformed Christian mind. The trouble with the blazing star was not that it could mean something, but that it did mean something.

A handful of publications concerning comets document an increased public interest in understanding stellar events and prognostication around the time of the 1577 comet.[7] At that time, writers composed new material that responded to the event and publishers reprinted earlier material. In considering how the blazing star would later emerge on the public stage, these texts offer some important theoretical considerations for the fleeting moments of pyrotechnical interruption. In Leonard Digges's guide to prognostication, the entry on comets is a brief and practical summation of nearly all other treatments of the subject: 'Comets signifie corruption of the ayre. They are signes of Earthquakes, of wars, changing of kingdomes, great dearth of Corne, yea a common death of man and beast'.[8] In this sense, the 'ayre' is an expanse of shared space, something that Stephanie Shirilan addresses in her own essay in this collection. Moreover, the 'corruption' is not the comet, but the comet signifies that some species of common rupture and harm is present and its effects are pending. This interpretation of the blazing star informs the first appearances of the device in three plays that feature the death of Thomas Stukeley.

Of all blasing starrs in general, by Frederick Nausea, offers the most comprehensive treatment of the natural and supernatural qualities of stellar phenomenon.[9] The composite view of the treatise is one in which the blazing star continually evolves in its meaning. This version of the blazing star especially informs the device in the five plays produced after the Stukeley plays. Nausea, who originally composed his treatise after the 1531 appearance of Halley's Comet over Mainz, turns to the matter of what blazing stars prognosticate. Nausea writes that while 'they can be signes or tokens ... they are no cause'.[10] However, it is possible, he concedes, that 'that which is the cause of warre and Pestilence' might also be the cause of the comet.[11] While Nausea ultimately counsels that 'it is not needfull that we stand in feare of the celestial signes', that to do so 'is extreame madnesse'; it is important to recognize how he privileges his own comet as a sign of the end.[12] Addressing the 1531 comet specifically, Nausea interprets it eschatologically as a sign that 'betokenes a heauie burthen of vengeaunce'.[13] The vengeance Nausea writes of is a collective one, the deserving punishment for a sinful humanity. In this sense, it provides a warning sign. Indeed, the minister Francis Shakelton interprets his own comet in a similar fashion. He writes that the blazing star is 'set on fire by gods prouidence to warne the whole worlde' to be 'moued to repentaunce'.[14] He also upholds the common understanding, summarized by Digges, that they 'dooe threaten some imminent euill'.[15] Although Shakleton is especially concerned with the comet of October 1580, he comments on the observable destruction after the Great Comet of 1577. The collective harm in this case took the form of shipwrecks, bad weather and crops, diseased livestock, sedition and Popish idolatry. In both cases, Nausea and Shakelton foreground their own encounters with blazing stars in offering empirical and eschatological interpretations. This privileging of individual witnesses as prime interpreters of the sign also surfaces in the five non-Stukeley plays.

Although some writers privileged their own perspectives of the blazing star, their explanations of its meaning remained directed towards collective and not individual experiences. The stars also were not supposed to be taken for signs of constant doomsaying, as a pamphlet composed by the satirical Simon Smel-Knave makes clear. Smel-Knave mocks the idea that individual people should link every unfavourable occurrence or accident to an appearance of a blazing star. Such a situation allows charlatans to take advantage of the gullible, a scenario that was later dramatized in the Cambridge University comedy *Albumazur* (1615).[16] The frontispiece of Smel-Knave's pamphlet displays an image of an astrological chart, the sort that appears throughout Simon Foreman's medical casebooks for the practice of judicial astrology, with the words 'Twelue a clocke at midnight' in a box at center. The difference between natural and judicial astrology bears on the scope of stellar prognostication as a whole. While natural astrology was widely accepted, judicial astrology was attacked on theological grounds as superstitious. Natural astrology considered 'the planetary influences on the terrestrial elements', such as the movement and alignment of the planets, stars, sun and moon.[17] That blazing stars signified the general coming of destructive collective events, such as war or famine, places them along the lines of natural astrology. It is a different matter entirely to consider what a comet prognosticates for an individual human life. That is the province of judicial astrology, which, 'sought to predict particular events, especially those that affected individual human lives'.[18] In his medical application of judicial astrology, Foreman first determined the current position of the stars in order to then prescribe a specific course of treatment for patients.[19] Unlike natural astrology, in which the activities of the stars announce but do not cause misfortune, judicial astrology posits that stars cause specific conditions. The specific relationship between the position of the stars and an individual life in judicial astrology characterizes the eventual use of the blazing star in early modern theatre. The stage versions respond to individual experience. While the blazing star might be collectively beheld by all characters, it serves as a reliable respondent to individuated problems of justice.

'Signes of Earthquakes, of wars, changing of kingdomes': The Stukeley plays

Over the course of three plays that premiered between c.1589 and c.1605, the theatre produced significations of the blazing star that drew on and departed from scientific and theological knowledge. The playhouse version of the blazing star first emerges in three plays that feature Thomas Stukeley: *The Battle of Alcazar* (c.1589), *Captain Thomas Stukeley* (1596) and 2 *If You Know Not Me, You Know Nobody* (c.1605).[20] The first two plays are traditionally recognized as 'the Stukeley plays', but all three are united through the device of the blazing star and the dramatic repetition of Stukeley's death in northern Morocco. While these plays remain understudied, scholars are currently revisiting them as part of an inquiry into race, empire and nostalgia.[21] Here, I show that the device of the blazing star is first associated with the battle depicted in *The Battle of Alcazar* and *Captain Thomas Stukeley* before becoming a sign more specifically associated with Stukeley's death in the third play, 2 *If You Know Not Me, You Know Nobody*. All three plays overlap in their representation of Stukeley, a buckling English opportunist with a reputation for pursuing fortune by playing both sides.[22] According to historical accounts, Stukeley was leading a papal expedition to re-Catholicize Ireland when the winds blew his ship to the Iberian Peninsula. From there, he was forced by King Sebastian of Portugal to lead Italian troops into the Battle of Three Kings at Ksar El-Kebir in 1578. Stukeley died there along with King Abd al-Malek of Morocco, Abu Abd Allah al-Mutawakkil, the king's nephew who challenged his uncle's claim to the throne and King Sebastian, who backed the nephew. *The Battle of Alcazar* focuses on the rivalry of Abdelmelec and Mahamet, as they are known on stage, whereas *Captain Thomas Stukeley* follows the title character from London to Ireland to Iberia and, finally, to Alcazar. Stukeley, himself, never appears in 2 *If You Know Not Me*, but the blazing star of the Alcazar battlefield appears when his death is discussed back in London.

The first two Stukeley plays draw their use of the blazing star from 2 *Tamburlaine*, the lesser known of Marlowe's two-part tragedy. As in Digges's explanation of the blazing star, it is a sign of destruction. Near the beginning of 2 *Tamburlaine*, the tyrant destroys the city of Larissa and delivers a speech that identifies the dramatic point he currently occupies: 'Over my zenith hang a blazing star/ That may endure till heaven be dissolved … . Threat'ning a death and famine to this land' (2.2.6–7, 9).[23] No comet actually appears, but as Stephen Greenblatt observes, in the 'charred soil and the blazing star, Tamburlaine seeks literally to make an enduring mark on the world, to stamp his image on time and space'.[24] In calling for the signal in the sky to remain for all time in defiance of its ephemerality, he identifies the comet as an annunciation of destruction. Tamburlaine's meta-historical narration during the razing of Larissa emphasizes a prognosticating historiography that tracks terrestrial and celestial events. These events, from wars to the Star of Bethlehem, serve as units of salvation and chronicle history. In the 'sons of *Tamburlaine*', as G. K. Hunter calls *The Battle of Alcazar* and *Captain Thomas Stukeley*, the blazing star appears to signal to audiences that destruction in Alcazar – and Stukeley's death – is nigh.[25]

The world of *The Battle of Alcazar* and *Captain Thomas Stukeley* is an occult one. In both, hidden forces cause natural elements to rise up based on Elizabethan Providential design. In addition, sympathetic forces drive characters together against their own agency. In *The Battle of Alcazar*, the treasonous Stukeley attempts to treat with King Sebastian at the edge of Catholic Christendom, but the Portuguese monarch rebukes him in occult terms for thinking he can retake Ireland with his fleet of 6,000 men in seven ships. In fact, Sebastian's description of Elizabeth's 'Sacred, imperial and holy ... seat' of Ireland sounds more appropriate for Tilbury in 1588 than in Lisbon a decade prior (2.4.109). The Portuguese king tells the English subject that his plans not only 'wrong the wonder of the highest God', but also that if he had a navy made of 'all the monarchs of the world/ To invade the island where her highness reigns,/ 'Twere all in vain, for heavens and destinies/ Attend and wait upon her majesty' (2.4.131; 2.4.105–8). King Sebastian seems to know what Stukeley tragically cannot sense: that a sacred order governs the world to protect Elizabeth and England from invasion. If necessary, that order overrides the normal properties of the elements. Stukeley pursues his vain excursions in vain. The tides, which are known to be governed by the moon, and winds redirect his journey. He is conscripted into Portugal's 'holy Christian wars' in north Africa (2.4.133). The seas, 'Whose raging floods do swallow up her [Elizabeth's] foes,/and on the rocks their ships in pieces split' thwart Stukeley as they later thwart the Spanish Armada (2.4.17–18). The sympathies of the ocean draw Stukeley to Portugal and the antipathies repel him from Elizabeth's islands.

The hidden forces that govern the defense of England through the waters do not necessarily extend to the rest of the world. Outside of England, as Tom Rutter notes, 'the actual incidents depicted in the play appear to take place in a fallen political world' in which Providence plays almost no role.[26] Indeed, the blazing star is drawn out in response to the confusing military alliances that lead to the battle at the end of the play. The comet appears in *The Battle of Alcazar* as part of an allegorical tableau that precedes the war. In the dumb show, Fame enters 'like an Angel', places three crowns on a tree and a blazing star appears while the chorus narrates that 'fiery stars and streaming comets blaze,/That threat the earth and princes of the same' (5 Prol. 15–16)[27]. More fireworks appear as the crowns of the three kings drop from the tree. Revising Marlowe, the chorus here explains that the star promises destruction to the kings (Mahamet, Abdelmelec and Sebastian), all of whom die in the subsequent battle. The dumb show with the blazing star gathers even more meaning for Mahamet and Stukeley as they near their deaths. Mahamet addresses the natural world and rails at the elements, both natural and supernatural, 'that wert at my birth predominate,/ Thou fatal star … . Spit out thy poison bad', for the way they 'bode a man' (5.1.81–3). Immediately after, Stukeley echoes Mahamet saying, 'since my stars bode me this tragic end … I must perish', and resigns himself to his death during an ambush (5.1.122–3). In referencing heavenly bodies and their particular stars that 'bode', this play materializes the blazing star as a determining device.

Captain Thomas Stukeley also depicts the politics of making, breaking and feigning military alliances. In addition, the language of occult symptoms similarly characterizes the inexplicable rivalry between Stukeley and Vernon, his sometimes friend and sometimes foe. In the early London scenes of the play, Vernon interrupts his own matchmaking with Nell Curtis so that Stukeley might have the merchant's daughter himself. Having proved profligate, Stukeley uses her entire dowry to pay debts before leaving for Ireland, then Spain and, finally, Morocco. At every further location, he encounters Vernon, who attempts, at every turn, to avoid him. When Vernon sees Stukeley in Spain, he wonders if some hidden force pulls his nemesis to him as his 'scourge/ Or I was born the foil to his fair haps,/ Or in our birth our stars were retrograde' (17.56–58). The language of antipathies and astrology is then dropped until the end of the play when it resurfaces as the two men near their fate. Moments before their shared death at the hands of vengeful Italian mercenaries near Alcazar, Vernon expresses his dismay that he 'could no way direct/ My course but always you were in my way', that is, that they could not be 'disjoined' (28.16–17; 28.19). They reconcile once they recognize that their multi-Continent rivalry derives from an overlooked and misunderstood sympathy. Stukeley is suddenly struck by the nature of their unavoidable attraction, which 'in our birth we two/ Were so ordained to be of one self heart,/To love one woman, breathe one country air' (28.24–5). With a clarity born of their imminent and shared death, Stukeley pronounces that they 'have sympathized/ In our affections', before the two are drawn together – the stage directions call for an embrace – in final harmony with nature.

In *Captain Thomas Stukeley*, the blazing star also appears in an extended dumb show sequence. Unlike the dumb show in *The Battle of Alcazar* that emblematically offered an abstracted version of the plot, this one uses blocking and pantomime to communicate a series of war plans between Spain, Portugal and the English Captain with his band of Italian troops. After Spain refuses to aid Portugal and King Sebastian conscripts Stukeley, the Englishman '*makes a show of persuading*' the Italians '*to join with the Portuguese .... when with a sudden thunder-clap the sky is on fire and the blazing star appears, which they prognosticating to be fortunate, depart very joyfully*' (17.21SD).[28] The play here employs a chorus to lock down the interpretation of the comet at the point in which the genre of the play pivots from City Comedy to Historical Tragedy. Curiously, the ominous blazing star is understood by the Portuguese and Italian soldiers to promise a 'fortunate' end. This interpretation goes against established precedent.

By the time *Captain Thomas Stukeley* premiered, the blazing star had been igniting above or across the stage for five to seven years in performances of *The Battle of Alcazar*. The star is a sure sign of destruction, yet *Captain Thomas Stukeley* extends the drama of the device in order to involve the audience in a game of knowing what the unfortunate characters do not. The Chorus intervenes to confirm the audience's expected interpretation of the device and narrates that 'heaven, displeased with their rash enterprise,/ Sent such a fatal comet in the air,/ Which they misconst'ring shone successfully' (20.42–4). In describing the 'comet in the air', the play categorizes the commonly beheld sky as a screen – a stage – of divine action. It also draws attention to the playhouse as a space of common beholding, hearing, smelling and breathing. The device of the blazing star literally and theatrically corrupts the air of the playhouse. While an actual comet is beheld through sight in the sky, the staged comet involves multiple senses. Early modern theatre makers likely accomplished the blazing star through pyrotechnics, perhaps by discharging squibs on a line or by discharging squibs on a mechanical rainbow device, such as the type developed by the Italian architects, Sebastiano Serlio and Nicolo Sabbatini.[29] As we know from our own live fireworks, the scattering of sparks and flames are accompanied by thunderous sound and followed by smoke. In fact, the chorus may have commented on the 'comet in the air', after its appearance, but its presence remained through the sight of dissipating smoke and odour. In tandem with this sensory experience, the chorus not only ensures that audiences know that the blazing star remains an ominous sign, but also it somewhat shifts the function of the blazing star from its previous iteration in *The Battle of Alcazar*. Heaven did not send the blazing star to cause, promise or warn of destruction. Rather, destructive action drew out the blazing star.

In the Stukeley plays, the blazing star of the Admiral's Men's theatrical practice becomes attached, first, to the war, and, then, to Stukeley's death. This second association occurs in 2 *If You Know Not Me, You Know Nobody*, which documents an additional theatrical connection between Stukeley and the blazing star. Unlike 1 *If You Know Not Me, You Know Nobody*, which contains a miraculous dumb show to sanctify Queen Elizabeth as a virgin martyr, the sequel does not feature supernatural staging. Nonetheless, 2 *If You Know Not Me, You Know Nobody* presents a providential version of English historiography in its depiction of the discovery of Dr Parry's plot against the Queen and the victory over the Spanish Armada. Stukeley doesn't actually appear as a character in this nostalgic city comedy that follows the merchant Thomas Greshem in the 1570s and 1580s, but the captain is discussed in a brief exchange that touches on mortality and memory. As Greshem vows that before he dies, 'The world shall see Ile leaue like memorie', the stage lights up with '*A blasing Starre*' (F2v).[30] Greshem and his associates marvel at the 'strange Comet' and repeat that such sights 'fore-tell of danger's immnent' (F2v). As they converse about astrology, they receive news of Stukeley's recent death at Alcazar. In this scene, the blazing star recalls the intertwined stories of Morocco, Portugal and Stukeley, as depicted in the two previous plays, and also acts as the present sign of an absent but remembered man.

In this almost apotheosis of Stukeley, the play presents a third and final version of the blazing star. In *The Battle of Alcazar*, the comet signifies a general foreboding that is also applicable to individual lives. In *Captain Thomas Stukeley*, the ominous star is drawn out by reprehensible violence. In this third play, the star comes to stand in, metonymically, for Stukeley and his fate. As the professional theatre continued to develop the blazing star, dramatists seized on the version in *Captain Thomas Stukeley* and transformed it into a device of justice.

Middleton's revenge tragedies and Rowley's British stars

In two sets of Jacobean plays that do not feature Thomas Stukeley, the blazing star is drawn out by grave conditions and reborn as a system of tragic interruption. In Freddie Rokem's recent work on interruption, he draws on Walter Benjamin's consideration of Brechtian devices. As Benjamin sees it, interruption in epic theatre 'is not so much to develop actions as to represent conditions' and 'to make them seem strange [*verfremden*]'.[31] In other words, it is a moment or, as Rokem puts it, a 'caesura or a rupture', that distances audiences from the developing action.[32] The interruption accomplished by the blazing star does not so much make the quotidian appear suddenly strange – these plays do not represent the bourgeois conditions of modern drama – but it does create a live moment of rupture between the developing action of the play and the audience. While the problem of justice unfolds over the course of these plays, the adjudication of the right to revenge ultimately rests with a universal theatricality rather than individual morality. The device serves as a boundary marker within particular conflicts and works with the natural elements to sort out, in divine or moral terms, the problems of revenge. No longer does the blazing star foretell of general destruction. Rather, it is drawn out, and only drawn out, by a true claim for vengeance.

In *The Revenger's Tragedy* (1606) and *The Bloody Banquet* (c.1608), theatrical liveness transforms the blazing star into an authorization of righteous revenge. *The Revenger's Tragedy*, originally attributed to Cyril Tourneur and now understood as the work of Thomas Middleton, and *The Bloody Banquet*, by Middleton and Thomas Dekker, stand out among the blazing star plays because they were both likely produced at the Globe and not at the Rose, Fortune or Red Bull, the sites most commonly addressed by literary critics and theatre historians for spectacular descents, sound effects and pyrotechnics. However, these revenge tragedies premiered during the period in which the King's Men began to incorporate increased effects and pageantry into their plays as a result of responding to the new repertoire of the Red Bull, roughly 1608–14. Unlike the two other Jacobean plays addressed below, much of the spectacle in *The Revenger's Tragedy* and *The*

Bloody Banquet turns on meta-dramatic disguising during formal and ceremonial occasions. However, the blazing star, like bouts of thunder, stand beyond these sorts of man-made theatrics.

The astrological and epoch-marking language present in the Stukeley plays is absent from the revenge tragedies. Instead, the blazing star portends righteous and individual revenge. Although the tyrant figures in both plays understand it as a generalizable ominous sign, the comet signals judgement against the irredeemably guilty. Towards the end of *The Revenger's Tragedy*, in which a pair of brothers pursue the downfall of a murderous Duke and his equally evil son, Lussurioso, the revenger Vindice begins to despair. He demands of 'almighty patience' to know whether 'there is no thunder left, or is't kept up/ In stock for heavier vengeance?' (4.2.197–8).[33] Justice answers Vindice's query with thunder. The sudden bout of noise does not reverberate throughout the playhouse to represent weather conditions, such as in a play of Noah or *The Tempest*. Rather, the theatre introduces thunder as part of a live vocabulary of a hidden world of signs that interrupt human action and override human judgement. The thunder – heard by the ears and, perhaps, felt in the body – alerts audiences that requirements for revenge are determined by a transcendent theatricality.

Although audiences may expect more immediate signs of justice, the blazing star does not materialize to confirm the righteousness of the brothers' revenge until the play nears its end. In fact, its absence is noted after Vindice has killed his first target, the duke, at the beginning of Act 5. There, a rival of the duke's family learns of the murder and demands, 'Over what roof hangs this prodigious comet/ In deadly fire?' (5.1.106–7). As Macdonald P. Jackson explains, this particular 'burst of metaphor is essentially a high-flown and hypocritical exclamation of horror at the calamity' (5.1.106N). While the theatre continues to withhold the blazing star for Vindice and Hippolito, it will never appear for their enemies. Vindice continues to pursue revenge against Lussorioso, the son of the murdered duke. On the verge of a masque of revenge, Vindice prays 'Let our hid flames break out as fire, as lightning/To blast this villainous dukedom vexed with sin' (5.2.5–6). When '*A blazing star appeareath*', Lussorioso curses 'that ill-knotted fire, That bushing, flaring star' but his hubris prevents him from retreating (5.3.15SD and 5.3.18–19).[34] As soon the masque begins, Vindice's thunder returns as the masked dancing turns bloody and the duke's remaining court is killed. In these moments, Vindice transitions from a character driven to revenge to an embodiment of revenge. He addresses the noise itself: 'Mark, thunder!/ Dost know thy cue,/ thou big-voiced crier? Dukes' groans are thunder's watchwords' (5.3.42–4). Afterwards, he offers presentational narration over the spectacle that he has stage-managed to emphasize that it is now accompanied by divine approval. As a choral figure, he outright explains the meaning of the 'cue' of thunder and live fire, that is, 'When thunder claps heaven likes the tragedy' (5.3.48). In doing so, *The Revenger's Tragedy* radically revises the previous uses of the device in the Stukeley plays. All new plays to feature the device centred on the necessity of revenge and produced iterations of the blazing star as tragic interruption.

Dumb shows, clown scenes, disguising and prop-laden punishment crowds the entirety of the grotesque *The Bloody Banquet* that out-bloodies *The Revenger's Tragedy's* own bloody banquet. As in the previous play, the meta-dramatic strategies of disguising and ceremony stage manage revenge, but celestial interference must validate the cause. At the beginning of Act Five, the tyrannical King of Cilicia has hung the limbs of Tymethes, son of the rival King of Lydia, around his banqueting hall. There, the tyrant forces his wife to eat Tymethes's flesh and drink from his skull 'as a penance' for her former love of him (5.1.180). Vengeful Lydian guards disguised as pilgrim visitors are also present waiting for the moment to strike. The blazing star does not appear, however, until the revenge part of the tragedy begins. Among the plots of dissembling, murder and vendetta are one that involve the tyrant's son and daughter. It ends, at the beginning of the banquet, when the daughter toasts with poisoned wine to kill both herself and her brother. Their death is marked with a combination of 'Thunder and lighting. A blazing star appears' (SD 5.1.110). The comet summons the tyrant who, like Lussorioso in *The Revenger's Tragedy*, addresses it directly. After hailing it as, 'thou blazing star,/I like not thy prodigious bearded fire', he finds his dead children (5.1.12–13). The blazing star does not appear to announce the death of the tyrant's children, but to mark the divinely sanctioned evisceration of the Cilician king, his court and all of his progeny. Afterwards, the pilgrims unveil themselves and carry out the vengeance authorized by the stream of fire.

The blazing star continues to serve as a device of moral delineation in *Thorney Abbey* (c.1615) by William Rowley. The play is an early medieval story with two plots in two different genres, revenge tragedy and tragicomedy, respectively. The first plot follows the contours of *Macbeth* and features the blazing star in the middle of the play when the murder-and-revenge plot concludes. The second plot, featuring a pregnant daughter and an angry father, runs the course of the play and does not conclude until an angel appears and the pair are reconciled at the end. Rowley retains the meaning of the blazing star as part of an epistemology of vengeance in placing it at the conclusion of the murder plot. As in *Macbeth*, the wife of the Earl of Coventry convinces her husband to kill the king in his bed and England is wracked with thunder and darkness until they are caught. The Earl knows that the evil 'deed call up the thunder' and the heavens have banished the sun and moon from the sky 'till this black deed of hell revealed be' (VII.24 and 28).[35] The Earl's conscience bears down on him as he attempts to hide his sin. He dares, 'Let Hell spit fire, I'le not accuse myself', which, of course, brings out an abundance of noise from the heavens – '*Thunder loud*' (IX.27 and SD IX.29).[36] When his wife is questioned by the late king's son, the thunder increases so much that it becomes audible to her interrogators. The external manifestation of her guilty conscience overrides her testimony. The court notices that 'Scarce had denial issued from' her 'lips/But thunder cryes aloud … .What else heaven will speak in miracles' (XI.43–5). She persists in denying the murder until the regicide is revealed by the appearance of a blazing star. Echoing the tyrants in Middleton's revenge tragedies, the Earl's wife demands of the damning sign, 'Why doth thy flaming train thus point at me?' and painfully begs the comet to 'hide thy branded fire, whose flaming beams/ Are shot into my brain', and ultimately causes her to confess (XI.66, 68–9). Soon after, the Earl is caught attempting to flee towards Ireland. The scenario somewhat recalls Stukeley's fortunes by sea in *The Battle of Alcazar*. In that play, the elements protected the queen's rightful sovereignty from Stukeley's treason. Similarly, in *Thorney Abbey*, the seas act against treason when 'the angry heavens call'd up the mounting waves' to ensure that the murderer's 'passage [is] thus denied by raging stormes' (XI.114 and 17). As the revenge plot concludes and the play shifts to the tragicomic mode, the 'heavenly' signs that verify the need for vengeance in the first half of the play are matched with an angelic apparition to validate true repentance at the play's end.

Alone of all the blazing star plays, *The Birth of Merlin* (c.1622), also by Rowley, contains a comet in its source narrative. According to Holinshed, who reiterates Geoffrey of Monmouth's account of Uther Pendragon, 'at the tyme of his natiuitie maruelously appeared … a blasing Starre'.[37] Yet, Rowley does not wholesale represent the comet from the myth. Rather, he re-interprets the comet in Uther's history through the citational practices of Jacobean drama. Marvel working appears throughout this tragicomedy in the form of miracle, necromancy and Merlin's magic. The sort of magic that characterizes magician plays, such as *Doctor Faustus* and *Friar Bacon and Friar Bungay*, also appears in this one that features a holy hermit, a Saxon magician and Merlin. At the beginning of the play, the hermit 'with his cross and his staff' orchestrates a victory over the Saxons by amazing the pagan army with a sky show of 'brightness' and 'glorious beams' (A4v). The hermit is later challenged to a show of supernatural power by the Saxons' magician, who conjures ancient spirits. Finally, Merlin detects two dragons fighting in a cave. All of these instances of supernatural activity occur through prayers or spells whereas the blazing star appears on its own. The star is drawn out, first, to validate Uther's defeat of his treacherous rival, Vortigern, and, second, as a glorious signal of the once and future king. Fearfully, Uther asks Merlin to 'declare at full this Constellation' and the Welsh magician prognosticates that 'War and Dissension strives to make division', and also announces the coming of Arthur through his father: 'He to the world shall add another Worthy, and as a Load-stone for his prowess, draw a train of Marshal Lovers to his Court' (G1v). Uther's fight against the Saxons draws down the star in congruence to the way in which Arthur will one day, 'like a load-stone', sympathetically draw great knights to the roundtable in the establishment of Britain. As materialized in the theatre, the hidden forces, which are observable in the sky and in magnetic stones, validate British legend based on the precedent of Jacobean revenge tragedy.

'The Heavens seeme on fire': Transformation and liveness

After *The Revenger's Tragedy* shifted the meaning of the blazing star, the use of the device held steady. All subsequent plays utilize it to affirm the right to revenge or mark the need for revenge. The critical excavation of the device functions somewhat like philology for performance. The blazing star and its attendant sights, sounds and smells, as a language and a vocabulary enter into dialogue with audiences in live performance. The device began as one thing and, through its several appearances, transitioned to adjacent iterations of meaning. Like other uses of language and signs, the most recently developed iteration might even determine the present encounter with earlier versions. For example, the audiences who encountered the blazing star in Caroline revivals of 2 *If You Know Not Me, You Know Nobody* may have understood it not simply as predetermined or fated, but also as a necessary and divinely ordained punishment for Stukeley's treacherous interest in re-Catholicizing Ireland. As I conclude this essay, I turn to two final plays that document the meaning and evolution of the blazing star. *Rollo, Duke of Normandy* (c.1617) by John Fletcher, Philip Massinger and others, and *The Courageous Turk* (1618) by Thomas Goffe stand apart from the other plays examined here in that the appearance of the blazing star is ambiguous in the former and the latter is not a professional play. Nonetheless, these plays further demonstrate how theatre makers depended on live audiences to interpolate the meaning of the blazing star.

In *Rollo, Duke of Normandy*, the play invokes the sudden appearance of the blazing star without actually materializing it through pyrotechnics. While the play is a revenge tragedy, it lacks textual references to stars or heavens that occurred in Middleton's and Rowley's plays. In addition, the special effects and extreme meta-theatricality of the other revenge plots are also absent. Yet, the sudden introduction of the idea of the blazing star at the end of *Rollo* offers a final iteration of the device's live evolution in early modern theatre. In Act Five, the young Edith arranges to distract the tyrannical Rollo to avenge her father's unjust execution. Edith arranges for a boy to sing verses to set the scene for seduction. Once distracted, Edith plans to murder the murderer. When Rollo hears the song, he does not respond to the sound, but instead becomes enchanted by a sight:

> What bright star, taking beauties forme upon her,
> In all the happy lustre of heavens glory,
> Ha's drop'd downe from the Skye to comfort me?

> Wonder of Nature, let it not prophane thee
> My rude hand touch thy beauty, nor this kisse
>
> (H4V)[38]

What is the 'bright star' to which Rollo refers? The stage directions are scant in this play, but given the documented pyrotechnics in other plays of the era, could Rollo's lines indicate that the blazing star materializes on stage? The question of whether the blazing star appeared in the theatre is one that gets at the crux of the conditions of liveness. Although it is ambiguous in the text and the King's Men could have included some special effects here, I want to suggest that the playwrights substituted Edith's body for the actual pyrotechnic device. At the most basic level, the 'bright star' refers to Edith. Not only do the final two lines indicate a touch and a kiss, but also Edith replies to Rollo that 'no diety [sic] dwells here', just her 'obedience' (H4v). Yet, in naming Edith herself the 'bright star' the play is not simply relying on a metaphorical meaning. Rather, it is relying on audiences' prior knowledge of blazing stars in live theatre and it is figuring Edith both as the avenger and the embodiment of rightful vengeance. It is an act of symbolic doubling up rather than a disappearing act. The blazing star appears materially and at the right moment in this revenge tragedy, but the sign has changed shape here. Put somewhat differently, if Rollo himself had watched *The Revenger's Tragedy* or *Thorney Abbey*, then he would know that his time was up if in his seductress he recognized a *bright star drop'd downe.*

Around the same time as *Rollo, Duke of Normandy* played in London, Goffe composed *The Courageous Turk* for the students of Christ Church Oxford. Set in the East and full of elaborate staging and music, the Islamophobic play combines a Tamburlaine figure with the devils of biblical drama. When the play reaches its climax, '*The Heavens seeme on fire, Comets and blazing Starres appeare*' as Amurath invokes '*Mahomet*' to crush his Christian foes (H1r).[39] As a university play and as a work that approaches something like *Tamburlaine* fan fiction, *The Courageous Turk* contrasts with the London revenge tragedies of the era. However, the use of the device does not reflect *Tamburlaine* or the sons of *Tamburlaine* plays, *The Battle of Alcazar* and *Captain Thomas Stukeley*. The blazing star in *The Courageous Turk* appears at the point at which Amurath's violence towards Christendom pulls down the heavens to oppose him. This use of the device in Jacobean Oxford suggests that the revenge tragedy iteration of the blazing star circulated legibly beyond the London playhouses. Even in an academic performance, the stage definition of the blazing star superseded scientific and theological signification.

In choosing sides, the theatricality of the blazing star is a Jacobean experiment in epistemology. The revenge tragedies that feature blazing stars also depict how everyday techniques of dramatization can achieve manipulating and entrapping through feigning and dissembling. The techniques at the center of theatrical representation – that is, professional pretending – become dishonest and sinister in everyday life. *The Revenger's Tragedy* features a re-costumed impersonating corpse and a masque, while *The Bloody Banquet* features clowning and unwelcome banqueters in disguise as welcomed guests. In Rowley's two plays, veiled identity and marvel-making extend the role of dramatic manipulation in disguising truth and require the interference of a force beyond the control or conjuring of human agency. The problem of knowing, therefore, must be settled through an external force. As a sign that cuts through the logics of the philosophical, the theological and the political, the blazing star interrupts the drama of thinking, feeling and choosing to demand one present action: revenge.

Notes

1 George Peele, *The Battell of Alcazar Fought in Barbarie* (Richard Bankworth: London, 1594), F1r, and T. W., *Thorny-Abbey in Gratiae theatrales* (R. D: London, 1662), 37. William Rowley is the recognized author of *Thorny-Abbey* and all subsequent references reflect his authorship.

2 *A Pleasant Conceited Historie, Called The Taming of a Shrew* (London, 1594), G1v, *All's Well That Ends Well* (London: Bloomsbury, 2018), 1.3.86, and *The School of Complement* (London, 1631), 30.

3 Deborah Harkness, *John Dee's Conversations With the Angels: Cabala, Alchemy, and the End of Nature* (Cambridge: Cambridge University Press, 1999), 68–9.

4 Ibid., 69.

5 *Occult Knowledge, Science, and Gender on the Shakespearean Stage* (Cambridge: Cambridge University Press, 2017), 3.

6 *Actes and Monuments* (London, 1570), 269.

7 In addition to the other texts discussed, Richard Jones received a license to print Thomas Twyne's *A View of Certain Wonderful Effects* on 16 January and Robert Walley registered Laurence Johnson's *Cometographia* on 20 February. See *A Transcript of the Registers of the Company of Stationers of London, 1554–1640*, ed. Edward Arber and Charles Robert Rivington (New York: P. Smith, 1950), 2: 145 and 146.

8 It was first printed in 1555 and was re-printed in 1578. *A Prognostication Euerlasting of Right Good Effect* (London, 1605), 6r.

9 It is unclear when exactly between March 1577 and March 1578 that Thomas Woodcocke published *Of All Blasing Starrs in General*. Because there is no mention of any recent comet in any of the paratextual matter, it may have been published prior to the November event. The 1577 (old style) publication is not recorded in the Stationer's Register. The treatise was published in 1577 and in 1618, the years of notable comets.

10 Frederich Nausea, *Of All Blasing Starrs in Generall* (London, 1577), E1r.

11 Ibid.

12 Ibid., E7v–E8r.

13 Ibid., E3v.

14 Francis Shakelton, *A Blazyng Starre or Burnyng Beacon* (London, 1580), C4r.

15 Ibid., C6r.

16 Simon Smel-Knave, *Fearful and Lamentable Effects of Two Dangerous Comets* (London, 1590). Don Cameron Allen summarizes Smel-knave's argument: 'He denounces hypocritical clergymen and officials hungry for bribes. With the utmost rigor he sketches the unhappy condition of the poor, who shall have no justice because they cannot pay and, who, since charity is wanting, will suffer more than other Englishmen from famine and cold'. *The Star-Crossed Renaissance: The Quarrel About Astrology and Its Influence in England* (London: Routledge, 1967), 222. In *Albumazur*, the title character, an astrologer, swindles his clients.

17 Robin B. Barnes, *Astrology and Reformation* (Oxford: Oxford University Press, 2015), 9.

18 Ibid.

19 See the explanation on medical judicial astrology at the *Casebooks* website. Lauren Kassell, Michael Hawkins, Robert Ralley, and

John Young, 'Early Modern Astrology', *A Critical Introduction to the Casebooks of Simon Forman and Richard Napier*, 1596–1634, https://casebooks.lib.cam.ac.uk/astrological-medicine/early-modern-astrology, accessed 8 February 2019.

20 All dates in the parentheticals in the main text are the dates of first performance, not playbook publication dates.

21 See especially Ambereen Dadabhoy, 'Barbarian Moors: Documenting Racial Formation in Early Modern England', in *The Cambridge Companion to Shakespeare and Race*, ed. Ayanna Thompson (Cambridge: Cambridge University Press, 2021), 30–46, and Amy Lidster, '"With Much Labour Out of Scattered Papers": The Caroline Reprints of Thomas Heywood's *1* and *2 If You Know Not Me You Know Nobody*',, *Renaissance Drama* 49, no. 2 (2021): 205–28.

22 For more on the life of Stukeley, see Charles Edelman's Introduction in *The Stukeley Plays: 'The Battle of Alcazar by George Peele and 'The Famous History of the Life and Death of Captain Thomas Stukeley'* (Manchester: Manchester University Press, 2011). Unless otherwise noted, all quotes from these two plays are taken from this edition.

23 Christopher Marlowe, *Tamburlaine*, ed. J. S. Cunningham (Manchester: Manchester University Press, 1999).

24 *Renaissance Self Fashioning: From More to Shakespeare* (Chicago: University of Chicago Press, 1980), 227.

25 *English Drama, 1586–1642: The Age of Shakespeare* (Oxford: Clarendon Press, 1997), 49.

26 *Shakespeare and the Admiral's Men* (Cambridge: Cambridge University Press, 2017), 110.

27 See note 1 above for all subsequent quotations from this edition.

28 For the specific stage direction of the 'sudden Thunder-clap the sky is one fire and the blazing star appears', see *The famous historye of the life and death of Captaine Thomas Stukeley* (London, 1605), K1r.

29 See also the discussion of blazing stars as theatrical lighting in R. B. Graves, *Lighting the Shakesperean Stage, 1567–1642* (Carbondale and Edwarsville: Southern Illinois University Press, 1999), 203–11.

30 Thomas Heywood, *The Second Part of, If You Know Not Me, You Know No Bodie* (London, 1606). All subsequent quotations taken from this edition.

31 Walter Benjamin qtd in Freddie Rokem, '"Suddenly a Stranger Comes into the Room": Interruptions in Brecht, Benjamin and Kafka', *Studies in Theatre and Performance* 36 (2016): 23.

32 Ibid., 22.
33 All citations from *The Revenger's Tragedy* and *The Bloody Banquet* are from *Thomas Middleton: The Collected Works*, ed. Gary Taylor and John Lavagnino (Oxford: Oxford University Press, 2010).
34 For the specific stage direction of the 'A blasing-star appeareth', see Cyril Tourneur, *The Reuenger's Traegedie* (London, 1607), 12v.
35 Unless otherwise noted, all quotes are taken from William M. Baillie, *A Choice Ternary of English Plays: Gratiae Theatrales (1662)* (Binghamton: Medieval & Renaissance Texts & Studies, 1984).
36 See note 1 for the location of the stage direction in the original playbook.
37 Raphael Holinshed, *The Chronicles of England, Scotlande, and Irelande* (London, 1577), I: 127.
38 B. J. F., *The Bloody Brother* (London, 1639). All subsequent citations are from this edition.
39 Thomas Goffe, *The Couragious Turke, or, Amurath the First* (London, 1632).

9

The apparitional audience

Prophesizing live collectives in modern India and early modern England

Jonathan Gil Harris

In the summer of 2001, I went to the Chanakyapuri Theatre, a massive single-screen cinema hall in New Delhi, to see the season's box-office smash, *Lagaan* (Tax).[1] The film was a historical drama about a ragtag crew of Indian villagers who, at the height of the British Raj, take on an English cricket team and, with some help from their female coach, win. Any film already has something of an apparitional quality: it magically conjures, here and now, a vision of a world beyond this one. But *Lagaan* was also an apparition in a way that the Shakespeare who wrote *Macbeth* would have recognized – it was a prophetic vision.[2] Even as the film depicted a fictionalized past (its subtitle was *Once Upon a Time in India*), its story presented itself as a prediction of the later anti-colonial struggle against the British, as well as modern India's status as a global cricketing power.

I very much enjoyed the film. But I enjoyed the experience of sitting in the Chanakyapuri Theatre even more. Thousands of people had crammed into the theatre; from their more expensive gallery seats, richer Anglophone types (including me) peered down at a human flood of poorer, largely Hindi-speaking people flowing into the pit. As the lights dimmed and the film's opening score started, the audience did not fall silent, as is customary in Western cineplexes. Instead a chorus of whistles and cheers began. This chorus then turned into a veritable hullaballoo when the star actor, Aamir Khan, made his first appearance as the villager who would eventually lead the cricket team to victory over the English. People whooped and stamped; some even threw coins at the screen. And as Aamir Khan started to lip-sync and dance to his first musical number, the human flood bubbled and boiled over: people jumped up, danced for joy and sang along with their idol.

This continued for the duration of the three-hour screening.

I remember thinking three things as I watched all this unfold. First, the Chanakyapuri Theatre may have been in India, but sitting in it called to mind the noisy capaciousness of the early modern English playhouse – the richer sort in the galleries, the groundlings in the pit, all visible and audible to each other. Second, I may have been watching a film, but it felt more like a religious event, with devotees entering into an ecstatic state in the presence of idols and magical apparitions. The dynamic human flood was, to my eyes, the most magical apparition of all, inasmuch as it appeared to be the result of some sublime conjuration that had transformed diverse filmgoers into a medium for something larger, something singular, something *live*: 'the' audience. They didn't behave uniformly as one; many of us in the gallery, for instance, watched the singers and dancers with wry amusement. But a spirit of togetherness was unleashed in the Chanakyapuri Theatre that day, one that animated the entire hall.

My third thought was political. *Lagaan* itself demonstrated what can happen when disparate individuals come together as a collective larger than the sum of its parts. One such collective was the film's cricket team; another was its equally diverse onscreen crowd of villagers, raja and courtiers who watched the cricket game for much of the film's second half. Uniting rich and poor, male and female, Hindu and Muslim and Sikh and Dalit, the onscreen crowd mirrored the diversity of the team. But their behaviour –

dancing, singing, cheering their heroes – closely mirrored what I was seeing in the pit of the Chanakyapuri Theatre. Crowd reflected team; audience reflected crowd. Disparate spectators, in other words, reconstituted themselves as a collective in response to the apparition of another collective. What was conjured in the process resisted tyranny in the postcolonial present as much as the colonial past: *Lagaan*'s onscreen apparitions from another age prophesized their offscreen audience *now*.

Two decades later, I remain haunted by my experience at the Chanakyapuri Theatre. So I ask here: what can prophetic apparitions, Indian and otherwise, teach us about the 'liveness' of the audience in the early modern English playhouse?

* * *

> Look, how the world's poor people are amazed
> At apparitions, signs and prodigies,
> Whereon with fearful eyes they long have gazed
> Infusing them with dreadful prophesies ...
>
> William Shakespeare, *Venus and Adonis* (925–8)[3]

Venus may be a pagan goddess. But when Shakespeare has her speak of 'apparitions, signs and prodigies', he anachronistically folds her into his English Protestant present. This was a present of invalidated supernatural presences. To 'infuse' apparitions and their ilk with the power of prophecy – to allow them to conjure presences beyond the physical world – was to resort to a magical thinking disallowed by the Reformation. Protestant clerics maintained that, although such miraculous 'prodigies' had taken place in biblical times, God no longer worked prophetic wonders 'above, beyond, or against the settled order and instinct of nature'.[4] As a result, lay writers such as Thomas Nashe denounced apparitions as nothing more than 'hot matter' that rises from our spleens to our brains, 'whereof many fearful visions are framed'.[5] Apparitions had now become 'fearful' perversions. Shakespeare's syntax underscores how Venus's belief in apparitions and their prophetic power overturns the natural order, lowering an immortal goddess to the level of 'the world's poor people'.[6]

Yet Shakespeare – typically – has it both ways. Venus's belief in apparitions is justified: treating the spectacle of Adonis's hounds bleeding from their encounter with the boar as a magical apparition, she correctly foretells his looming end. Apparitions, Shakespeare seems to say, are indeed fearful perversions; yet they also conjure *something* of the future that can be felt with extraordinary intensity. Adonis's future death, in this apparitional instant, becomes a live event, a vivid mediated presence that takes over Venus's present.

Belief in apparitions blurs into what many Protestants stigmatized as idolatry: the mistake of seeing in a present object the supernumerary presence of some other life beyond it.[7] This effect of double presence is crucial to the seeming magic of the apparition. By vividly conjuring something beyond itself, it presents itself both of this world and out of this world. The apparition, then, is always a mediating entity. As Venus shows us, something else – something live, even if it predicts death – speaks through and as the apparition: without that something else, it is no longer an apparition but, rather, just an image or empty sign.

We might also note in Venus's speech a second, more theatrical, dimension of the apparition. Venus helps us realize how apparitions are not just magical visions: they can also be collective events. Extrapolating from her own situation as an individual confronted with a possible apparition, Venus conjures a larger singularity that becomes more than the sum of its parts, and that can be prefixed with a definite article: '*the* world's poor people'. The phrase 'poor people' might seem class coded, but it also acquires something of the universalizing sense of 'the commons'. And Venus too is subsumed within this commons. Which is to say, those who are 'amazed' by apparitions are in turn magically apparitionalized as members of a *global collective*, a live entity that mirrors Venus's own position as a gazer. And that collective derives its very existence from the apparitions it regards.

Spectators of the world unite, Venus says: you have nothing to lose but your apparitions.

Venus's collective recalls that produced by another institution. Within the living memory of many of Shakespeare's readers, the Roman Catholic Church had made an apparitional experience the centrepiece of its Mass. The customary English term for the sacrament of the Eucharist, 'Communion', derives from the Latin for 'sharing in common'; it marks a collective experience of the Host, the consecrated wafer, that apparitionalizes not just the object but also its audience. When the priest raises the Host before the assembled faithful and says 'hoc est corpus meum' (this is my body) his Latin formula magically transubstantiates the wafer into the living presence of Jesus Christ. But the formula also makes the wafer the portal to another apparitional body that knits together diverse churchgoers into a collectivity indifferent to distinctions of class, gender or ethnicity: the universal, mystical body of Christ as the Catholic Church.[8] The two apparitions may not have been hallucinatory visions like Venus's. But they both magically supplemented physical entities with intensely felt spiritual ones.

Communion had no doubt been one of the most powerful elements of Catholic ritual. The Mass had offered its English celebrants the pleasure of being subsumed into something magically bigger, something 'common', something live. In doing so, they experienced a mirror stage of sorts – though one rather different from that theorized by Jacques Lacan. His account of the mirror stage was concerned with the phantasmic promise of the individuated whole self; Communion, by contrast, promised the phantasm of the collective. Yet both located the source of their phantasm in an externality – the image in the mirror in the case of Lacan, the consecrated wafer in the case of Communion. Both these externalities prophesized another living presence – the 'I', the *corpus mysticum* of Christ. And both captioned their object with a version of the formula: 'this is my body'.

The experience of Communion was only enhanced by the shared synesthetic rituals that accompanied the performance of the Mass: seeing the priest's brightly coloured robes, feeling the sprinkling of holy water, tasting the Communion wine, smelling the incense, hearing the bells. The reformed early modern English church not only dispensed with most of these rituals, however, seeing them as idolatrous; it also treated the consecrated wafer as a symbol rather than a prophetic apparition of living presence.[9] As a result, English churchgoers were no longer magically transformed by Communion into a dynamic mystical body. They were now an assembly of devout individuals, disabled from entering the apparitional live collectivity that the old rituals of smells and bells used to induce.

Many must have experienced this as a significant loss.[10] Theatre, however, provided a powerful consolation and even replacement for the lost Catholic Communion.

* * *

Stephen Greenblatt has noted how the commercial theatre of post-Reformation London inherited many of the materials of the recently disestablished Catholic Church.[11] Playing companies not only took possession of priests' discarded vestments, repurposing these as costumes; they also staged, in plays like *King Lear*, magical Catholic rituals such as exorcism discredited under the new disposition. Stripped of their former spiritual lives, these materials were now empty signifiers, consigned to the playhouses as forms of theatre. Greenblatt argues that this inheritance served a double end. It upheld the Protestant view that the rituals and accessories of Catholicism were no more than mere scripts and stage properties. But it also capitalized on their residual magical power to astonishing, subversive effect.

Greenblatt considers the remnants of the Catholic Church onstage, on the bodies of actors and in the language and practices given to them by the playwrights. But Catholic remnants were to be found also in the playhouse's pit and its galleries. Affective longings proscribed by the Reformation were brought by theatregoers to performances of plays. These most certainly included the desire for Communion – the desire not just to witness the magical transformation of mere matter into something live, but also to be magically apparitionalized as a common live body, joined together in ritual activity that involved stimulation of the senses.

Thomas Middleton and Thomas Dekker's comedy, *The Roaring Girl*, illuminates both facets of the desire for Communion. In a remarkable scene, Sir Alexander Wengrave takes Sir Davy Dapper on a tour of his house:

> Nay when you look into my galleries,
> How bravely they are trimmed up, you all shall swear
> Y' are highly pleased to see what's set down there:
> Stories of men and women (mixed together
> Fair ones with foul, like sunshine in wet weather)
> Within one square a thousand heads are laid
> So close, that all of heads, the room seems made,
> As many faces there (filled with blithe looks)
> Show like the promising titles of new books,
> (Writ merrily) the Readers being their own eyes,
> Which seem to move and to give plaudities,
> And here and there (whilst with obsequious ears,

Thronged heaps do listen) a cutpurse thrusts and leers
With hawk's eyes for his prey: I need not show him,
By a hanging villainous look, yourselves may know him,
The face is drawn so rarely. Then sir below,
The very floor (as 'twere) waves to and fro,
And like a floating Island, seems to move,
Upon a sea bound in with shores above.[12]

This speech captures with haunting vividness an early modern actor's view, from the stage, of commercial playgoers. The actor playing Sir Alexander describes the richer sort in the gallery, the tightly packed groundlings in the pit, even the 'cutpurses' or pickpockets who would prey on them. Peering over his shoulder, we see playgoers of all classes listening intently to his lines and applauding them.

But the speech is much more than just a snapshot of those who went to see plays at the Fortune Theatre, where *The Roaring Girl* was staged sometime between 1607 and 1610. It also discloses the process of theatrical conjuration by which mere matter magically could turn into an apparition and individual playgoers into a collective audience. In an extraordinary manoeuvre, Sir Alexander turns the physical space of his library into something *live*. He begins by describing for Sir Davy his books, enlisting the individual men and women in the playhouse gallery to double as them. These playgoer-books are diverse, a blend of 'fair' and 'foul', 'sunshine' and 'wet weather'. The personification works in two directions. Even as Sir Alexander makes his 'books' out of living men and women, he also makes a live audience out of his 'library' – a structuring metaphor that collates different elements into a whole. And Sir Alexander's is a self-aware, or self-regarding, 'library'. His playgoer-books' 'Readers' are the 'eyes' of the playgoers themselves, meaning that the latter are looking not just at the actor playing Sir Alexander, but also at each other, mediated by images of themselves reflected back at them from the stage. This allows them to take stock of themselves *as a collective* – an event that Sir Alexander's speech would have enacted in performance, inasmuch as it demanded that the diverse playgoers recognize themselves in, and as, the apparitional audience conjured by him. Note the Eucharist-like resolution: a massive plurality consisting of disparate elements has now become, through a process of mediation, a fantastical live singularity.[13] The formula for its conjuration might be paraphrased as 'this is my library'.

By the conclusion of Sir Alexander's speech, his self-regarding library-cum-audience has become even more dynamic, its groundlings metaphorically morphing into a 'floating Island' in constant motion. It is as magical a transformation as that which would later, in performances of *The Tempest*, turn the bare stage of the Globe Theatre into an island, making its timber alternate between the 'tawny' strips that Antonio and Sebastian see and the 'green' that Gonzalo ascribes to it (2.1.55–6).[14] The difference is that *The Roaring Girl*'s apparitional island takes shape in the pit rather than on the stage.

What Sir Alexander describes here, then, is the performance of a profane Communion. It works to produce magical live presences both onstage and off it: a library, an audience. Yet, although the performance may have ritual and affective roots in the Catholic sacrament of the Eucharist, it is also by now sufficiently detached from its predecessor that there is no echo of religious language in Sir Alexander's speech. His shaping metaphors are of books and floating islands, not of bread and feasting. The scene he enacts, therefore, isn't simply a post-Reformation substitute for Communion. It is also a theoretical exposition of how 'the' audience is apparitionalized as a self-aware, live singularity, channelling its spirit from what it gazes at. And that's why Sir Alexander's speech can help illuminate the liveness of the audience not just in the Fortune Theatre in early modern London but also in the Chanakyapuri Theatre in millennial New Delhi.

* * *

Let's be clear: the human-flood audience called forth by the screening of *Lagaan* was not the floating-island audience of *The Roaring Girl*. Nor was it the apparitional Indian grandchild of the Catholic mystical body of the Church, conjured by the sacrament of the Eucharist. Nevertheless, Sir Alexander's speech highlights an element of live performance whose kernel resides in a type of apparitional religious experience by no means confined to Catholicism and Communion.

The idol, as we have seen, is an apparitional entity. It is marked by two presences: that of its material form, and that of the divine spirit it mediates. In India, religious devotion usually entails vivid experiences of an idol or sacred object's double presence. And religious devotion has shaped habits of film viewing throughout the subcontinent.[15] In the case of the Chanakyapuri Theatre screening of *Lagaan*, a variety of subcontinental devotional traditions spanning various forms of Hinduism, and to a lesser extent Islam, had laid the performative and affective foundations for the filmgoers' response to what they saw and heard onscreen. These traditions may not have been theologically discredited for Indian filmgoers the way Catholic rituals had been for early modern playgoers. But there was, I would venture, a shared sense of longing for such rituals in the face of their loss.

A significant portion of the Chanakyapuri Theatre filmgoers – certainly those who had bought cheaper tickets in the pit – were migrant labourers from villages, who had come to Delhi in search of economic opportunity. Devotional practices remain much more central to everyday life in Indian villages than they do in the big cities; and in villages, these practices are also tethered to a strong sense of community. In most Hindu traditions, and some Indian Islamic ones, the focal expression of devotion takes place during the *darshan*, or ceremonial showing, of divinity – for Hindus, in the form of the idol of a *devta* (god) or *devi* (goddess) displayed in temples and processions through the streets; for Muslims, at least those of a Sufi bent, in the *dargah* (shrine) of a *pir* (saint-teacher). The *darshan* has an apparitional dimension, inasmuch as a transcendent spiritual power operates through, and beyond, the sacred object of devotion. It also creates the apparition of the devotional community. For the *darshan* is not a private but a public audience with divinity; it demands that its devotees – rich and poor, male and female, sometimes multi-faith – respond as something larger than themselves. More often than not they are united by noisy adulation, cheering, dancing and singing together.

But such experiences of live collectivity stand to be sacrificed when one moves from the village to the city. In this regard, the experience of migrant labourers who have swollen the populations of India's mega-cities parallel those of the large number of citizens in early modern London who had – like Shakespeare himself – migrated from their villages. All sought economic opportunity in the city, but they did so at the expense of belonging to a community pinned together by the performance of common rituals.[16] If playhouses like the Fortune Theatre offered London's migrant labourers a substitute for lost experiences of community and Communion, modern Indian cinema halls have likewise provided compensatory spaces in which something of the village *darshan* might be re-enacted.

A further point of similarity between the early modern London playhouse and the modern Indian cinema hall is the detachment of their apparitional audiences from any singular religious tradition. The early modern theatre allowed playgoers to access ancient longings for Communion in a venue that, as Greenblatt notes, also paid lip service to the Protestant critique of Catholicism as mere theatre. That is why the early modern English apparitional audience, in *Venus and Adonis* as much as in *The Roaring Girl*, is a 'floating Island' in a religious as well as a spatial sense: it moves between denominational adversaries and settles on neither. Likewise, the apparitional audience of modern Indian popular cinema cross-hatches Hindu and Muslim devotional practices. Both playhouse and cinema hall, in short, make space for religiously mixed constituencies – a pluralism born in part from the commercial imperative to appeal to as broad a range of paying customers as possible.[17] But in India, the pluralism of the cinema hall has deeper historical roots.

The power of the Hindu *darshan* had been appropriated in the sixteenth century by the Mughal emperor Akbar, a Muslim. In a ritual called the *jharokha darshan* (window showing) the emperor ceremonially presented himself to his Hindu and Muslim subjects for viewing, framed within a window from on high. The ritual, which Akbar's Mughal successors also made part of their ceremonial self-presentations, had a strongly religious dimension. The emperor presented not just his physical body, but also his *baraka* – an Arabic term for blessing that described the divine charismatic energy flowing through him onto his subjects, both commanding them as his devotees and sustaining them as a polity.[18] The emperor's *baraka*, mediated through the *jharokha darshan*, animated the apparition of a common political body fashioned out of its diverse constituent Muslim and Hindu parts.[19]

Something of both the village *darshan* and the Mughal *jharokha darshan* survives in modern popular Indian films and audience responses to them. Although the term 'idol' as a synonym for a film star is of Western provenance, it seems particularly appropriate in India, where leading actors are frequently venerated as gods: the leading star of the 1970s and 1980s, Amitabh Bachchan, even became the *devta* of a temple consecrated to him in Kolkata.[20] Film stars are also venerated in terms that recall those used to represent the Mughals: Bachchan is popularly known as the *Shahenshah* or Emperor, and his successor idol Shah Rukh Khan as the *Badshah*, another term for Emperor. The standard introductory 'reveal' shot of a leading actor in Indian popular film is not unlike the *darshan* of an idol; it recalls even more the Mughal *jharokha darshan*, particularly when the – often Muslim – star makes his charismatic first appearance framed within a suddenly opened door, light streaming from behind him, high above his multi-faith devotees cheering in the pit.

In a crucial way, though, the star is incidental to the live audience response. The cinema hall *darshan* is arguably just a pretext for filmgoers' deeper compulsion to come together as an audience in a spirit of adulation, performing the same rites, singing the same songs, dancing the same steps. As befits a polytheistic and multi-faith society, filmgoers' devotion is promiscuous, and the performance of idol-adulation in the Indian cinema hall can be readily transferred from one idol to another. But any such performance will entail a doubly apparitional experience: an experience of *baraka*-like charismatic power that emanates from the star, which commands the experience of the live human-flood collective, the dancing and singing and whistling and cheering version of Middleton and Dekker's 'floating island'.

What I witnessed in the Chanakyapuri Theatre, then, was a subcontinental counterpart to Communion. The sacrament of the Eucharist knitted together people from different backgrounds within an apparitional body, fulfilling the promise of Christ's word. The public *darshan* of *Lagaan* and its idol likewise brought together people across divides of class, religion and gender, mirroring the vision of the film, in which Aamir Khan's character assembles a multi-caste, multi-faith team of men coached by a woman. That mirroring not only made the Chanakyapuri Theatre audience apparitional; it also made the audience the fulfilment of a prophecy. The filmgoers didn't simply see *Lagaan* as individuals. As I have noted, they also saw themselves in its team and onscreen crowd as a live collective, and responded accordingly. Channelling a higher power – the charismatic uniting power of the idol on screen above them – the filmgoers collectively acted out the film's vision of collectivity, making that vision a living presence in the equally apparitional shape of 'the' audience.

* * *

How might the prophetic dimension of the Chanakyapuri Theatre's relation between onscreen apparition and apparitional audience help illuminate the liveness of Shakespeare's playhouses, the Globe and the Blackfriars?

Macbeth stands unsurpassed among Shakespeare's works for its capacity to frighten. It doesn't just feature scary Witches who predict the future in riddles, a murderous tyrant who strikes terror into every corner of his kingdom, and his cruelly butchered friend who returns as a horrifying ghost. Much of the power of the play derives also from its staging of eerie, unsettling apparitions – in particular, a series of visions that emerge from the Witches' cauldron in Act 4 scene 1: a bloody head, an infant, a child carrying a tree, a procession of kings. All these apparitions are prophetic visions.

Macbeth's apparitions are presented in ways that seem to affirm a Reformation sensibility. Apparitions, under Catholicism, had once covered a spectrum that ranged from divine revelations and expressions of Christ's living presence to Satanic deceptions – opposing poles represented by Hamlet's confused response to the Ghost as a 'spirit of health' and 'goblin damned' (1.4.40).[21] After the Reformation, the spectrum shifted: apparitions were now the result of bad melancholy humours, demonic deception or both. The apparitions that materialize out of the Witches' cauldron seem to have something of this diabolical quality: they are sinister riddles that trick Macbeth into an unearned confidence that he will survive all threats to his life and rule. Conspiring to produce this confidence seems part of the Witches' malevolent plan: 'Security', Hecate says, 'Is mortals' chiefest enemy' (3.5.32–3).[22] And so the Witches' apparitions prove deadly to Macbeth.

Yet the play's apparitions do generate powerful effects of prophecy. Banquo asks the Witches if they 'can look into the seeds of time,/ And say which grain will grow, and which not' (1.3.58–9); the play answers his question in the affirmative. Macbeth resorts to the same metaphor when he asks the Witches to reveal 'the treasure/ Of Nature's germen' (4.1.57–8), which they proceed to do. The word 'germen' – a collective noun related to 'germ' and 'germinate'

– refers to seeds or, more generally, future life-generating materials.[23] *Macbeth*'s apparitions afford its characters synchronous glimpses of potential 'treasure' within present 'germen' – or, as Lady Macbeth says, of 'the future in the instant' (1.5.58).

Most of the onstage apparitions that conjure potential futures, however, are apprehended by the Macbeths (and briefly Banquo) alone, even when they experience them in seemingly public places. Other characters cannot see or hear them. The stains of blood on Lady Macbeth's hands, which she too invests with apparitional power as signs of her looming damnation in Hell, are invisible to her onlookers. Likewise, Macbeth alone sees the terrifying apparition of the murdered Banquo's ghost at his dinner party; other characters see nothing – or they see an empty joint stool in Banquo's place, which, as James L. Calderwood has noted, translates the live presence of Banquo's ghost into an inert stage property.[24] A playgoer gazes on these apparitions with a kind of baffled double vision: she both senses the otherworldliness of the apparitions and recognizes their sheer theatricality. They may generate in spectators a feeling of eerie uncanniness.[25] But they do not, as yet, prompt the collective live experience of profane Communion produced by *The Roaring Girl*. If anything, they conduce to a playgoer's feeling distanced from the apparition-enthralled Macbeths on stage, of being shut out – for good or for bad – from an audience experience of liveness.

Yet amid this enforced Protestant-friendly distancing of playgoers from its theatrical apparitions, *Macbeth* generates another, more haunting apparition. Or rather, a ghost of an apparition: the ghost of the memory of the apparitional collective.

In a fascinating analysis, Jonathan Hope and Michael Witmore have noted that the word 'the' appears with much higher frequency in *Macbeth* than in any other play by Shakespeare.[26] It is a seemingly insignificant word, but its repeated use in the play has powerful effects. Hope and Witmore single out Lady Macbeth's remark about the source of a sudden noise: 'It was the owl that screeched, the fatal bellman' (2.2.3–4). As Hope and Witmore note, we would expect Lady Macbeth to say 'It was *an* owl that screeched, *a* fatal bellman'. Her double use of the definite article has an apparitional effect. It creates an uncanny sense of this owl being not any owl, but *the* owl – an owl not only invested with a prophetic 'fatal' power, but also known to a community who can recognize it as 'the' owl. The apparition generated here is not just of an ominous night bird but also of insider knowledge, of a convention from which the playgoers cannot help but feel themselves discomfortingly excluded.[27] And what is a 'convention', in its literal etymological sense, other than a coming together of many? The apparition of the collective is invoked, then, only to exclude those watching the play. In *Macbeth*, there is collectivity, no end of collectivity – just not, it would seem, for its playgoers.

Such moments do not simply exclude playgoers. They are active disincentives to playgoers' collective transubstantiation into a live apparitional audience. The creepiness of '*the* owl' underlines the illicitness, the evil, of the apparition. Here as elsewhere, the play deals in the currency of apparitional collectives conjured by definite articles just as *the* 'world's poor people' does for Venus and *the* 'library' does for Sir Alexander in *The Roaring Girl*. But in the case of *Macbeth*, playgoers are discouraged from joining such collectives. This points to how the apparition of an *im*possibility lurks in the play. The impossibility is more precisely a spectre than an apparition: an apparition tends to predict the future, whereas a spectre is a visitation from the past of an entity now erased by its death.[28] In *Macbeth*, this spectre is the apparitional collectivity of the Catholic Communion.

We can catch a whiff of this spectre in the first scene with the Witches. The stench of cheap squibs detonated at the start of the play in its first performances, as called for by the stage direction of '*Thunder and Lightning*' and materialized in that scene's stifling 'fog and filthy air' (1.1.10), would have been the first significant sensory experience playgoers had during the performance of the play.[29] The smell might have recalled earlier morality plays where fireworks were used to evoke the aroma of devils. The stinking odour of cheap gunpowder – usually made from pig excrement – may have also evoked the apparition of the recent failed Gunpowder plot of 1605, connecting the medieval setting of the play to a later age, centuries beyond its own. But even as the stench of gunpowder evoked the 'future' of Shakespeare's present, it also pointed back to a lost past. To enter into an enclosed, seated assembly so awash with the foul smell of excremental smoke must have conjured a memory of the fair smell of holy smoke in the Catholic Church. As the Witches say: 'Fair is foul and foul is fair' (1.1.9). In the Catholic Church, incense and candles made the air thick with fumes, but in a way that promised divine spirit as opposed to the diabolical associations prompted by the fumes of gunpowder in the Globe and Blackfriars playhouses, where *Macbeth* was most likely first performed.[30] The play mediated the memory of Catholic devotion through a demonic spectre, a 'goblin damned' that had returned with the scandalous smell of sulphur.

The smell of gunpowder that accompanies each of the Witches' scenes would have certainly struck the man who was the ostensible target of the Gunpowder plot – and the titular patron of Shakespeare's company, The King's Men: King James I of England and VI of Scotland. But the king wasn't just a possible spectator/ olfactor of an early performance of *Macbeth*.[31] He was also one of the most powerful apparitions haunting the whole play. Author of a treatise on demonology and witchcraft that devoted an entire book to the question of apparitions and their prophesies of the future, King James was himself quite literally a prophetic apparition conjured by the play – if his image was, as some have speculated, the one visible in the 'glass' held up at the end of the Witches' final vision: the '*show of eight kings*' (4.1.111) descended from Banquo.

This is how many have understood the image in the glass at the end of the apparitional kings' procession. Countless critics have read Macbeth's description of 'the two-fold balls and treble scepters' (4.1.120) that he sees in the glass as a reference to King James – the twofold balls marking the king's union of Scottish and English crowns, the three sceptres alluding to the kingdoms of Great Britain, Ireland and France.[32] Having likewise infused the glass with a prophecy of King James, Jonathan Goldberg treats the scene as a devilishly subversive meditation on reflection itself. The king who wrote passionately in his *Demonology* against witchcraft is now conjured by the Witches, Goldberg compellingly argues, his reign not only predicted by them but also incorporated into their apparitional regime of representation.[33]

There are problems, though, with reading King James as the image captured in the glass. To do so projects from his presence at a hypothetical, singular court performance the enduring telos of the Witches' procession of kings. This is a dubious move. For one, Macbeth remarks that the eighth king 'bears a glass/ Which shows me many more' (4.1.118–19); he sees not an individual king but a plurality. The insistence on placing King James in the glass is all the more dubious given that the script that we have inherited was crafted for public performances of *Macbeth* that he would never have attended. The Folio edition, particularly in Act 4 scene 1, contains interpolations by Thomas Middleton – the playwright who wrote Sir Alexander Wengrave's speech about the audience in *The Roaring Girl*.[34] Even if *Macbeth* was performed at court and James caught a glimpse of himself in the mirror, the stage property was almost certainly a piece of theatrical business that would have been employed in public performances. Who or what was visible in it, given that King James wouldn't have been present for performances of *Macbeth* at the Globe or the Blackfriars?

The 'many more' that Macbeth spies in the glass would have certainly reflected the many people seated in the playhouse. Gazing at the glass held up the last figure in the procession of kings, these people would have glimpsed themselves framed in one image as 'the' audience. In a visual version of Sir Alexander's speech in *The Roaring Girl*, then, the procession of the kings becomes a prophecy not just of future rulers of Scotland but also of an apparitional audience in a time to come.

It is this image, not just of the descendants of Banquo but also of the audience, that causes Macbeth so much consternation. This audience has a collective power – and playgoers would have *seen* themselves as an audience invested with it. But what is this power? Why should it frighten Macbeth so? The view of the kings affirms that his own power, for all its tyranny, will be supplanted. But how would the seventeenth-century apparitional audience captured in the glass have had power over the singular, single-minded medieval tyrant? Macbeth's 'many more' gives us a clue – 'the' audience is a collective that comprises 'many', with the 'more' suggesting an ellipsis that extends to embrace a potentially infinite number of future members. Does the power of the 'many more' of the audience reside in the Leviathan plurality that comprises the English King's body politic (itself a reworking of the *corpus mysticum* of the Catholic Church[35])? In the Anglo-Scottish union that King James sought to produce? In the Catholic-Protestant plurality out of which Shakespeare's audience was comprised? Or – as this procession of questions rather than kings might suggest – does the power of the 'many more' reside in the radically plural uncertainties of the audience, catching itself in an instant of collective questioning?

The play 'reflects' the King, but also conjures the audience in his place, imagining it as the fellow spawn, midwifed by the Witches, of Banquo – the fugitive from tyranny, the seeker of alternative futures, the pursuer of an elsewhere. The audience is hailed by the Witches as an apparitional *corpus mysticum* that is both impossible in the time of the Reformation yet always possible as a live anti-tyrannical collective in a time to come. This is not the jubilant audience of the Chanakyapuri Theatre, or the dynamic audience of the Fortune Theatre. But it is a version of *the* audience, apparitionalized in the Globe and the Blackfriars as the fulfilment of *Macbeth*'s prophecy of 'many more'.

* * *

The apparitional audiences of *Macbeth* and of modern Indian cinema intriguingly merge in Vishal Bhardwaj's 2003 film *Maqbool*. The film is an Indian adaptation of *Macbeth*, set in the gangster underworld of 1990s Bombay. *Maqbool* is more art house movie than popular Hindi film; as a result, it was first screened not in vast cinema halls like the Chanakyapuri Theatre, but in the new, smaller and more upmarket multiplexes of urban shopping malls. Multiplex filmgoers in the early 2000s were far more homogeneously middle-class and restrained than those of the single-screen cinema hall. Still, the film self-consciously reflects on an apparitional audience's diversity, in a way that speaks uncannily to *Macbeth* and taps into the subcontinent's devotional traditions in religion and popular entertainment alike.[36]

The song 'Tu Mere Rubaru Hai' (You Are in Front of Me) appears early in *Maqbool*. The picturization of the song, and its lyrics by the poet Gulzar, is important in establishing the romance between mafia captain Maqbool and Nimmi, the Macbeth and Lady Macbeth of the film. The twist is that this romance is a forbidden one: Nimmi is the paramour of Abbu Ji, Maqbool's don, and the Duncan of the film. The song's lyrics initially seem to frame the desire of Maqbool for Nimmi. We see them both walking in a large procession of devotees; the occasion is an 'urs mela', the anniversary festival for a Sufi saint. Maqbool, walking behind Nimmi who is literally in front of him, gazes at her in longing as we hear the words of the song, sung by the Sikh singer Daler Mendi.

But the lines' applicability to Maqbool's personal longing is displaced by the occasion. The song is sung live by a *qawwali* ensemble – a group of Muslim Sufi singers – at a *dargah* next to a *pir*'s (or Sufi seer's) covered shrine. In this context, the lyrics apply to the *qawwali* singers addressing the *pir* in front of them and, through him, God. There is another, third application. Gathered in front of the *qawwali* ensemble is a large audience of devotees; they include Abbu Ji and his daughter – both Muslims – and her secret Hindu lover. The song now describes the devotees, including the interfaith couple. Finally, this image on screen presents the filmgoers with a specular image of themselves as an audience: they witness, in front of them, a multi-faith collective listening to a devotional song, and recognize themselves in it. The song's lyrics connect the apparitional audience to its onscreen counterpart in front of it – and vice versa. The apparitional audience becomes the song's prayer seated in front of the screen, the realization of *Maqbool*'s Sufi prophecy.

This mirrored relationship of screen and audience is powerfully captured by the Urdu word 'rubaru' in the song's title. I have translated it as 'in front of' – but it means, more specifically, face to face with a live apparition of divinity. And in Sufi poetic tradition, to be 'rubaru roshni' – face to face with the light – means that one both loses oneself and finds oneself anew, reconstituted by, and as an extension of, that light. The song's lyrics and picturization, with the multilayered playfulness typical of Sufi devotional poetry, allows us to see how 'rubaru' describes the apparitional encounter that mediates not only devotee and divinity or lover and beloved, but also performance and audience.

Vishal Bhardwaj and his lyricist Gulzar may not have been attentive to the apparitional audience of *Macbeth*, or its affective and performative roots in proscribed Catholic rituals of Communion. But they didn't need to be. They were already highly conscious of the relations between popular Hindi film and spiritual devotion, and the ways in which these allowed for formations of live collectives across seeming differences of religion, gender and class. 'Tu Mere Rubaru Hai' – sung by a Sikh, lip-synced by a Sufi *qawwali* ensemble, heard by an interfaith Muslim–Hindu couple – is just as much a brilliant performative theorization of the diverse, live apparitional audience as is *Lagaan*'s cricket game, *The Roaring Girl*'s library and *Macbeth*'s mirror of 'many more'.

* * *

The apparitional audience, in modern India as in early modern England, demonstrates the power of the live collective. This power is extraordinary to witness, as my experience watching *Lagaan* in the Chanakyapuri Theatre makes clear. The power can also be frightening; its religious antecedents suggest how it derives from unquestioning surrender to a higher power – the idol, the *devta*, God, the living presence. The apparitional audience is *possessed* by this higher power, a relation hinted at in Sir Alexander Wengrave's proprietorial metaphor of the audience as his library. As such, the apparitional audience might seem a more benign form of the mob, acting out the will of its charismatic master. But there is a difference. In the theatre, the apparitional audience is aware of itself as comprised out of diverse, even disparate, parts. The mob demands the erasure of difference; the apparitional audience, in all the instances I have examined here, celebrates coming together across difference.

We scholars of early modern English theatre and of Shakespeare are the heirs of the Reformation in ways that we don't always realize. We assume that an audience is a little like us – individuals who diligently 'read' the play in a variety of ways.[37] We try not to reify 'the' audience; we are urged to remember that it includes individuals from many different backgrounds, who potentially interpreted spectacles differently from each other. That remains true. But this fear of reification overlooks the desire of early modern English playgoers, or that of modern Indian filmgoers, for collective audience experience. We forget the extent to which early modern playgoers did not sit in atomized contemplation. As *The Roaring Girl* makes clear, the playhouse was populated by dynamic floating islands. Rethinking the audience through modern India's cinema halls can help us better understand the ways in which Shakespeare's and Middleton's playhouses were less scenes of private scholarly reading than of ecstatic collective devotion, self-regarding liveness on the part of 'the' audience, and prophecies of solidarity against the singular stories of tyrants.

Notes

1 I have written about my experience of watching *Lagaan* also in *Masala Shakespeare: How A Firangi Writer Became Indian* (New Delhi: Aleph Books, 2018), 1–17.

2 Although Shakespeare elsewhere uses the word 'apparition' to refer to ghosts from the past – Julius Caesar, Hamlet's father, Posthumus's

father – in *Macbeth* the three apparitions of Act 4 scene 1 are predictions of the future.

3 All references to *Venus and Adonis* are to Katherine Duncan-Jones and H. R. Woudhuysen, eds, *Shakespeare's Poems*, Arden Third Series (London: Bloomsbury, 2007).

4 This is the classic formulation of St Thomas Aquinas. See Alexandra Walsham, 'Miracles in Post-Reformation England', *Studies in Church History* 41 (2005): 273–306, 273.

5 Thomas Nashe, *Terrors of the Night, Or, A Discourse of Apparitions* (London, 1594), 9.

6 Kenneth Burke, *A Rhetoric of Motives* (Berkeley: University of California Press, 1969), 217.

7 For a useful discussion of the Protestant discourse of idolatry in early modern England, see David Hawkes, *Idols of the Marketplace: Idolatry and Commodity Fetishism in English Literature, 1580–1680* (New York: Palgrave, 2001).

8 My thinking about the apparitional power of the formula 'hoc est corpus meum' has been shaped by Louis Marin, *Food for Thought*, trans Mette Hjort (Baltimore: Johns Hopkins University Press, 1997).

9 There was a wide spectrum within continental Protestant thought on transubstantiation. But the twenty-eighth article of the *Thirty-Nine Articles of Religion* of the Church of England (1563) declares that the doctrine of transubstantiation 'overthroweth the sacrament'.

10 Jennifer R. Rust offers a brilliant discussion of the loss of the *corpus mysticum*, and its reconstitution in Protestant discourses of martyrdom and the theatre, in *The Body in Mystery: The Political Theology of the Corpus Mysticum in the Literature of Reformation England* (Evanston, IL: Northwestern University, 2014).

11 Stephen Greenblatt, *Shakespearean Negotiations: The Circulation of Social Energy in Renaissance England* (Oxford: Clarendon University Press, 2018), and *Hamlet in Purgatory* (Princeton: Princeton University Press, 2001).

12 Thomas Middleton and Thomas Dekker, *The Roaring Girl*, ed. Elizabeth Cook (London: A & C Black, 2001), 1.2.14–32.

13 Antony Dawson also sees the early modern theatre audience as drawing on the experience of the Eucharist; see Dawson and Paul Yachnin, *The Culture of Playgoing in Shakespeare's England: A Collaborative Debate* (Cambridge: Cambridge University Press, 2001), 29–45.

14 Virginia Mason Vaughan and Alden T. Vaughan, eds., *The Tempest*, Arden Third Series (London: Bloomsbury, 2011).

15 See Rachel Dwyer, *Filming the Gods: Religion and Indian Cinema* (London: Routledge, 2006).

16 Andrew Gurr, *Playgoing in Shakespeare's London* (Cambridge: Cambridge University Press, 2004), 63.

17 I develop the links between the diversity of audiences in Shakespeare's playhouse and Indian cinema in *Masala Shakespeare*, 5–6.

18 Josef W. Meri, *Medieval Islamic Civilization: An Encyclopedia*, Vol. 1 (London: Routledge, 2006), 98.

19 Malika Mohammada, *The Foundations of the Composite Culture in India* (New Delhi: Aakar Books, 2007), esp. 310.

20 On the Amitabh Bachchan temple in Kolkata, see https://www.indiatimes.com/news/india/one-massive-fan-of-big-b-built-a-temple-for-him-in-kolkata-this-is-his-story-273785.html, accessed 5 February 2022.

21 References to *Hamlet* are from Ann Thompson and Neil Taylor (eds.), *Hamlet*, Arden Third Series (London: Bloomsbury, 2006).

22 All references to *Macbeth* are from Sandra Clark and Pamela Mason (eds.), *Macbeth*, Arden Third Series (London: Bloomsbury, 2015).

23 See Rhodri Lewis, 'Polychronic *Macbeth*', *Modern Philology* 117 (2020): 323–46.

24 James L. Calderwood, *Shakespearean Metadrama* (London: Oxford University Press, 1971), 12–14.

25 Andrew Sofer discusses the eerie power of invisible entities – or entities seen differently by characters from how audiences see them – in *Dark Matter: Invisibility in Drama, Theatre and Performance* (Ann Arbor, MI: University of Michigan Press, 2023).

26 Jonathan Hope and Michael Witmore, 'The Language of *Macbeth*', in *Macbeth: The State of Play*, ed. Ann Thompson (London: Bloomsbury, 2014), 183–214.

27 Compare Nashe, *Terrors of the Night*, 30: 'the scritch-owl ... might overawe us from any insolent transgression at that time. ... for her lavish blabbing of forbidden secrets being forever ordained to be a blab of ill news and misfortune, still is crying out in our ears that we are mortal, and must die'.

28 My thoughts here are shaped by those of Jacques Derrida in his reading of *Hamlet* through Marx in *Spectres of Marx: The State of*

the Debt, the Work of Mourning, and the New International, trans. Peggy Kamuf (London and New York: Routledge, 1993).

29 I have discussed these ideas at greater length in Jonathan Gil Harris, 'The Smell of *Macbeth*', *Shakespeare Quarterly* 58 (2007): 465–86.

30 Where was *Macbeth* first performed? There are records of its performance at the Globe in 1611 – Simon Forman saw a performance there – but so much of the play, particularly its pyrotechnics and night-time scenes, seems to demand the resources of an indoor theatre like the Blackfriars, which Shakespeare's company took over in 1609. See Will Tosh, 'Darkness Doth the Face of Earth Entomb', *Shakespeare's Globe* blog, https://www.shakespearesglobe.com/discover/blogs-and-features/2020/11/04/darkness-does-the-face-of-earth-entomb/

31 The idea that the play was staged for King James has been popular since Lewis Theobald; it acquired particular influence in Henry N. Paul, *The Royal Play of Macbeth* (New York: Macmillan, 1950).

32 The meaning of the two balls and three scepters has been much disputed. See E. B. Lyle, 'The "Twofold Balls and Treble Scepters" in *Macbeth*', *Shakespeare Quarterly* 28 (1977): 516–19.

33 Jonathan Goldberg, 'Speculations: *Macbeth* and Source', in *Shakespeare Reproduced: The Text in History and Ideology*, ed. Jean E. Howard and Marion F. O'Connor (New York: Methuen, 1987), 242–64.

34 On Middleton's interpolations, see Inga-Stina Ewbank, 'The Middle of Middleton', in *The Arts of Performance in Elizabethan and Early Stuart Drama*, ed. Murray Biggs et al. (Edinburgh, 1991), 156–72.

35 Christopher Pye, *The Regal Phantasm: Shakespeare and the Politics of Spectacle* (New York: Routledge, 1989).

36 For a discussion of Indian 'gangster' film Shakespeares, see *Masala Shakespeare*, 164–9.

37 See Ralph Berry, *Shakespeare and the Awareness of Audience* (New York: Routledge, 1985).

INDEX

Page numbers in *italics* refer to figures; 'n.' to chapter notes.

absence   39, 41–4, 49–52, 55 n.11, 58 n.40
accessibility, audience   30, 91–3
acting   27, 29, 30, 61, 69–70, 74–5, 78–83
Adamson, Henry   44
Aebischer, Pascale   7, 18, 39, 74–5, 78
agency   23, 75, 90, 99, 106, 108
Ahmadinejad, Tara   30
air   38, 40, 49, 204, 230
aliveness   7, 61–3, 76–7, 82–3
All's Well That Ends Well (Shakespeare)   196
American Shakespeare Center (ASC)   22, 114, 115
animation   95–6
Antony and Cleopatra (Shakespeare)   46–52, 58 n.40
apparitions, prophetic   217–35 n.2
Arslanköy Theatre Company, *Kraliçe Lear* (2019)   151–8, *154*
Artaud, Antonin   179–80, 193
asynchronicity   42, 46, 52
audience(s), *see also* engagement; interactivity; shared experience
    accessibility   30, 91–3
    apparitional   217–35 n.2
    co-creation   66–9, 75, 90, 105, 108
    emotional involvement   97–9, 108
    feedback   89, 91–3, 97–100, 104–7
    Indian film   217–19, 224–8, 233–5
augmented reality (AR)   89–108
Auslander, Philip   2, 3, 7, 16–18, 31, 56 n.22, 68, 76
authenticity   114–15
avatars   1–2, 21, 22, 27, 28, 30, 95, 103–4, 106–7

Back Room Shakespeare Project   114–15
Barker, Martin   63
Bay-Cheng, Sarah   3–4
BBC iPlayer   24
Belsey, Catherine   58 n.40
Benjamin, Walter   206
Bhardwaj, Vishal, *Maqbool* (film, 2003)   233–4
Big Telly Theatre Company
    Macbeth (2020)   62–3, 73–81, *81*
    Recipe for Disaster (2021)   45–7, *47*
    The Tempest (2020)   74, 76, 78
Bisṭāmī, Abū Yazīd   178
Blackfriars, London   228, 231, 232, 238 n.30

Black Lives Matter movement 103
Blau, Herbert 82
blazing star, the 196–213
Bloom, Gina 18, 20
body(ies) 29–30, 97, 174–80, 189–90
  at a distance 41–4
  and heart 178–9, 184–6, 190, 191
Borsuk, Amy 74
breath 38, 41, 48–52, 174, 180–90
Breen, Philip 15, 19
Broadbridge, Helen 105
Broadribb, Benjamin 76
Brook, Peter 192–3
Buchanan, Judith 64–5, 67–8, 84 n.10

Calderwood, James L. 229
Carter, Elizabeth 35 n.41
Caserini, Mario, *Macbeth* (1909) 65, 67, 68
'catch' theatre game 41, 46
Catholicism, Holy Communion 220–8, 230–1
Chanakyapuri Theatre, *Lagaan* screening 217–19, 225, 227–8, 235
Chironis, Katie 21
Christianity 39–40, 44–5, 198, *see also* Catholicism; Protestant
  metaphysics 39–40, 44
  theology 175–7, 192
chromakey 61, 63–73, 73, 82
climate crisis 103
co-creation 66–9, 75, 90, 105, 108
collaboration 112, 119–22, 126
collectivity 20, 217–35

Comedy of Errors, The (Shakespeare)
  Original Practice Shakespeare Festival (OPSF) 117, 128
  Royal Shakespeare Company (RSC, 2021) 15
comets
  the blazing star 196–213
  Great Comet of 1577 196–200, 214 n.9
Commonwealth Shakespeare Company 22, 35 n.35
conferencing software, *see* Zoom
Conkie, Rob 5, 112, 116
contemporaneity 25, 76, 77
co-presence 44–6, 75, 90, 99, 100, 108
cosmos 186–7
Covid-19 pandemic 15–16, 24–31, 38, 40–3, 45, 50–2, 62, 73, 77, 89, 101, 103, 145, 146, 148, 149, 151–3, 155, 157–9, 164, 164 n.2, 167 n.39
  social distance 39, 101–3
Creation Theatre Company, *The Tempest* (2020) 74, 76, 78
CREW
  Hamlet Encounters (2018) 92
  Hamlet's Lunacy (2019) 92
  Hands-on-Hamlet (2017) 89–100
  Terra Nova (2011) 92
Crystal, David 5, 7

death 50, 52, 173–4, 182, 191, 193
Dee, John 197
Dekker, Thomas, and Middleton
  The Bloody Banquet 206–8
  The Roaring Girl 222–4, 226, 232, 235

INDEX

Deleuze, Gilles 179–80
Derrida, Jacques 39, 41, 43, 180, 193
Digges, Leonard 198, 199
direct address 26, 35 n.41, 40, 79
disorientation 40, 95–7
distance 39–49, 51, 52, 56 n.17
distraction 97, 100
dramaturgy 90–2, 96–7, 113
  institutional 115, 116, 122
Dustagheer, Sarah 115

early modern theatre, as term 6–8
Edward's Boys 112, 118
ekphrasis 39, 48–9
Elizabeth I 197
Elsinore (game) 21–2
embodiment 8, 16, 29, 99, 178, 192, 212
emotional involvement 97–9, 108
engagement, audience
  in digital mediums 61, 67, 68, 70, 76, 81, 82
  in virtual performances 17–20, 23
  in virtual reality (VR) and augmented reality (AR) adaptations 91, 100, 104, 108
environment(s) 103, 108, 154
  cinematic 61, 63, 64
  digital 69, 95, 96, 99, 104
  shared 116–18, 123
  virtual 28, 29, 96–7, 99, 108
Epic Games 26
Erasmus 44
Erdenk, Barış 147
Erikson, Jon 42
Esmer, Pelin
  Kraliçe Lear (2019) 146, 151–8, *154*
  Oyun (2005) 155

Expertise Centre for Digital Media, University of Hasselt 90

faith 44–5, *see also* religiosity
Fallon, Connor 21
Falocco, Joe 19
Fawkner, Harald 50
feedback, audience 89, 91–3, 97–100, 104–7
Ficino, Marsilio 44
filmed productions 17, 24–6, 64–5, 68–72, 100, *see also* live streaming
Fletcher, John, and Massinger, *Rollo, Duke of Normandy* 211–12
Floyd-Wilson, Mary 197
Foreman, Simon 199–200
Foxe, John 198
funding 91, 92

gaming/gamification 16, 20–4, 26–30, 66, 76, 99
gaps 41–3, 47, 49, 51, 56 n.18
gender
  identities 120, 129–30, 154, 160
  relations 127, 146, 152, 155–7, 162
gesture 30, 40, 41
al-Ghazālī, Abū Ḥamid Muḥammad 176, 193
Giannachi, Gabriella 19, 42, 48
Globe Theatre, London 4, 19, 24, 116
  Hamlet 228, 231, 232, 238 n.30
  Middleton's revenge tragedies 206
  Original Shakespeare Company (OSC) 113–14
  Read Not Dead 112
  Romeo and Juliet 5

Goffe, Thomas, *The Courageous Turk* 211–13
Goldberg, Jonathan 231
Golden Glitch 21
Gorman, Tom 56 n.17
Green, Morgan 24, 25
Greenblatt, Stephen 201, 222, 226
green screen, *see* chromakey
Gurr, Andrew 4, 7

Hamlet (Shakespeare) 22
   Dream of Hamlet (Hülagu/Karagöz, 2020–1) 146, 158–64, *161*, 169 nn.80–1
   Elsinore (game) 21–2
   Fat Ham (Wilma Theatre, 2020) 24–6
   Hamlet 360: Thy Father's Spirit (Maler, 2019) 22–4
   Hamlet Encounters (CREW, 2018) 92
   Hamlet's Lunacy (CREW, 2019) 92
   Hands-on-Hamlet (CREW, 2017) 89–100
Hanson, Christopher 20
Hayles, N. Katherine 71
Helmont, Jan Baptise Van 43–4
Henry, Akiya 82
Henry IV, Part One (Shakespeare), Original Practice Shakespeare Festival (OPSF) 129–30
Heywood, Thomas, *Apology for Actors* 6–7
Hindu devotion 225–7, 234
Hope, Jonathan 229
Hove, Ivo van 121
Hülagu, Ayhan, *Dream of Hamlet* (2020–21) 146, 158–64, *161*, 169 nn.80–1
humour 128–31, 157, 160–2

Hunter, Lindsay Brandon 2–3
hybridity 74, 77, 102
hypertextuality 69, 73, 119

idols 224–8, 235
Ijames, James 24
imagination 40–1, 43, 45, 49, 51, 52, 96, 118, 184, 186
immediacy 18, 24, 26, 29
immersion 22, 27, 29, 63, 71
improvisation 116, 118–31
Indian film audiences 217–19, 224–8, 233–5
innovation, digital 90–3
interactivity 1, 4, 8
   of body and theatre 178
   in digital mediums 61, 66–7, 74, 76, 82
   online 41, 45
   in Turkish Shakespeares 152, 159–60
   in virtual performances 16–20, 31
   in virtual reality (VR) and augmented reality (AR) adaptations 90, 92, 95, 99–102, 104–8
International Theatre Amsterdam (ITA) 121
interruptions 119, 123–4, 127, 206, 208, *see also* unexpected, the
intimacy 7, 97–8
iPhones/iPads 92–3, 103, 105
Islam 182–5, 191–2
   devotion 225–7, 234
isolation 19, 78–9, 82, 99, 103, 108

Jackson, Macdonald P. 207
James I of England and VI of Scotland 231–3, 238 n.31
Jāmī, 'Abd al-Raḥmān 173, 177, 182–4

Jonson, Ben, *Bartholomew Faire* 8
Joris, Eric 90
Julius Caesar (Shakespeare), Original Practice Shakespeare Festival (OPSF) 119, *120*, 124
Juul, Jesper 21

Kanninen, Mikko 56 n.17
Karagöz Theatre Company, *Dream of Hamlet* (2020–21) 146, 158–64, *161*, 169 nn.80–1
Kāshifī, Ḥusayn Wā'iẓ 178–9, 182–5, 189, 193
Kattenbelt, Chiel 96–7
Kaye, Nick 42, 48
Keenan, Siobhan 117
Kiarostomi, Abbas 66
King Lear (Shakespeare) 8, 26, 35 n.41, 56 n.17, 222
  Kraliçe Lear (Esmer, 2019) 146, 151–8, *154*
King's Men 206
Kubrā, Najm al-Dīn 181–2

Lacan, Jacques 221
Lehman, Hans-Thies 50, 52
Lewis, C.S., *Discarded Image* 93
Lewis, Helen 121
life and liveness, relationship between 173–8, 193
Lindelof, Anja Mølle 19
live chat 19, 20, 26
liveness 1–8
  as aliveness 63, 75, 76, 83
  and apparitional audiences 219, 224, 227, 229, 235
  and atmospheric presence 38–43, 45, 46, 50–2
  and life 173–8, 193

in mixed reality contexts 89–90, 92, 93, 97–100, 104–8
Naqshbandī theory of 176, 180–4, 188–90
and production systems 112
and transformation 196, 206, 210–13
in virtual theatre 16–21, 24–6, 29, 31, 159, 164
live streaming 16–27, 74, 158–64, *161*
Lopez, Jeremy 114

Macbeth (Shakespeare) 209
  apparitions in 228–33, 235 n.2, 238 nn.30–1
  Big Telly Theatre Company (2020) 62–3, 73–81, *81*
  Caserini (1909) 65, 67, 68
  İkinci Katil (Yiğit, 2017) 146–51, *148*
  Maqbool (Bhardwaj, 2003) 233–4
  Monkman (2018) 61, 63–73, *73*, 82, 84 n.10
  Original Practice Shakespeare Festival (OPSF) 116
McCutcheon, Rebecca 101
MacMahon, Henry 72
magic 30, 39–40, 43–4, 210, 218–24
Maler, Steven, *Hamlet 360: Thy Father's Spirit* (VR film, 2019) 22–4
Manchester International Festival 26
Marlowe, Christopher, *2 Tamburlaine* 201–3
Marshmallow Laser Feast 26
Massey, Doreen 71
Massinger, Philip, and Fletcher, *Rollo, Duke of Normandy* 211–12

mediatization   2–3, 16, 56 n.22
medium convergence   62, 65, 71–4
medium specificity   61–2, 65, 71–4, 108
Merry Wives of Windsor, The (Shakespeare), Original Practice Shakespeare Festival (OPSF)   121, 128, 132–3, *133*
metaphysics   39–40, 44
metatheatricality   8, 158, 207, 208, 211
Me Too movement   127
Middleton, Thomas
  and Dekker, *The Roaring Girl*   222–4, 226, 232, 235
  revenge tragedies of   206–8, 211
Midsummer Night's Dream, A (Shakespeare), *Dream* (RSC, 2021)   1–3, 16, 26–7, 104
mimesis   2–3, 6, 45–50, 52, 192
Monkman, Kit, *Macbeth* (2018)   61, 63–73, *73*, 82, 84 n.10
motion capture technology   1, 70, 85 n.14, 93, 95, 96, 102, 103
Much Ado About Nothing (Shakespeare), Original Practice Shakespeare Festival (OPSF)   *123*, *125*, *126*
music   153, 154, 156, 159

Nancy, Jean Luc   42
Naqshbandī theory of liveness   176, 180–4, 188–90
Nashe, Thomas   219
National Theatre, NT Live   20
natural philosophy   39, 43, 196, 197

Nausea, Frederich   198–9
Nedelkopoulou, Eirini   20
Nelson, Richard   74
Nelson, Robin   93–4, 97, 102
New England Shakespeare Festival   114
New York Times, The   72
Nexus Studios, *The Tempest* (2020)   90–3, 101–8
nostalgia   4, 7, 116, 152, 200

objects at a distance   41–4, 48
O'Donovan, Crissy   75–6
online streaming, *see* live streaming
Oregon ArtsWatch   122, 125
Oregon Shakespeare Festival   129
Original Practices (OP)   4–6, 111–33
Original Practice Shakespeare Festival (OPSF)   113–33
  The Comedy of Errors   117, 128
  Henry IV, Part One   129–30
  Julius Caesar   119, *120*, 124
  Macbeth   116
  The Merry Wives of Windsor   121, 128, 132–3, *133*
  Much Ado About Nothing   *123*, *125*, *126*
  Othello   120
  Prompters in   113–26, *126*, 130–3
  Romeo and Juliet   117, 119, 124–5, 132–3
  The Taming of the Shrew   126–9
  The Tempest   124, 128
  Twelfth Night   124
  WIL Fest   118–23, *123*, 126–7, 143 n.25

appendix of performances 134–41
Original Pronunciation (OP) 5–6
Original Shakespeare Company (OSC) 113–14
Othello (Shakespeare), Original Practice Shakespeare Festival (OPSF) 5, 120
Owens, Sinéad 74, 76

Padden, Matt 103
Palfrey, Simon 113
Papadinis, Demitra 114
Pārsā, Khwāja Muḥammad 176–7
perception 8, 23, 41, 45, 90, 97, 101, 105, 108
Pericles (Shakespeare) 26
Persian theatre 173–93
Phelan, Peggy 2, 16, 17, 175–7, 179
plot pathways 69–71
pneumatic enargeia 39, 41, 48–52
poetry/poetics 6, 7, 44, 48–9, 51, 234
politics 127–30, 218–19, 226, 232
Popat, Sita 16
power 50–2
Practice as Research (PaR) 93–108
Prescott, Paul 114, 115
presence 25, 29, 39, 76–7, 97, 98, 101, 106, 108, 174, 192
  co-presence 44–6, 75, 90, 99, 100, 108
  at a distance 39–49
  divine 44, 220, 221, 224–5, 228, 235
  pneumatic 49–52
Prime, John 44
prompters, in Original Practice Shakespeare Festival (OPSF) performance 113–26, *126*, 130–3
prophetic apparitions 217–35 n.2
Protestant Reformation 219–22, 228, 233, 235, 236 n.9
proximity 19, 26, 31, 38–45, 51, 52, 97–8, 108
Purcell, Stephen 112, 114, 115
pyrotechnics 197–8, 204, 206, 211–12, 238 n.30

Qāsim-i Anwār 186–9

racial inequality 52, 103, 120, 128, 129
Read Not Dead 112
reality(ies) 2–3, 5, 8, 16, 95–6, 178, 188, *see also* augmented reality (AR); virtual reality (VR)
  'as if' 177, 193
  digital 15–16, 19
real-time technology 90–2, 104–8
Reason, Matthew 19
religiosity 218–26, 235, *see also* faith; *specific religions*
remembrance(s) 146, 151, 155, 164, 181–3
remote theatre 39–41, 44, 45, 52, 54 n.10, 56 n.17
repertory scheduling 111–22, 131–3, 143 n.25
revenge, right to 206–13
ritual(s) 221–2, 225–6
Rokem, Freddie 206
Romeo and Juliet (Shakespeare)
  Globe Theatre, London 5
  Original Practice Shakespeare Festival (OPSF) *117*, 119, 124–5, 132–3
Rosvally, Danielle 35 n.35
Rowe, Katherine 62
Rowley, William
  The Birth of Merlin 210, 213

Thorney Abbey 208–9, 213
Royal Holloway, University of London 91
Royal Shakespeare Company (RSC) 15, 20, 24
  The Comedy of Errors (2021) 15
  Dream (2021) 1–3, 16, 26–7, 104
  The Tempest (2016) 3, 70, 85 n.14
Rubin, Peter 22
rūḥ (spirit) 187–8
Rutter, Tom 202

Ṣafī 'Alī, Fahr al-Dīn 180–1, 184
San Francisco Shakespeare Festival 26
Schmitt, Carl 94
screenality 164, 177–8, 188
  screens as barriers 158–9
Seaton, Zoë 74–81
senses, the 41, 97, 101, 204, 222
Sensorium 22
Shakelton, Francis 199
Shakespeare, William, *see specific titles of works*
Shakespeare in the Park 114, 116
Shakespeare's Tavern 115
shared experience 15, 24, 38, 151, 160
Shirley, James, *The School of Complaint* 196–7
Sidney, Philip 6, 7
Smel-Knave, Simon 199
sociability 90, 99, 101
social criticism 158, 160, 163
social inequality 146–9, 151–3, 165 n.4
social media 16, 17, 20, 24, *see also* live chat
Soloski, Alexis 30

Sonnet 55 (Shakespeare) 44
Sorgun, Hüseyin 158
soul 44, 174, 189
spatiality 22, 97, 102, 104, 106–7
  distanced 39–42
spirit 187–90
  respiratory 50–2, 174, 180
State Theatre, Ankara 146, 151, 165 n.4
Steichen, James 115
Stern, Tiffany 113
StoryFutures 91, 101
Stukeley plays 200–5, 209
Sufism 176, 179, 180, 233–4
Sullivan, Erin 20, 29, 30
superstition 197–8
sympathy 43, 44, 202, 203
synchronicity 16, 20, 24–6, 29, 31, 40–3, 75
  asynchronicity 42, 46, 52
Syrjä, Tiina 56 n.17

Taming of A Shrew (Anonymous) 196
Taming of the Shrew, The (Shakespeare), Original Practice Shakespeare Festival (OPSF) 126–9
taqlīn (narrative) 173–4
tawajjuh (regarding/turning to) 184, 186, 188, 193
ta'ziyeh (Persian play form) 183–4, 191, 192
telematic theatre 39–41, 44, 45, 52, 54 n.10, 56 n.17
Tempest, The (Shakespeare) 102–3, 224
  Big Telly Theatre Company (2020) 74, 76, 78
  Nexus Studios (2020) 90–3, 101–8
  Original Practice Shakespeare Festival (OPSF) 124, 128

Royal Shakespeare Company
   (RSC, 2016)   3, 70, 85 n.14
'Under Presents' *Tempest* (VR
   game)   27–8, 30
temporality   8, 17–19, 21–2, 25,
   29
   distanced   39–42, 50
Tender Claws, 'Under Presents'
   Tempest (VR game)   27–8,
   30
360-degree video
   experiences   22–4, 95–6
togetherness, feelings of   100–2,
   218
touring/travelling
   productions   117, 122,
   146, 151–8, *154*
transitionality   61–2, 72, 211
Tucker, Patrick   113, 114
Turkish shadow theatre
   (Karagöz)   146, 158–64,
   161
Turkish Shakespeares   145–64
Twelfth Night (Shakespeare)   7
   Original Practice Shakespeare
   Festival (OPSF)   124
uncanniness   29, 52, 229
unexpected, the   116–19, *see also*
   interruptions

Unreal Engine   3

Venus and Adonis
   (Shakespeare)   219–20
Vermigli, Peter Martyr   45

video games, *see* gaming/
   gamification
virtual performances   8, 15–31,
   39, 42, 44, 62–3, *see also*
   live streaming; Zoom
virtual reality (VR)   17, 22–4,
   27–30, 35 n.35, 66, 70, 71,
   89–108
vMix software   76
voids   41–2

Wagner, Matthew   19
Wanamaker, Sam   4
weather conditions   207–8
Weimann, Robert   18, 22
   locus and *platea*   18, 22, 25
Weingust, Don   113, 115
Whipday, Emma   132
WIL Fest   118–23, 126–7,
   143 n.25
   appendix of
   performances   134–41
Wilma Theatre, Philadelphia, *Fat
   Ham* (2020)   24–6
witchcraft   231
Witmore, Michael   229
Worthen, William (W.B.)   3, 19,
   122
Wynants, Nele   95–6

Yiğit, Serhat, *İkinci Katil*
   (2017)   146–51, *148*

Zoom   24, 26, 40–1, 46, 62,
   73–6, 79–82

www.ingramcontent.com/pod-product-compliance
Lightning Source LLC
Chambersburg PA
CBHW062134300426
44115CB00012BA/1913